NON SANZ DROICT.

As you Like it.

Actus primus. Scæna Prima.

William Shakespeare

As You Like It

With New and Updated Critical Essays and a Revised Bibliography

Edited by Albert Gilman

THE SIGNET CLASSIC SHAKESPEARE
General Editor: Sylvan Barnet

A SIGNET CLASSIC

SIGNET CLASSIC
Published by New American Library, a division of
Penguin Group (USA) Inc., 375 Hudson Street,
New York, New York 10014, USA
Penguin Group (Canada), 10 Alcorn Avenue, Toronto,
Ontario M4V 3B2, Canada (a division of Pearson Penguin Canada Inc.)
Penguin Books Ltd., 80 Strand, London WC2R 0RL, England
Penguin Ireland, 25 St. Stephen's Green, Dublin 2,
Ireland (a division of Penguin Books Ltd.)
Penguin Group (Australia), 250 Camberwell Road, Camberwell, Victoria 3124,
Australia (a division of Pearson Australia Group Pty. Ltd.)
Penguin Books India Pvt. Ltd., 11 Community Centre, Panchsheel Park,
New Delhi - 110 017, India
Penguin Group (NZ), cnr Airborne and Rosedale Roads, Albany,
Auckland 1310, New Zealand (a division of Pearson New Zealand Ltd.)
Penguin Books (South Africa) (Pty.) Ltd., 24 Sturdee Avenue,
Rosebank, Johannesburg 2196, South Africa

Penguin Books Ltd., Registered Offices:
80 Strand, London WC2R 0RL, England

Published by Signet Classic, an imprint of New American Library, a division of
Penguin Group (USA) Inc. The Signet Classic Edition of *As You Like It* was
first published in 1963, and an updated edition was published in 1986.

First Signet Classic Printing (Second Revised Edition), April 1998
20 19 18 17 16 15 14 13 12 11 10

Library of Congress Catalog Card Number: 97-69246

Printed in the United States of America

Contents

Shakespeare: An Overview

Biographical Sketch

Between the record of his baptism in Stratford on 26 April 1564 and the record of his burial in Stratford on 25 April 1616, some forty official documents name Shakespeare, and many others name his parents, his children, and his grandchildren. Further, there are at least fifty literary references to him in the works of his contemporaries. More facts are known about William Shakespeare than about any other playwright of the period except Ben Jonson. The facts should, however, be distinguished from the legends. The latter, inevitably more engaging and better known, tell us that the Stratford boy killed a calf in high style, poached deer and rabbits, and was forced to flee to London, where he held horses outside a playhouse. These traditions are only traditions; they may be true, but no evidence supports them, and it is well to stick to the facts.

Mary Arden, the dramatist's mother, was the daughter of a substantial landowner; about 1557 she married John Shakespeare, a tanner, glove-maker, and trader in wool, grain, and other farm commodities. In 1557 John Shakespeare was a member of the council (the governing body of Stratford), in 1558 a constable of the borough, in 1561 one of the two town chamberlains, in 1565 an alderman (entitling him to the appellation of "Mr."), in 1568 high bailiff—the town's highest political office, equivalent to mayor. After 1577, for an unknown reason he drops out of local politics. What *is* known is that he had to mortgage his wife's property, and that he was involved in serious litigation.

The birthday of William Shakespeare, the third child and the eldest son of this locally prominent man, is unrecorded, but the Stratford parish register records that the infant was baptized on 26 April 1564. (It is quite possible that he was born on 23 April, but this date has probably been assigned by tradition because it is the date on which, fifty-two years later, he died, and perhaps because it is the feast day of St. George, patron saint of England.) The attendance records of the Stratford grammar school of the period are not extant, but it is reasonable to assume that the son of a prominent local official attended the free school—it had been established for the purpose of educating males precisely of his class—and received substantial training in Latin. The masters of the school from Shakespeare's seventh to fifteenth years held Oxford degrees; the Elizabethan curriculum excluded mathematics and the natural sciences but taught a good deal of Latin rhetoric, logic, and literature, including plays by Plautus, Terence, and Seneca.

On 27 November 1582 a marriage license was issued for the marriage of Shakespeare and Anne Hathaway, eight years his senior. The couple had a daughter, Susanna, in May 1583. Perhaps the marriage was necessary, but perhaps the couple had earlier engaged, in the presence of witnesses, in a formal "troth plight" which would render their children legitimate even if no further ceremony were performed. In February 1585, Anne Hathaway bore Shakespeare twins, Hamnet and Judith.

That Shakespeare was born is excellent; that he married and had children is pleasant; but that we know nothing about his departure from Stratford to London or about the beginning of his theatrical career is lamentable and must be admitted. We would gladly sacrifice details about his children's baptism for details about his earliest days in the theater. Perhaps the poaching episode is true (but it is first reported almost a century after Shakespeare's death), or perhaps he left Stratford to be a schoolmaster, as another tradition holds; perhaps he was moved (like Petruchio in *The Taming of the Shrew*) by

> Such wind as scatters young men through the world,
> To seek their fortunes farther than at home
> Where small experience grows.   (1.2.49–51)

In 1592, thanks to the cantankerousness of Robert Greene, we have our first reference, a snarling one, to Shakespeare as an actor and playwright. Greene, a graduate of St. John's College, Cambridge, had become a playwright and a pamphleteer in London, and in one of his pamphlets he warns three university-educated playwrights against an actor who has presumed to turn playwright:

> There is an upstart crow, beautified with our feathers, that with his *tiger's heart wrapped in a player's hide* supposes he is as well able to bombast out a blank verse as the best of you, and being an absolute Johannes-factotum [i.e., jack-of-all-trades] is in his own conceit the only Shake-scene in a country.

The reference to the player, as well as the allusion to Aesop's crow (who strutted in borrowed plumage, as an actor struts in fine words not his own), makes it clear that by this date Shakespeare had both acted and written. That Shakespeare is meant is indicated not only by *Shake-scene* but also by the parody of a line from one of Shakespeare's plays, *3 Henry VI*: "O, tiger's heart wrapped in a woman's hide" (1.4.137). If in 1592 Shakespeare was prominent enough to be attacked by an envious dramatist, he probably had served an apprenticeship in the theater for at least a few years.

In any case, although there are no extant references to Shakespeare between the record of the baptism of his twins in 1585 and Greene's hostile comment about "Shake-scene" in 1592, it is evident that during some of these "dark years" or "lost years" Shakespeare had acted and written. There are a number of subsequent references to him as an actor. Documents indicate that in 1598 he is a "principal comedian," in 1603 a "principal tragedian," in 1608 he is one of the "men players." (We do not have, however, any solid information about which roles he may have played; later traditions say he played Adam in *As You Like It* and the ghost in *Hamlet*, but nothing supports the assertions. Probably his role as dramatist came to supersede his role as actor.) The profession of actor was not for a gentleman, and it occasionally drew the scorn of university men like Greene who resented writing speeches for persons less educated than themselves, but it was respectable enough; players, if prosperous, were in effect members of the bourgeoisie, and there is nothing to suggest that Stratford considered William Shakespeare less than a solid citizen. When, in 1596, the Shakespeares were granted a coat of arms—i.e., the right to be considered gentlemen—the grant was made to Shakespeare's father, but probably William Shakespeare had arranged the matter on his own behalf. In subsequent transactions he is occasionally styled a gentleman.

Although in 1593 and 1594 Shakespeare published two narrative poems dedicated to the Earl of Southampton, *Venus and Adonis* and *The Rape of Lucrece*, and may well have written most or all of his sonnets in the middle nineties, Shakespeare's literary activity seems to have been almost entirely devoted to the theater. (It may be significant that the two narrative poems were written in years when the plague closed the theaters for several months.) In 1594 he was a charter member of a theatrical company called the Chamberlain's Men, which in 1603 became the royal company, the King's Men, making Shakespeare the king's playwright. Until he retired to Stratford (about 1611, apparently), he was with this remarkably stable company. From 1599 the company acted primarily at the Globe theater, in which Shakespeare held a one-tenth interest. Other Elizabethan dramatists are known to have acted, but no other is known also to have been entitled to a share of the profits.

Shakespeare's first eight published plays did not have his name on them, but this is not remarkable; the most popular play of the period, Thomas Kyd's *The Spanish Tragedy*, went through many editions without naming Kyd, and Kyd's authorship is known only because a book on the profession of acting happens to quote (and attribute to Kyd) some lines on the interest of Roman emperors in the drama. What is remarkable is that after 1598 Shakespeare's name commonly appears on printed plays—some of which are not his. Presumably his name was a drawing card, and publishers used it to attract potential buyers. Another indication of his popularity comes from Francis Meres, author of *Palladis Tamia: Wit's Treasury* (1598). In this anthology of snippets accompanied by an essay on literature, many playwrights are mentioned, but Shakespeare's name occurs more often than any other, and Shakespeare is the only playwright whose plays are listed.

From his acting, his play writing, and his share in a playhouse, Shakespeare seems to have made considerable money. He put it to work, making substantial investments in Stratford real estate. As early as 1597 he bought New Place, the second-largest house in Stratford. His family moved in soon afterward, and the house remained in the family until a granddaughter died in 1670. When Shakespeare made his will in 1616, less than a month before he died, he sought to leave his property intact to his descendants. Of small bequests to relatives and to friends (including three actors, Richard Burbage, John Heminges, and Henry Condell), that to his wife of the second-best bed has provoked the most comment. It has sometimes been taken as a sign of an unhappy marriage (other supposed signs are the apparently hasty marriage, his wife's seniority of eight years, and his residence in London without his family). Perhaps the second-best bed was the bed the couple had slept in, the best bed being reserved for visitors. In any case, had Shakespeare not excepted it, the bed would have gone (with the rest of his household possessions) to his daughter and her husband.

On 25 April 1616 Shakespeare was buried within the chancel of the church at Stratford. An unattractive monument to his memory, placed on a wall near the grave, says that he died on 23 April. Over the grave itself are the lines, perhaps by Shakespeare, that (more than his literary fame) have kept his bones undisturbed in the crowded burial ground where old bones were often dislodged to make way for new:

> Good friend, for Jesus' sake forbear
> To dig the dust enclosed here.
> Blessed be the man that spares these stones
> And cursed be he that moves my bones.

A Note on the Anti-Stratfordians, Especially Baconians and Oxfordians

Not until 1769—more than a hundred and fifty years after Shakespeare's death—is there any record of anyone expressing doubt about Shakespeare's authorship of the plays and poems. In 1769, however, Herbert Lawrence nominated Francis Bacon (1561–1626) in *The Life and Adventures of Common Sense*. Since then, at least two dozen other nominees have been offered, including Christopher Marlowe, Sir Walter Raleigh, Queen Elizabeth I, and Edward de Vere, 17th earl of Oxford. The impulse behind all anti-Stratfordian movements is the scarcely concealed snobbish opinion that "the man from Stratford" simply could not have written the plays because he was a country fellow without a university education and without access to high society. Anyone, the argument goes, who used so many legal terms, medical terms, nautical terms, and so forth, and who showed some familiarity with classical writing, must have attended a university, and anyone who knew so much about courtly elegance and courtly deceit must himself have moved among courtiers. The plays do indeed reveal an author whose interests were exceptionally broad, but specialists in any given field—law, medicine, arms and armor, and so on—soon find that the plays do not reveal deep knowledge in specialized matters; indeed, the playwright often gets technical details wrong.

The claim on behalf of Bacon, forgotten almost as soon as it was put forth in 1769, was independently reasserted by Joseph C. Hart in 1848. In 1856 it was reaffirmed by W. H. Smith in a book, and also by Delia Bacon in an article; in 1857 Delia Bacon published a book, arguing that Francis Bacon had directed a group of intellectuals who wrote the plays.

Francis Bacon's claim has largely faded, perhaps because it was advanced with such evident craziness by Ignatius Donnelly, who in *The Great Cryptogram* (1888) claimed to break a code in the plays that proved Bacon had written not only the plays attributed to Shakespeare but also other Renaissance works, for instance the plays of Christopher Marlowe and the essays of Montaigne.

Consider the last two lines of the Epilogue in *The Tempest*:

> As you from crimes would pardoned be,
> Let your indulgence set me free.

What was Shakespeare—sorry, Francis Bacon, Baron Verulam—*really* saying in these two lines? According to Baconians, the lines are an anagram reading, "Tempest of Francis Bacon, Lord Verulam; do ye ne'er divulge me, ye words." Ingenious, and it is a pity that in the quotation the letter *a* appears only twice in the cryptogram, whereas in the deciphered message it appears three times. Oh, no problem; just alter "Verulam" to "Verul'm" and it works out very nicely.

Most people understand that with sufficient ingenuity one can torture any text and find in it what one wishes. For instance: Did Shakespeare have a hand in the King James Version of the Bible? It was nearing completion in 1610, when Shakespeare was forty-six years old. If you look at the 46th Psalm and count forward for forty-six words, you will find the word *shake*. Now if you go to the end of the psalm and count backward forty-six words, you will find the word *spear*. Clear evidence, according to some, that Shakespeare slyly left his mark in the book.

Bacon's candidacy has largely been replaced in the twentieth century by the candidacy of Edward de Vere (1550–1604), 17th earl of Oxford. The basic ideas behind the Oxford theory, advanced at greatest length by Dorothy and Charlton Ogburn in *This Star of England* (1952, rev. 1955), a book of 1297 pages, and by Charlton Ogburn in *The Mysterious William Shakespeare* (1984), a book of 892 pages, are these: (1) The man from Stratford could not possibly have had the mental equipment and the experience to have written the plays—only a courtier could have written them; (2) Oxford had the requisite background (social position, education, years at Queen Elizabeth's court); (3) Oxford did not wish his authorship to be known for two basic reasons: writing for the public theater was a vulgar pursuit, and the plays show so much courtly and royal disreputable behavior that they would have compromised Oxford's position at court. Oxfordians offer countless details to support the claim. For example, Hamlet's phrase "that ever I was born to set it right" (1.5.89) barely conceals "E. Ver, I was born to set it right," an unambiguous announcement of de Vere's authorship, according to *This Star of England* (p. 654). A second example: Consider Ben

Jonson's poem entitled "To the Memory of My Beloved Master William Shakespeare," prefixed to the first collected edition of Shakespeare's plays in 1623. According to Oxfordians, when Jonson in this poem speaks of the author of the plays as the "swan of Avon," he is alluding not to William Shakespeare, who was born and died in Stratford-on-Avon and who throughout his adult life owned property there; rather, he is alluding to Oxford, who, the Ogburns say, used "William Shakespeare" as his pen name, and whose manor at Bilton was on the Avon River. Oxfordians do not offer any evidence that Oxford took a pen name, and they do not mention that Oxford had sold the manor in 1581, forty-two years before Jonson wrote his poem. Surely a reference to the Shakespeare who was born in Stratford, who had returned to Stratford, and who had died there only seven years before Jonson wrote the poem is more plausible. And exactly why Jonson, who elsewhere also spoke of Shakespeare as a playwright, and why Heminges and Condell, who had acted with Shakespeare for about twenty years, should speak of Shakespeare as the author in their dedication in the 1623 volume of collected plays is never adequately explained by Oxfordians. Either Jonson, Heminges and Condell, and numerous others were in on the conspiracy, or they were all duped—equally unlikely alternatives. Another difficulty in the Oxford theory is that Oxford died in 1604, and some of the plays are clearly indebted to works and events later than 1604. Among the Oxfordian responses are: At his death Oxford left some plays, and in later years these were touched up by hacks, who added the material that points to later dates. *The Tempest*, almost universally regarded as one of Shakespeare's greatest plays and pretty clearly dated to 1611, does indeed date from a period after the death of Oxford, but it is a crude piece of work that should not be included in the canon of works by Oxford.

The anti-Stratfordians, in addition to assuming that the author must have been a man of rank and a university man, usually assume two conspiracies: (1) a conspiracy in Elizabethan and Jacobean times, in which a surprisingly large number of persons connected with the theater knew that the actor Shakespeare did not write the plays attributed to him but for some reason or other pretended that he did; (2) a conspiracy of today's Stratfordians, the professors who teach Shakespeare in the colleges and universities, who are said to have a vested interest in preserving Shakespeare as the author of the plays they teach. In fact, (1) it is inconceivable that the secret of Shakespeare's non-authorship could have been preserved by all of the people who supposedly were in on the conspiracy, and (2) academic fame awaits any scholar today who can disprove Shakespeare's authorship.

The Stratfordian case is convincing not only because hundreds or even thousands of anti-Stratford arguments—of the sort that say "ever I was born" has the secret double meaning "E. Ver, I was born"—add up to nothing at all but also because irrefutable evidence connects the man from Stratford with the London theater and with the authorship of particular plays. The anti-Stratfordians do not seem to understand that it is not enough to dismiss the Stratford case by saying that a fellow from the provinces simply couldn't have written the plays. Nor do they understand that it is not enough to dismiss all of the evidence connecting Shakespeare with the plays by asserting that it is perjured.

The Shakespeare Canon

We return to William Shakespeare. Thirty-seven plays as well as some nondramatic poems are generally held to constitute the Shakespeare canon, the body of authentic works. The exact dates of composition of most of the works are highly uncertain, but evidence of a starting point and/or of a final limiting point often provides a framework for informed guessing. For example, *Richard II* cannot be earlier than 1595, the publication date of some material to which it is indebted; *The Merchant of Venice* cannot be later than 1598, the year Francis Meres mentioned it. Sometimes arguments for a date hang on an alleged topical allusion, such as the lines about the unseasonable weather in *A Midsummer Night's Dream*, 2.1.81–117, but such an allusion, if indeed it is an allusion to an event in the real world, can be variously interpreted, and in any case there is always the possibility that a topical allusion was inserted years later, to bring the play up to date. (The issue of alterations in a text between the time that Shakespeare drafted it and the time that it was printed—alterations due to censorship or playhouse practice or Shakespeare's own second thoughts—will be discussed in "The Play Text as a Collaboration" later in this overview.) Dates are often attributed on the basis of style, and although conjectures about style usually rest on other conjectures (such as Shakespeare's development as a playwright, or the appropriateness of lines to character), sooner or later one must rely on one's literary sense. There is no documentary proof, for example, that *Othello* is not as early as *Romeo and Juliet*, but one feels that *Othello* is a later, more mature work, and because the first record of its performance is 1604, one is glad enough to set its composition at that date and not push it back into Shakespeare's early years. (*Romeo and Juliet* was first published in 1597, but evidence suggests that it was written a little earlier.) The following chronology, then, is indebted not only to facts but also to informed guesswork and sensitivity. The dates, necessarily imprecise for some works, indicate something like a scholarly consensus concerning the time of original composition. Some plays show evidence of later revision.

Plays. The first collected edition of Shakespeare, published in 1623, included thirty-six plays. These are all accepted as Shakespeare's, though for one of them, *Henry VIII*, he is thought to have had a collaborator. A thirty-seventh play, *Pericles*, published in 1609 and attributed to Shakespeare on the title page, is also widely accepted as being partly by Shakespeare even though it is not included in the 1623 volume. Still another play not in the 1623 volume, *The Two Noble Kinsmen*, was first published in 1634, with a title page attributing it to John Fletcher and Shakespeare. Probably most students of the subject now believe that Shakespeare did indeed have a hand in it. Of the remaining plays attributed at one time or another to Shakespeare, only one, *Edward III*, anonymously published in 1596, is now regarded by some scholars as a serious candidate. The prevailing opinion, however, is that this rather simple-minded play is not Shakespeare's; at most he may have revised some passages, chiefly scenes with the Countess of

Salisbury. We include *The Two Noble Kinsmen* but do not include *Edward III* in the following list.

1588–94	*The Comedy of Errors*
1588–94	*Love's Labor's Lost*
1589–91	*2 Henry VI*
1590–91	*3 Henry VI*
1589–92	*1 Henry VI*
1592–93	*Richard III*
1589–94	*Titus Andronicus*
1593–94	*The Taming of the Shrew*
1592–94	*The Two Gentlemen of Verona*
1594–96	*Romeo and Juliet*
1595	*Richard II*
1595–96	*A Midsummer Night's Dream*
1596–97	*King John*
1594–96	*The Merchant of Venice*
1596–97	*1 Henry IV*
1597	*The Merry Wives of Windsor*
1597–98	*2 Henry IV*
1598–99	*Much Ado About Nothing*
1598–99	*Henry V*
1599	*Julius Caesar*
1599–1600	*As You Like It*
1599–1600	*Twelfth Night*
1600–1601	*Hamlet*
1601–1602	*Troilus and Cressida*
1602–1604	*All's Well That Ends Well*
1603–1604	*Othello*
1604	*Measure for Measure*
1605–1606	*King Lear*
1605–1606	*Macbeth*
1606–1607	*Antony and Cleopatra*
1605–1608	*Timon of Athens*
1607–1608	*Coriolanus*
1607–1608	*Pericles*
1609–10	*Cymbeline*
1610–11	*The Winter's Tale*
1611	*The Tempest*

| 1612–13 | *Henry VIII* |
| 1613 | *The Two Noble Kinsmen* |

Poems. In 1989 Donald W. Foster published a book in which he argued that "A Funeral Elegy for Master William Peter," published in 1612, ascribed only to the initials W.S., *may* be by Shakespeare. Foster later published an article in a scholarly journal, *PMLA* 111 (1996), in which he asserted the claim more positively. The evidence begins with the initials, and includes the fact that the publisher and the printer of the elegy had published Shakespeare's *Sonnets* in 1609. But such facts add up to rather little, especially because no one has found any connection between Shakespeare and William Peter (an Oxford graduate about whom little is known, who was murdered at the age of twenty-nine). The argument is based chiefly on statistical examinations of word patterns, which are said to correlate with Shakespeare's known work. Despite such correlations, however, many readers feel that the poem does not sound like Shakespeare. True, Shakespeare has a great range of styles, but his work is consistently imaginative and interesting. Many readers find neither of these qualities in "A Funeral Elegy."

1592–93	*Venus and Adonis*
1593–94	*The Rape of Lucrece*
1593–1600	*Sonnets*
1600–1601	*The Phoenix and the Turtle*

Shakespeare's English

1. Spelling and Pronunciation. From the philologist's point of view, Shakespeare's English is modern English. It requires footnotes, but the inexperienced reader can comprehend substantial passages with very little help, whereas for the same reader Chaucer's Middle English is a foreign language. By the beginning of the fifteenth century the chief grammatical changes in English had taken place, and the final unaccented -*e* of Middle English had been lost (though it survives even today in spelling, as in *name*); during the fifteenth century the dialect of London, the commercial and political center, gradually displaced the provincial dialects, at least in writing; by the end of the century, printing had helped to regularize and stabilize the language, especially spelling. Elizabethan spelling may seem erratic to us (there were dozens of spellings of *Shakespeare*, and a simple word like *been* was also spelled *beene* and *bin*), but it had much in common with our spelling. Elizabethan spelling was conservative in that for the most part it reflected an older pronunciation (Middle English) rather than the sound of the language as it was then spoken, just as our spelling continues to reflect medieval pronunciation—most obviously in the now silent but formerly pronounced letters in a word such as *knight*. Elizabethan pronunciation, though not identical with ours, was much closer to ours than to that of the Middle Ages. Incidentally, though no one can be certain about what Elizabethan English sounded like, specialists tend to believe it was rather like the speech of a modern stage Irishman (*time* apparently was pronounced *toime*, *old* pronounced *awld*, *day* pronounced *die*, and *join* pronounced *jine*) and not at all like the Oxford speech that most of us think it was.

An awareness of the difference between our pronunciation and Shakespeare's is crucial in three areas—in accent, or number of syllables (many metrically regular lines may look irregular to us); in rhymes (which may not look like rhymes); and in puns (which may not look like puns). Examples will be useful. Some words that were at least on occasion stressed differently from today are *aspèct*, *còmplete*, *fòrlorn*, *revènue*, and *sepùlcher*. Words that sometimes had an additional syllable are *emp[e]ress*, *Hen[e]ry*, *mon[e]th*, and *villain* (three syllables, *vil-lay-in*). An additional syllable is often found in possessives, like *moon*'s (pronounced *moones*) and in words ending in *-tion* or *-sion*. Words that had one less syllable than they now have are *needle* (pronounced *neel*) and *violet* (pronounced *vilet*). Among rhymes now lost are *one* with *loan*, *love* with *prove*, *beast* with *jest*, *eat* with *great*. (In reading, trust your sense of metrics and your ear, more than your eye.) An example of a pun that has become obliterated by a change in pronunciation is Falstaff's reply to Prince Hal's "Come, tell us your

reason" in *1 Henry IV*: "Give you a reason on compulsion?
If reasons were as plentiful as blackberries, I would give no
man a reason upon compulsion, I" (2.4.237–40). The *ea* in
reason was pronounced rather like a long *a*, like the *ai* in
raisin, hence the comparison with blackberries.

Puns are not merely attempts to be funny; like metaphors
they often involve bringing into a meaningful relationship
areas of experience normally seen as remote. In *2 Henry IV*,
when Feeble is conscripted, he stoically says, "I care not. A
man can die but once. We owe God a death" (3.2.242–43),
punning on *debt*, which was the way *death* was pronounced.
Here an enormously significant fact of life is put into simple
commercial imagery, suggesting its commonplace quality.
Shakespeare used the same pun earlier in *1 Henry IV*, when
Prince Hal says to Falstaff, "Why, thou owest God a death,"
and Falstaff replies, " 'Tis not due yet: I would be loath
to pay him before his day. What need I be so forward with
him that calls not on me?" (5.1.126–29).

Sometimes the puns reveal a delightful playfulness;
sometimes they reveal aggressiveness, as when, replying to
Claudius's "But now, my cousin Hamlet, and my son,"
Hamlet says, "A little more than kin, and less than kind!"
(1.2.64–65). These are Hamlet's first words in the play, and
we already hear him warring verbally against Claudius.
Hamlet's "less than kind" probably means (1) Hamlet is not
of Claudius's family or nature, *kind* having the sense it still
has in our word *mankind*; (2) Hamlet is not kindly (affec-
tionately) disposed toward Claudius; (3) Claudius is not
naturally (but rather unnaturally, in a legal sense incestu-
ously) Hamlet's father. The puns evidently were not put in
as sops to the groundlings; they are an important way of
communicating a complex meaning.

2. *Vocabulary.* A conspicuous difficulty in reading Shakespeare is rooted in the fact that some of his words are no
longer in common use—for example, words concerned with
armor, astrology, clothing, coinage, hawking, horsemanship, law, medicine, sailing, and war. Shakespeare had a
large vocabulary—something near thirty thousand words—
but it was not so much a vocabulary of big words as a
vocabulary drawn from a wide range of life, and it is partly

his ability to call upon a great body of concrete language that gives his plays the sense of being in close contact with life. When the right word did not already exist, he made it up. Among words thought to be his coinages are *accommodation, all-knowing, amazement, bare-faced, countless, dexterously, dislocate, dwindle, fancy-free, frugal, indistinguishable, lackluster, laughable, overawe, premeditated, sea change, star-crossed*. Among those that have not survived are the verb *convive*, meaning to feast together, and *smilet*, a little smile.

Less overtly troublesome than the technical words but more treacherous are the words that seem readily intelligible to us but whose Elizabethan meanings differ from their modern ones. When Horatio describes the Ghost as an "erring spirit," he is saying not that the ghost has sinned or made an error but that it is wandering. Here is a short list of some of the most common words in Shakespeare's plays that often (but not always) have a meaning other than their most usual modern meaning:

'a	he
abuse	deceive
accident	occurrence
advertise	inform
an, and	if
annoy	harm
appeal	accuse
artificial	skillful
brave	fine, splendid
censure	opinion
cheer	(1) face (2) frame of mind
chorus	a single person who comments on the events
closet	small private room
competitor	partner
conceit	idea, imagination
cousin	kinsman
cunning	skillful
disaster	evil astrological influence
doom	judgment
entertain	receive into service

envy	malice
event	outcome
excrement	outgrowth (of hair)
fact	evil deed
fancy	(1) love (2) imagination
fell	cruel
fellow	(1) companion (2) low person (often an insulting term if addressed to someone of approximately equal rank)
fond	foolish
free	(1) innocent (2) generous
glass	mirror
hap, haply	chance, by chance
head	army
humor	(1) mood (2) bodily fluid thought to control one's psychology
imp	child
intelligence	news
kind	natural, acting according to nature
let	hinder
lewd	base
mere(ly)	utter(ly)
modern	commonplace
natural	a fool, an idiot
naughty	(1) wicked (2) worthless
next	nearest
nice	(1) trivial (2) fussy
noise	music
policy	(1) prudence (2) stratagem
presently	immediately
prevent	anticipate
proper	handsome
prove	test
quick	alive
sad	serious
saw	proverb
secure	without care, incautious
silly	innocent

sensible	capable of being perceived by the senses
shrewd	sharp
so	provided that
starve	die
still	always
success	that which follows
tall	brave
tell	count
tonight	last night
wanton	playful, careless
watch	keep awake
will	lust
wink	close both eyes
wit	mind, intelligence

All glosses, of course, are mere approximations; sometimes one of Shakespeare's words may hover between an older meaning and a modern one, and as we have seen, his words often have multiple meanings.

3. Grammar. A few matters of grammar may be surveyed, though it should be noted at the outset that Shakespeare sometimes made up his own grammar. As E.A. Abbott says in *A Shakespearian Grammar,* "Almost any part of speech can be used as any other part of speech": a noun as a verb ("he childed as I fathered"); a verb as a noun ("She hath made compare"); or an adverb as an adjective ("a seldom pleasure"). There are hundreds, perhaps thousands, of such instances in the plays, many of which at first glance would not seem at all irregular and would trouble only a pedant. Here are a few broad matters.

Nouns: The Elizabethans thought the *-s* genitive ending for nouns (as in *man's*) derived from *his*; thus the line " 'gainst the count his galleys I did some service," for "the count's galleys."

Adjectives: By Shakespeare's time adjectives had lost the endings that once indicated gender, number, and case. About the only difference between Shakespeare's adjectives and ours is the use of the now redundant *more* or *most* with the comparative ("some more fitter place") or superlative

("This was the most unkindest cut of all"). Like double comparatives and double superlatives, double negatives were acceptable; Mercutio "will not budge for no man's pleasure."

Pronouns: The greatest change was in pronouns. In Middle English *thou, thy,* and *thee* were used among familiars and in speaking to children and inferiors; *ye, your,* and *you* were used in speaking to superiors (servants to masters, nobles to the king) or to equals with whom the speaker was not familiar. Increasingly the "polite" forms were used in all direct address, regardless of rank, and the accusative *you* displaced the nominative *ye.* Shakespeare sometimes uses *ye* instead of *you,* but even in Shakespeare's day *ye* was archaic, and it occurs mostly in rhetorical appeals.

Thou, thy, and *thee* were not completely displaced, however, and Shakespeare occasionally makes significant use of them, sometimes to connote familiarity or intimacy and sometimes to connote contempt. In *Twelfth Night* Sir Toby advises Sir Andrew to insult Cesario by addressing him as *thou:* "If thou thou'st him some thrice, it shall not be amiss" (3.2.46–47). In *Othello* when Brabantio is addressing an unidentified voice in the dark he says, "What are you?" (1.1.91), but when the voice identifies itself as the foolish suitor Roderigo, Brabantio uses the contemptuous form, saying, "I have charged thee not to haunt about my doors" (93). He uses this form for a while, but later in the scene, when he comes to regard Roderigo as an ally, he shifts back to the polite *you,* beginning in line 163, "What said she to you?" and on to the end of the scene. For reasons not yet satisfactorily explained, Elizabethans used *thou* in addresses to God—"O God, thy arm was here," the king says in *Henry V* (4.8.108)—and to supernatural characters such as ghosts and witches. A subtle variation occurs in *Hamlet.* When Hamlet first talks with the Ghost in 1.5, he uses *thou,* but when he sees the Ghost in his mother's room, in 3.4, he uses *you,* presumably because he is now convinced that the Ghost is not a counterfeit but is his father.

Perhaps the most unusual use of pronouns, from our point of view, is the neuter singular. In place of our *its, his* was often used, as in "How far that little candle throws *his* beams." But the use of a masculine pronoun for a neuter noun came to seem unnatural, and so *it* was used for the possessive as well as the nominative: "The hedge-sparrow fed the cuckoo so long / That it had it head bit off by it young." In the late sixteenth century the possessive form *its* developed, apparently by analogy with the *-s* ending used to indicate a genitive noun, as in *book*'s, but *its* was not yet common usage in Shakespeare's day. He seems to have used *its* only ten times, mostly in his later plays. Other usages, such as "you have seen Cassio and she together" or the substitution of *who* for *whom*, cause little problem even when noticed.

Verbs, Adverbs, and Prepositions: Verbs cause almost no difficulty: The third person singular present form commonly ends in *-s*, as in modern English (e.g., "He blesses"), but sometimes in *-eth* (Portia explains to Shylock that mercy "blesseth him that gives and him that takes"). Broadly speaking, the *-eth* ending was old-fashioned or dignified or "literary" rather than colloquial, except for the words *doth, hath,* and *saith*. The *-eth* ending (regularly used in the King James Bible, 1611) is very rare in Shakespeare's dramatic prose, though not surprisingly it occurs twice in the rather formal prose summary of the narrative poem *Lucrece*. Sometimes a plural subject, especially if it has collective force, takes a verb ending in *-s*, as in "My old bones aches." Some of our strong or irregular preterites (such as *broke*) have a different form in Shakespeare (*brake*); some verbs that now have a weak or regular preterite (such as *helped*) in Shakespeare have a strong or irregular preterite (*holp*). Some adverbs that today end in *-ly* were not inflected: "grievous sick," "wondrous strange." Finally, prepositions often are not the ones we expect: "We are such stuff as dreams are made on," "I have a king here to my flatterer."

Again, none of the differences (except meanings that have substantially changed or been lost) will cause much difficulty. But it must be confessed that for some elliptical passages there is no widespread agreement on meaning. Wise editors resist saying more than they know, and when they are uncertain they add a question mark to their gloss.

Shakespeare's Theater

In Shakespeare's infancy, Elizabethan actors performed wherever they could—in great halls, at court, in the courtyards of inns. These venues implied not only different audiences but also different playing conditions. The innyards must have made rather unsatisfactory theaters: on some days they were unavailable because carters bringing goods to London used them as depots; when available, they had to be rented from the innkeeper. In 1567, presumably to avoid such difficulties, and also to avoid regulation by the Common Council of London, which was not well disposed toward theatricals, one John Brayne, brother-in-law of the carpenter turned actor James Burbage, built the Red Lion in an eastern suburb of London. We know nothing about its shape or its capacity; we can say only that it may have been the first building in Europe constructed for the purpose of giving plays since the end of antiquity, a thousand years earlier. Even after the building of the Red Lion theatrical activity continued in London in makeshift circumstances, in marketplaces and inns, and always uneasily. In 1574 the Common Council required that plays and playing places in London be licensed because

> sundry great disorders and inconveniences have been found to ensue to this city by the inordinate haunting of great multitudes of people, specially youth, to plays, interludes, and shows, namely occasion of frays and quarrels, evil practices of incontinency in great inns having chambers and secret places adjoining to their open stages and galleries.

The Common Council ordered that innkeepers who wished licenses to hold performance put up a bond and make contributions to the poor.

The requirement that plays and innyard theaters be licensed, along with the other drawbacks of playing at inns and presumably along with the success of the Red Lion, led James Burbage to rent a plot of land northeast of the city walls, on property outside the jurisdiction of the city. Here he built England's second playhouse, called simply the Theatre. About all that is known of its construction is that it was wood. It soon had imitators, the most famous being the Globe (1599), essentially an amphitheater built across the Thames (again outside the city's jurisdiction), constructed with timbers of the Theatre, which had been dismantled when Burbage's lease ran out.

Admission to the theater was one penny, which allowed spectators to stand at the sides and front of the stage that jutted into the yard. An additional penny bought a seat in a covered part of the theater, and a third penny bought a more comfortable seat and a better location. It is notoriously difficult to translate prices into today's money, since some things that are inexpensive today would have been expensive in the past and vice versa—a pipeful of tobacco (imported, of course) cost a lot of money, about three pennies, and an orange (also imported) cost two or three times what a chicken cost—but perhaps we can get some idea of the low cost of the penny admission when we realize that a penny could also buy a pot of ale. An unskilled laborer made about five or sixpence a day, an artisan about twelve pence a day, and the hired actors (as opposed to the sharers in the company, such as Shakespeare) made about ten pence a performance. A printed play cost five or sixpence. Of course a visit to the theater (like a visit to a baseball game today) usually cost more than the admission since the spectator probably would also buy food and drink. Still, the low entrance fee meant that the theater was available to all except the very poorest people, rather as movies and most athletic events are today. Evidence indicates that the audience ranged from apprentices who somehow managed to scrape together the minimum entrance fee and to escape from their masters for a few hours, to prosperous members of the middle class and aristocrats who paid the additional fee for admission to the galleries. The exact proportion of men to women cannot be determined, but women of all classes certainly were present. Theaters were open every afternoon but Sundays for much of the year, except in times of plague, when they were closed because of fear of infection. By the way, no evidence suggests the presence of toilet facilities. Presumably the patrons relieved themselves by making a quick trip to the fields surrounding the playhouses.

There are four important sources of information about the

structure of Elizabethan public playhouses—drawings, a contract, recent excavations, and stage directions in the plays. Of drawings, only the so-called de Witt drawing (c. 1596) of the Swan—really his friend Aernout van Buchell's copy of Johannes de Witt's drawing—is of much significance. The drawing, the only extant representation of the interior of an Elizabethan theater, shows an amphitheater of three tiers, with a stage jutting from a wall into the yard or

Johannes de Witt, a Continental visitor to London, made a drawing of the Swan theater in about the year 1596. The original drawing is lost; this is Aernout van Buchell's copy of it.

center of the building. The tiers are roofed, and part of the stage is covered by a roof that projects from the rear and is supported at its front on two posts, but the groundlings, who paid a penny to stand in front of the stage or at its sides, were exposed to the sky. (Performances in such a playhouse were held only in the daytime; artificial illumination was not used.) At the rear of the stage are two massive doors; above the stage is a gallery.

The second major source of information, the contract for the Fortune (built in 1600), specifies that although the Globe (built in 1599) is to be the model, the Fortune is to be square, eighty feet outside and fifty-five inside. The stage is to be forty-three feet broad, and is to extend into the middle of the yard, i.e., it is twenty-seven and a half feet deep.

The third source of information, the 1989 excavations of the Rose (built in 1587), indicate that the Rose was fourteen-sided, about seventy-two feet in diameter with an inner yard almost fifty feet in diameter. The stage at the Rose was about sixteen feet deep, thirty-seven feet wide at the rear, and twenty-seven feet wide downstage. The relatively small dimensions and the tapering stage, in contrast to the rectangular stage in the Swan drawing, surprised theater historians and have made them more cautious in generalizing about the Elizabethan theater. Excavations at the Globe have not yielded much information, though some historians believe that the fragmentary evidence suggests a larger theater, perhaps one hundred feet in diameter.

From the fourth chief source, stage directions in the plays, one learns that entrance to the stage was by the doors at the rear (*"Enter one citizen at one door, and another at the other"*). A curtain hanging across the doorway—or a curtain hanging between the two doorways—could provide a place where a character could conceal himself, as Polonius does, when he wishes to overhear the conversation between Hamlet and Gertrude. Similarly, withdrawing a curtain from the doorway could "discover" (reveal) a character or two. Such discovery scenes are very rare in Elizabethan drama, but a good example occurs in *The Tempest* (5.1.171), where a stage direction tells us, *"Here Prospero discovers Ferdinand and Miranda playing at chess."* There was also some sort of playing space "aloft" or "above" to represent, for instance, the top of a city's walls or a room above the street. Doubtless each theater had its own peculiarities, but perhaps we can talk about a "typical" Elizabethan theater if we realize that no theater need exactly fit the description, just as no mother is the average mother with 2.7 children.

This hypothetical theater is wooden, round, or polygonal (in *Henry V* Shakespeare calls it a "wooden *O*") capable of holding some eight hundred spectators who stood in the yard around the projecting elevated stage—these spectators were the "groundlings"—and some fifteen hundred additional spectators who sat in the three roofed galleries. The stage, protected by a "shadow" or "heavens" or roof, is entered from two doors; behind the doors is the "tiring house" (attiring house, i.e., dressing room), and above the stage is some sort of gallery that may sometimes hold spectators but can be used (for example) as the bedroom from which Romeo—according to a stage direction in one text—"goeth down." Some evidence suggests that a throne can be lowered onto the platform stage, perhaps from the "shadow"; certainly characters can descend from the stage through a trap or traps into the cellar or "hell." Sometimes this space beneath the stage accommodates a sound-effects man or musician (in *Antony and Cleopatra* "*music of the hautboys* [oboes] *is under the stage*") or an actor (in *Hamlet* the "*Ghost cries under the stage*"). Most characters simply walk on and off through the doors, but because there is no curtain in front of the platform, corpses will have to be carried off (Hamlet obligingly clears the stage of Polonius's corpse, when he says, "I'll lug the guts into the neighbor room"). Other characters may have fallen at the rear, where a curtain on a doorway could be drawn to conceal them.

Such may have been the "public theater," so called because its inexpensive admission made it available to a wide range of the populace. Another kind of theater has been called the "private theater" because its much greater admission charge (sixpence versus the penny for general admission at the public theater) limited its audience to the wealthy or the prodigal. The private theater was basically a large room, entirely roofed and therefore artificially illuminated, with a stage at one end. The theaters thus were distinct in two ways: One was essentially an amphitheater that catered to the general public; the other was a hall that catered to the wealthy. In 1576 a hall theater was established in Blackfriars, a Dominican priory in London that had been suppressed in 1538 and confiscated by the Crown and thus was not under the city's jurisdiction. All the actors in this Blackfriars theater were boys about eight to thirteen years old (in the public theaters similar boys played female parts; a boy Lady Macbeth played to a man Macbeth). Near the end of this section on Shakespeare's theater we will talk at some length about possible implications in this convention of using boys to play female roles, but for the moment we should say that it doubtless accounts for the relative lack of female roles in Elizabethan drama. Thus, in *A Midsummer Night's Dream*, out of twenty-one named roles, only four are female; in *Hamlet*, out of twenty-four, only two (Gertrude and Ophelia) are female. Many of Shakespeare's characters have fathers but no mothers—for instance, King Lear's daughters. We need not bring in Freud to explain the disparity; a dramatic company had only a few boys in it.

To return to the private theaters, in some of which all of the performers were children—the "eyrie of . . . little eyases" (nest of unfledged hawks—2.2.347–48) which Rosencrantz mentions when he and Guildenstern talk with Hamlet. The theater in Blackfriars had a precarious existence, and ceased operations in 1584. In 1596 James Burbage, who had already made theatrical history by building the Theatre, began to construct a second Blackfriars theater. He died in 1597, and for several years this second Blackfriars theater was used by a troupe of boys, but in 1608 two of Burbage's sons and five other actors (including Shakespeare) became joint operators of the theater, using it in the winter when the open-air Globe was unsuitable. Perhaps such a smaller theater, roofed, artificially illuminated, and with a tradition of a wealthy audience, exerted an influence in Shakespeare's late plays.

Performances in the private theaters may well have had intermissions during which music was played, but in the public theaters the action was probably uninterrupted, flowing from scene to scene almost without a break. Actors would enter, speak, exit, and others would immediately enter and establish (if necessary) the new locale by a few properties and by words and gestures. To indicate that the scene took place at night, a player or two would carry a torch. Here are some samples of Shakespeare establishing the scene:

This is Illyria, lady.   (*Twelfth Night*, 1.2.2)

Well, this is the Forest of Arden.   (*As You Like It*, 2.4.14)

This castle has a pleasant seat; the air
Nimbly and sweetly recommends itself
Unto our gentle senses.   (*Macbeth*, 1.6.1–3)

The west yet glimmers with some streaks of day.

(*Macbeth*, 3.3.5)

Sometimes a speech will go far beyond evoking the minimal setting of place and time, and will, so to speak, evoke the social world in which the characters move. For instance, early in the first scene of *The Merchant of Venice* Salerio suggests an explanation for Antonio's melancholy. (In the following passage, *pageants* are decorated wagons, floats, and *cursy* is the verb "to curtsy," or "to bow.")

Your mind is tossing on the ocean,
There where your argosies with portly sail—
Like signiors and rich burghers on the flood,
Or as it were the pageants of the sea—
Do overpeer the petty traffickers
That cursy to them, do them reverence,
As they fly by them with their woven wings.   (1.1.8–14)

Late in the nineteenth century, when Henry Irving produced the play with elaborate illusionistic sets, the first scene showed a ship moored in the harbor, with fruit vendors and dock laborers, in an effort to evoke the bustling and exotic life of Venice. But Shakespeare's words give us this exotic, rich world of commerce in his highly descriptive language when Salerio speaks of "argosies with portly sail" that fly with "woven wings"; equally important, through Salerio Shakespeare conveys a sense of the orderly, hierarchical society in which the lesser ships, "the petty traffickers," curtsy and thereby "do . . . reverence" to their superiors, the merchant prince's ships, which are "Like signiors and rich burghers."

On the other hand, it is a mistake to think that except for verbal pictures the Elizabethan stage was bare. Although Shakespeare's Chorus in *Henry V* calls the stage an "unworthy scaffold" (Prologue 1.10) and urges the spectators to "eke out our performance with your mind" (Prologue 3.35), there was considerable spectacle. The last act of *Macbeth,* for instance, has five stage directions calling for *"drum and colors,"* and another sort of appeal to the eye is indicated by the stage direction *"Enter Macduff, with Macbeth's head."* Some scenery and properties may have been substantial; doubtless a throne was used, but the pillars supporting the roof would have served for the trees on which Orlando pins his poems in *As You Like It*.

Having talked about the public theater—"this wooden *O*"—at some length, we should mention again that Shakespeare's plays were performed also in other locales. Alvin Kernan, in *Shakespeare, the King's Playwright: Theater in the Stuart Court 1603–1613* (1995) points out that "several of [Shakespeare's] plays contain brief theatrical performances, set always in a court or some noble house. When Shakespeare portrayed a theater, he did not, except for the choruses in *Henry V*, imagine a public theater" (p. 195). (Examples include episodes in *The Taming of the Shrew*, *A Midsummer Night's Dream*, *Hamlet*, and *The Tempest*.)

A Note on the Use of Boy Actors in Female Roles

Until fairly recently, scholars were content to mention that the convention existed; they sometimes also mentioned that it continued the medieval practice of using males in female roles, and that other theaters, notably in ancient Greece and in China and Japan, also used males in female roles. (In classical Noh drama in Japan, males still play the female roles.) Prudery may have been at the root of the academic failure to talk much about the use of boy actors, or maybe there really is not much more to say than that it was a convention of a male-centered culture (Stephen Greenblatt's view, in *Shakespearean Negotiations* [1988]). Further, the very nature of a convention is that it is not thought about: Hamlet is a Dane and Julius Caesar is a Roman, but in Shakespeare's plays they speak English, and we in the audience never give this odd fact a thought. Similarly, a character may speak in the presence of others and we understand, again without thinking about it, that he or she is not heard by the figures on the stage (the aside); a character alone on the stage may speak (the soliloquy), and we do not take the character to be unhinged; in a realistic (box) set, the fourth wall, which allows us to see what is going on, is miraculously missing. The no-nonsense view, then, is that the boy actor was an accepted convention, accepted unthinkingly—just as today we know that Kenneth Branagh is not Hamlet, Al Pacino is not Richard III, and Denzel Washington is not the Prince of Aragon. In this view, the audience takes the performer for the role, and that is that; such is the argument we now make for race-free casting, in which African-Americans and Asians can play roles of persons who lived in medieval Denmark and ancient Rome. But gender perhaps is different, at least today. It is a matter of abundant academic study: The Elizabethan theater is now sometimes called a transvestite theater, and we hear much about cross-dressing.

Shakespeare himself in a very few passages calls attention to the use of boys in female roles. At the end of *As You Like It* the boy who played Rosalind addresses the audience, and says, "O men, . . . if I were a woman, I would kiss as many of you as had beards that pleased me." But this is in the Epilogue; the plot is over, and the actor is stepping out of the play and into the audience's everyday world. A second reference to the practice of boys playing female roles occurs in *Antony and Cleopatra*, when Cleopatra imagines that she and Antony will be the subject of crude plays, her role being performed by a boy:

> The quick comedians
> Extemporally will stage us, and present
> Our Alexandrian revels: Antony
> Shall be brought drunken forth, and I shall see
> Some squeaking Cleopatra boy my greatness.   (5.2.216–20)

In a few other passages, Shakespeare is more indirect. For instance, in *Twelfth Night* Viola, played of course by a boy, disguises herself as a young man and seeks service in the house of a lord. She enlists the help of a Captain, and (by way of explaining away her voice and her beardlessness) says,

> I'll serve this duke
> Thou shalt present me as an eunuch to him.   (1.2.55–56)

In *Hamlet*, when the players arrive in 2.2, Hamlet jokes with the boy who plays a female role. The boy has grown since Hamlet last saw him: "By'r Lady, your ladyship is nearer to heaven than when I saw you last by the altitude of a chopine" (a lady's thick-soled shoe). He goes on: "Pray God your voice . . . be not cracked" (434–38).

Exactly how sexual, how erotic, this material was and is, is now much disputed. Again, the use of boys may have been unnoticed, or rather not thought about—an unexamined convention—by most or all spectators most of the time, perhaps *all* of the time, except when Shakespeare calls the convention to the attention of the audience, as in the passages just quoted. Still, an occasional bit seems to invite erotic thoughts. The clearest example is the name that Rosalind takes in *As You Like It*, Ganymede—the beautiful youth whom Zeus abducted. Did boys dressed to play female roles carry homoerotic appeal for straight men (Lisa Jardine's view, in *Still Harping on Daughters* [1983]), or for gay men, or for some or all women in the audience? Further, when the boy actor played a woman who (for the purposes of the plot) disguised herself as a male, as Rosalind, Viola, and Portia do—so we get a boy playing a woman playing a man—what sort of appeal was generated, and for what sort of spectator?

Some scholars have argued that the convention empowered women by letting female characters display a freedom unavailable in Renaissance patriarchal society; the convention, it is said, undermined rigid gender distinctions. In this view, the convention (along with plots in which female characters for a while disguised themselves as young men) allowed Shakespeare to say what some modern gender critics say: Gender is a constructed role rather than a biological given, something we make, rather than a fixed binary opposition of male and female (see Juliet Dusinberre, in *Shakespeare and the Nature of Women* [1975]). On the other hand, some scholars have maintained that the male disguise assumed by some female characters serves only to reaffirm traditional social distinctions since female characters who don male garb (notably Portia in *The Merchant of Venice* and Rosalind in *As You Like It*) return to their female garb and at least implicitly (these critics say) reaffirm the status quo. (For this last view, see Clara Claiborne Park, in an essay in *The Woman's Part*, ed. Carolyn Ruth Swift Lenz et al. [1980].) Perhaps no one answer is right for all plays; in *As You Like It* cross-dressing empowers Rosalind, but in *Twelfth Night* cross-dressing comically traps Viola.

Shakespeare's Dramatic Language: Costumes, Gestures and Silences; Prose and Poetry

Because Shakespeare was a dramatist, not merely a poet, he worked not only with language but also with costume, sound effects, gestures, and even silences. We have already discussed some kinds of spectacle in the preceding section, and now we will begin with other aspects of visual language; a theater, after all, is literally a "place for seeing." Consider the opening stage direction in *The Tempest*, the first play in the first published collection of Shakespeare's plays: *"A tempestuous noise of thunder and Lightning heard: Enter a Ship-master, and a Boteswain."*

Costumes: What did that shipmaster and that boatswain wear? Doubtless they wore something that identified them as men of the sea. Not much is known about the costumes that Elizabethan actors wore, but at least three points are clear: (1) many of the costumes were splendid versions of contemporary Elizabethan dress; (2) some attempts were made to approximate the dress of certain occupations and of antique or exotic characters such as Romans, Turks, and Jews; (3) some costumes indicated that the wearer was supernatural. Evidence for elaborate Elizabethan clothing can be found in the plays themselves and in contemporary comments about the "sumptuous" players who wore the discarded clothing of noblemen, as well as in account books that itemize such things as "a scarlet cloak with two broad gold laces, with gold buttons down the sides."

The attempts at approximation of the dress of certain occupations and nationalities also can be documented from the plays themselves, and it derives additional confirmation from a drawing of the first scene of Shakespeare's *Titus Andronicus*—the only extant Elizabethan picture of an identifiable episode in a play. (See pp. xxxviii–xxxix.) The drawing, probably done in 1594 or 1595, shows Queen Tamora pleading for mercy. She wears a somewhat medieval-looking robe and a crown; Titus wears a toga and a wreath, but two soldiers behind him wear costumes fairly close to Elizabethan dress. We do not know, however, if the drawing represents an actual stage production in the public theater, or perhaps a private production, or maybe only a reader's visualization of an episode. Further, there is some conflicting evidence: In *Julius Caesar* a reference is made to Caesar's doublet (a close-fitting jacket), which, if taken literally, suggests that even the protagonist did not wear Roman clothing; and certainly the lesser characters, who are said to wear hats, did not wear Roman garb.

It should be mentioned, too, that even ordinary clothing can be symbolic: Hamlet's "inky cloak," for example, sets him apart from the brightly dressed members of Claudius's court and symbolizes his mourning; the fresh clothes that are put on King Lear partly symbolize his return to sanity. Consider, too, the removal of disguises near the end of some plays. For instance, Rosalind in *As You Like It* and Portia and Nerissa in *The Merchant of Venice* remove their male attire, thus again becoming fully themselves.

Gestures and Silences: Gestures are an important part of a dramatist's language. King Lear kneels before his daughter Cordelia for a benediction (4.7.57–59), an act of humility that contrasts with his earlier speeches banishing her and that contrasts also with a comparable gesture, his ironic

kneeling before Regan (2.4.153–55). Northumberland's failure to kneel before King Richard II (3.3.71–72) speaks volumes. As for silences, consider a moment in *Coriolanus*: Before the protagonist yields to his mother's entreaties (5.3.182), there is this stage direction: *"Holds her by the hand, silent."* Another example of "speech in dumbness" occurs in *Macbeth*, when Macduff learns that his wife and children have been murdered. He is silent at first, as Malcolm's speech indicates: "What, man! Ne'er pull your hat upon your brows. Give sorrow words" (4.3.208–09). (For a discussion of such moments, see Philip C. McGuire's *Speechless Dialect: Shakespeare's Open Silences* [1985].)

Of course when we think of Shakespeare's work, we think primarily of his language, both the poetry and the prose.

Prose: Although two of his plays (*Richard II* and *King John*) have no prose at all, about half the others have at least one quarter of the dialogue in prose, and some have notably more: *1 Henry IV* and *2 Henry IV*, about half; *As You Like It*

and *Twelfth Night*, a little more than half; *Much Ado About Nothing*, more than three quarters; and *The Merry Wives of Windsor*, a little more than five sixths. We should remember that despite Molière's joke about M. Jourdain, who was amazed to learn that he spoke prose, most of us do not speak prose. Rather, we normally utter repetitive, shapeless, and often ungrammatical torrents; prose is something very different—a sort of literary imitation of speech at its most coherent.

Today we may think of prose as "natural" for drama; or even if we think that poetry is appropriate for high tragedy we may still think that prose is the right medium for comedy. Greek, Roman, and early English comedies, however, were written in verse. In fact, prose was not generally considered a literary medium in England until the late fifteenth century; Chaucer tells even his bawdy stories in verse. By the end of the 1580s, however, prose had established itself on the English comic stage. In tragedy, Marlowe made some use of prose, not simply in the speeches of clownish servants but even in the speech of a tragic hero, Doctor Faustus. Still, before Shakespeare, prose normally was used in the theater only for special circumstances: (1) letters and proclamations, to set them off from the poetic dialogue; (2) mad characters, to indicate that normal thinking has become disordered; and (3) low comedy, or speeches uttered by clowns even when they are not being comic. Shakespeare made use of these conventions, but he also went far beyond them. Sometimes he begins a scene in prose and then shifts into verse as the emotion is heightened; or conversely, he may shift from verse to prose when a speaker is lowering the emotional level, as when Brutus speaks in the Forum.

Shakespeare's prose usually is not prosaic. Hamlet's prose includes not only small talk with Rosencrantz and Guildenstern but also princely reflections on "What a piece of work is a man" (2.2.312). In conversation with Ophelia, he shifts from light talk in verse to a passionate prose denunciation of women (3.1.103), though the shift to prose here is perhaps also intended to suggest the possibility of madness. (Consult Brian Vickers, *The Artistry of Shakespeare's Prose* [1968].)

Poetry: Drama in rhyme in England goes back to the Middle Ages, but by Shakespeare's day rhyme no longer dominated poetic drama; a finer medium, blank verse (strictly speaking, unrhymed lines of ten syllables, with the stress on every second syllable) had been adopted. But before looking at unrhymed poetry, a few things should be said about the chief uses of rhyme in Shakespeare's plays. (1) A couplet (a pair of rhyming lines) is sometimes used to convey emotional heightening at the end of a blank verse speech; (2) characters sometimes speak a couplet as they leave the stage, suggesting closure; (3) except in the latest plays, scenes fairly often conclude with a couplet, and sometimes, as in *Richard II*, 2.1.145–46, the entrance of a new character within a scene is preceded by a couplet, which wraps up the earlier portion of that scene; (4) speeches of two characters occasionally are linked by rhyme, most notably in *Romeo and Juliet*, 1.5.95–108, where the lovers speak a sonnet between them; elsewhere a taunting reply occasionally rhymes with the previous speaker's last line; (5) speeches with sententious or gnomic remarks are sometimes in rhyme, as in the duke's speech in *Othello* (1.3.199–206); (6) speeches of sardonic mockery are sometimes in rhyme—for example, Iago's speech on women in *Othello* (2.1.146–58)—and they sometimes conclude with an emphatic couplet, as in Bolingbroke's speech on comforting words in *Richard II* (1.3.301–2); (7) some characters are associated with rhyme, such as the fairies in *A Midsummer Night's Dream*; (8) in the early plays, especially *The Comedy of Errors* and *The Taming of the Shrew*, comic scenes that in later plays would be in prose are in jingling rhymes; (9) prologues, choruses, plays-within-the-play, inscriptions, vows, epilogues, and so on are often in rhyme, and the songs in the plays are rhymed.

Neither prose nor rhyme immediately comes to mind when we first think of Shakespeare's medium: It is blank verse, unrhymed iambic pentameter. (In a mechanically exact line there are five iambic feet. An iambic foot consists of two syllables, the second accented, as in *away*; five feet make a pentameter line. Thus, a strict line of iambic pentameter contains ten syllables, the even syllables being stressed more heavily than the odd syllables. Fortunately, Shakespeare usually varies the line somewhat.) The first speech in *A Midsummer Night's Dream*, spoken by Duke Theseus to his betrothed, is an example of blank verse:

> Now, fair Hippolyta, our nuptial hour
> Draws on apace. Four happy days bring in
> Another moon; but, O, methinks, how slow
> This old moon wanes! She lingers my desires,
> Like to a stepdame, or a dowager,
> Long withering out a young man's revenue.   (1.1.1–6)

As this passage shows, Shakespeare's blank verse is not mechanically unvarying. Though the predominant foot is the iamb (as in *apace* or *desires*), there are numerous variations. In the first line the stress can be placed on "fair," as the regular metrical pattern suggests, but it is likely that "Now" gets almost as much emphasis; probably in the second line "Draws" is more heavily emphasized than "on," giving us a trochee (a stressed syllable followed by an unstressed one); and in the fourth line each word in the phrase "This old moon wanes" is probably stressed fairly heavily, conveying by two spondees (two feet, each of two stresses) the oppressive tedium that Theseus feels.

In Shakespeare's early plays much of the blank verse is end-stopped (that is, it has a heavy pause at the end of each line), but he later developed the ability to write iambic pentameter verse paragraphs (rather than lines) that give the illusion of speech. His chief techniques are (1) enjambing, i.e., running the thought beyond the single line, as in the first three lines of the speech just quoted; (2) occasionally replacing an iamb with another foot; (3) varying the position of the chief pause (the caesura) within a line; (4) adding an occasional unstressed syllable at the end of a line, traditionally called a feminine ending; (5) and beginning or ending a speech with a half line.

Shakespeare's mature blank verse has much of the rhythmic flexibility of his prose; both the language, though richly figurative and sometimes dense, and the syntax seem natural. It is also often highly appropriate to a particular character. Consider, for instance, this speech from *Hamlet*, in which Claudius, King of Denmark ("the Dane"), speaks to Laertes:

> And now, Laertes, what's the news with you?
> You told us of some suit. What is't, Laertes?
> You cannot speak of reason to the Dane
> And lose your voice. What wouldst thou beg, Laertes,
> That shall not be my offer, not thy asking?   (1.2.42–46)

Notice the short sentences and the repetition of the name "Laertes," to whom the speech is addressed. Notice, too, the shift from the royal "us" in the second line to the more intimate "my" in the last line, and from "you" in the first three lines to the more intimate "thou" and "thy" in the last two lines. Claudius knows how to ingratiate himself with Laertes.

For a second example of the flexibility of Shakespeare's blank verse, consider a passage from *Macbeth*. Distressed by the doctor's inability to cure Lady Macbeth and by the imminent battle, Macbeth addresses some of his remarks to the doctor and others to the servant who is arming him. The entire speech, with its pauses, interruptions, and irresolution (in "Pull't off, I say," Macbeth orders the servant to remove the armor that the servant has been putting on him), catches Macbeth's disintegration. (In the first line, *physic* means "medicine," and in the fourth and fifth lines, *cast the water* means "analyze the urine.")

> Throw physic to the dogs, I'll none of it.
> Come, put mine armor on. Give me my staff.
> Seyton, send out.—Doctor, the thanes fly from me.—
> Come, sir, dispatch. If thou couldst, doctor, cast
> The water of my land, find her disease
> And purge it to a sound and pristine health,
> I would applaud thee to the very echo,
> That should applaud again.—Pull't off, I say.—
> What rhubarb, senna, or what purgative drug,
> Would scour these English hence? Hear'st thou of them?
>
> (5.3.47–56)

Blank verse, then, can be much more than unrhymed iambic pentameter, and even within a single play Shakespeare's blank verse often consists of several styles, depending on the speaker and on the speaker's emotion at the moment.

The Play Text as a Collaboration

Shakespeare's fellow dramatist Ben Jonson reported that the actors said of Shakespeare, "In his writing, whatsoever he penned, he never blotted out line," i.e., never crossed out material and revised his work while composing. None of Shakespeare's plays survives in manuscript (with the possible exception of a scene in *Sir Thomas More*), so we cannot fully evaluate the comment, but in a few instances the published work clearly shows that he revised his manuscript. Consider the following passage (shown here in facsimile) from the best early text of *Romeo and Juliet*, the Second Quarto (1599):

Ro. Would I were sleepe and peace so sweet to rest
The grey eyde morne smiles on the frowning night,
Checkring the Easterne Clouds with streaks of light,
And darknesse fleckted like a drunkard reeles,
From forth daies pathway, made by *Tytans* wheeles.
Hence will I to my ghostly Friers close cell,
His helpe to craue, and my deare hap to tell.

                                                    Exit.

Enter Frier alone with a basket.   (night,
Fri. The grey-eyed morne smiles on the frowning
Checking the Easterne clowdes with streaks of light:
And fleckeld darknesse like a drunkard reeles,
From forth daies path, and *Titans* burning wheeles:
Now ere the sun aduance his burning eie,

Romeo rather elaborately tells us that the sun at dawn is
dispelling the night (morning is smiling, the eastern clouds
are checked with light, and the sun's chariot—Titan's
wheels—advances), and he will seek out his spiritual father,
the Friar. He exits and, oddly, the Friar enters and says pretty
much the same thing about the sun. Both speakers say that
"the gray-eyed morn smiles on the frowning night," but there
are small differences, perhaps having more to do with the
business of printing the book than with the author's
composition: For Romeo's "checkring," "fleckted," and
"pathway," we get the Friar's "checking," "fleckeld," and
"path." (Notice, by the way, the inconsistency in Elizabethan
spelling: Romeo's "clouds" become the Friar's "clowdes.")
    Both versions must have been in the printer's copy, and it
seems safe to assume that both were in Shakespeare's manuscript. He must have written one version—let's say he first
wrote Romeo's closing lines for this scene—and then he
decided, no, it's better to give this lyrical passage to the
Friar, as the opening of a new scene, but he neglected to
delete the first version. Editors must make a choice, and they
may feel that the reasonable thing to do is to print the text as
Shakespeare intended it. But how can we know what he
intended? Almost all modern editors delete the lines from

Romeo's speech, and retain the Friar's lines. They don't do this because they know Shakespeare's intention, however. They give the lines to the Friar because the first published version (1597) of *Romeo and Juliet* gives only the Friar's version, and this text (though in many ways inferior to the 1599 text) is thought to derive from the memory of some actors, that is, it is thought to represent a performance, not just a script. Maybe during the course of rehearsals Shakespeare—an actor as well as an author—unilaterally decided that the Friar should speak the lines; if so (remember that we don't know this to be a fact) his final intention was to give the speech to the Friar. Maybe, however, the actors talked it over and settled on the Friar, with or without Shakespeare's approval. On the other hand, despite the 1597 version, one might argue (if only weakly) on behalf of giving the lines to Romeo rather than to the Friar, thus: (1) Romeo's comment on the coming of the daylight emphasizes his separation from Juliet, and (2) the figurative language seems more appropriate to Romeo than to the Friar. Having said this, in the Signet edition we have decided in this instance to draw on the evidence provided by earlier text and to give the lines to the Friar, on the grounds that since Q1 reflects a production, in the theater (at least on one occasion) the lines were spoken by the Friar.

A playwright sold a script to a theatrical company. The script thus belonged to the company, not the author, and author and company alike must have regarded this script not as a literary work but as the basis for a play that the actors would create on the stage. We speak of Shakespeare as the author of the plays, but readers should bear in mind that the texts they read, even when derived from a single text, such as the First Folio (1623), are inevitably the collaborative work not simply of Shakespeare with his company—doubtless during rehearsals the actors would suggest alterations—but also with other forces of the age. One force was governmental censorship. In 1606 parliament passed "an Act to restrain abuses of players," prohibiting the utterance of oaths and the name of God. So where the earliest text of *Othello* gives us "By heaven" (3.3.106), the first Folio gives "Alas," presumably reflecting the compliance of stage practice with the law. Similarly, the 1623 version of *King Lear* omits the oath "Fut" (probably from "By God's foot") at 1.2.142, again presumably reflecting the line as it was spoken on the stage. Editors who seek to give the reader the play that Shakespeare initially conceived—the "authentic" play conceived by the solitary Shakespeare— probably will restore the missing oaths and references to God. Other editors, who see the play as a collaborative work, a construction made not only by Shakespeare but also by actors and compositors and even government censors, may claim that what counts is the play as it was actually performed. Such editors regard the censored text as legitimate, since it is the play that was (presumably) finally put on. A performed text, they argue, has more historical reality than a text produced by an editor who has sought to get at what Shakespeare initially wrote. In this view, the text of a play is rather like the script of a film; the script is not the film, and the play text is not the performed play. Even if we want to talk about the play that Shakespeare "intended," we will find ourselves talking about a script that he handed over to a company with the intention that it be implemented by actors. The "intended" play is the one that the actors—we might almost say "society"—would help to construct.

Further, it is now widely held that a play is also the work of readers and spectators, who do not simply receive meaning, but who create it when they respond to the play. This idea is fully in accord with contemporary post-structuralist critical thinking, notably Roland Barthes's "The Death of the Author," in *Image-Music-Text* (1977) and Michel Foucault's "What Is an Author?," in *The Foucault Reader* (1984). The gist of the idea is that an author is not an isolated genius; rather, authors are subject to the politics and other social structures of their age. A dramatist especially is a worker in a collaborative project, working most obviously with actors—parts may be written for particular actors—but working also with the audience. Consider the words of Samuel Johnson, written to be spoken by the actor David Garrick at the opening of a theater in 1747:

> The stage but echoes back the public voice;
> The drama's laws, the drama's patrons give,
> For we that live to please, must please to live.

The audience—the public taste as understood by the playwright—helps to determine what the play is. Moreover, even members of the public who are not part of the playwright's immediate audience may exert an influence through censorship. We have already glanced at governmental censorship, but there are also other kinds. Take one of Shakespeare's most beloved characters, Falstaff, who appears in three of Shakespeare's plays, the two parts of *Henry IV* and *The Merry Wives of Windsor*. He appears with this name in the earliest printed version of the first of these plays, *1 Henry IV*, but we know that Shakespeare originally called him (after an historical figure) Sir John Oldcastle. Oldcastle appears in Shakespeare's source (partly reprinted in the Signet edition of *1 Henry IV*), and a trace of the name survives in Shakespeare's play, 1.2.43–44, where Prince Hal punningly addresses Falstaff as "my old lad of the castle." But for some reason—perhaps because the family of the historical Oldcastle complained—Shakespeare had to change the name. In short, the play as we have it was (at least in this detail) subject to some sort of censorship. If we think that a text should present what we take to be the author's intention, we probably will want to replace *Falstaff* with *Oldcastle*. But if we recognize that a play is a collaboration, we may welcome the change, even if it was forced on Shakespeare. Somehow *Falstaff*, with its hint of *false-staff*, i.e., inadequate prop, seems just right for this fat knight who, to our delight, entertains the young prince with untruths. We can go as far as saying that, at least so far as a play is concerned, an insistence on the author's original intention (even if we could know it) can sometimes impoverish the text.

The tiny example of Falstaff's name illustrates the point that the text we read is inevitably only a version—something in effect produced by the collaboration of the playwright with his actors, audiences, compositors, and editors—of a fluid text that Shakespeare once wrote, just as the *Hamlet* that we see on the screen starring Kenneth Branagh is not the *Hamlet* that Shakespeare saw in an open-air playhouse starring Richard Burbage. *Hamlet* itself, as we shall note in a moment, also exists in several versions. It is not surprising that there is now much talk about the *instability* of Shakespeare's texts.

Because he was not only a playwright but was also an actor and a shareholder in a theatrical company, Shakespeare probably was much involved with the translation of the play from a manuscript to a stage production. He may or may not have done some rewriting during rehearsals, and he may or may not have been happy with cuts that were made. Some plays, notably *Hamlet* and *King Lear*, are so long' that it is most unlikely that the texts we read were acted in their entirety. Further, for both of these plays we have more than one early text that demands consideration. In *Hamlet*, the Second Quarto (1604) includes some two hundred lines not found in the Folio (1623). Among the passages missing from the Folio are two of Hamlet's reflective speeches, the "dram of evil" speech (1.4.13–38) and "How all occasions do inform against me" (4.4.32–66). Since the Folio has more numerous and often fuller stage directions, it certainly looks as though in the Folio we get a theatrical version of the play, a text whose cuts were probably made—this is only a hunch, of course—not because Shakespeare was changing his conception of Hamlet but because the playhouse demanded a modified play. (The problem is complicated, since the Folio not only cuts some of the Quarto but adds some material. Various explanations have been offered.)

Or take an example from *King Lear*. In the First and Second Quarto (1608, 1619), the final speech of the play is given to Albany, Lear's surviving son-in-law, but in the First Folio version (1623), the speech is given to Edgar. The Quarto version is in accord with tradition—usually the highest-ranking character in a tragedy speaks the final words. Why does the Folio give the speech to Edgar? One possible answer is this: The Folio version omits some of Albany's speeches in earlier scenes, so perhaps it was decided (by Shakespeare? by the players?) not to give the final lines to so pale a character. In fact, the discrepancies are so many between the two texts, that some scholars argue we do not simply have texts showing different theatrical productions. Rather, these scholars say, Shakespeare substantially revised the play, and we really have two versions of *King Lear* (and of *Othello* also, say some)—two different plays—not simply two texts, each of which is in some ways imperfect.

In this view, the 1608 version of *Lear* may derive from Shakespeare's manuscript, and the 1623 version may derive from his later revision. The Quartos have almost three hundred lines not in the Folio, and the Folio has about a hundred lines not in the Quartos. It used to be held that all the texts were imperfect in various ways and from various causes—some passages in the Quartos were thought to have been set from a manuscript that was not entirely legible, other passages were thought to have been set by a compositor who was new to setting plays, and still other passages were thought to have been provided by an actor who misremembered some of the lines. This traditional view held that an editor must draw on the Quartos and the Folio in order to get Shakespeare's "real" play. The new argument holds (although not without considerable strain) that we have two authentic plays, Shakespeare's early version (in the Quarto) and Shakespeare's—or his theatrical company's—revised version (in the Folio). Not only theatrical demands but also Shakespeare's own artistic sense, it is argued, called for extensive revisions. Even the titles vary: Q1 is called *True Chronicle Historie of the life and death of King Lear and his three Daughters*, whereas the Folio text is called *The Tragedie of King Lear*. To combine the two texts in order to produce what the editor thinks is the play that Shakespeare intended to write is, according to this view, to produce a text that is false to the history of the play. If the new view is correct, and we do have texts of two distinct versions of *Lear* rather than two imperfect versions of one play, it supports in a textual way the poststructuralist view that we cannot possibly have an unmediated vision of (in this case) a play by Shakespeare; we can only recognize a plurality of visions.

Editing Texts

Though eighteen of his plays were published during his lifetime, Shakespeare seems never to have supervised their publication. There is nothing unusual here; when a playwright sold a play to a theatrical company he surrendered his ownership to it. Normally a company would not publish the play, because to publish it meant to allow competitors to acquire the piece. Some plays did get published: Apparently hard-up actors sometimes pieced together a play for a publisher; sometimes a company in need of money sold a play; and sometimes a company allowed publication of a play that no longer drew audiences. That Shakespeare did not concern himself with publication is not remarkable; of his contemporaries, only Ben Jonson carefully supervised the publication of his own plays.

In 1623, seven years after Shakespeare's death, John Heminges and Henry Condell (two senior members of Shakespeare's company, who had worked with him for about twenty years) collected his plays—published and unpublished—into a large volume, of a kind called a folio. (A folio is a volume consisting of large sheets that have been folded once, each sheet thus making two leaves, or four pages. The size of the page of course depends on the size of the sheet—a folio can range in height from twelve to sixteen inches, and in width from eight to eleven; the pages in the 1623 edition of Shakespeare, commonly called the First Folio, are approximately thirteen inches tall and eight inches wide.) The eighteen plays published during Shakespeare's lifetime had been issued one play per volume in small formats called quartos. (Each sheet in a quarto has been folded twice, making four leaves, or eight pages, each page being about nine inches tall and seven inches wide, roughly the size of a large paperback.)

Heminges and Condell suggest in an address "To the great variety of readers" that the republished plays are presented in better form than in the quartos:

> Before you were abused with diverse stolen and surreptitious copies, maimed and deformed by the frauds and stealths of injurious impostors that exposed them; even those, are now offered to your view cured and perfect of their limbs, and all the rest absolute in their numbers, as he [i.e., Shakespeare] conceived them.

There is a good deal of truth to this statement, but some of the quarto versions are better than others; some are in fact preferable to the Folio text.

Whoever was assigned to prepare the texts for publication

in the first Folio seems to have taken the job seriously and yet not to have performed it with uniform care. The sources of the texts seem to have been, in general, good unpublished copies or the best published copies. The first play in the collection, *The Tempest*, is divided into acts and scenes, has unusually full stage directions and descriptions of spectacle, and concludes with a list of the characters, but the editor was not able (or willing) to present all of the succeeding texts so fully dressed. Later texts occasionally show signs of carelessness: in one scene of *Much Ado About Nothing* the names of actors, instead of characters, appear as speech prefixes, as they had in the Quarto, which the Folio reprints; proofreading throughout the Folio is spotty and apparently was done without reference to the printer's copy; the pagination of *Hamlet* jumps from 156 to 257. Further, the proofreading was done while the presses continued to print, so that each play in each volume contains a mix of corrected and uncorrected pages.

Modern editors of Shakespeare must first select their copy; no problem if the play exists only in the Folio, but a considerable problem if the relationship between a Quarto and the Folio—or an early Quarto and a later one—is unclear. In the case of *Romeo and Juliet*, the First Quarto (Q1), published in 1597, is vastly inferior to the Second (Q2), published in 1599. The basis of Q1 apparently is a version put together from memory by some actors. Not surprisingly, it garbles many passages and is much shorter than Q2. On the other hand, occasionally Q1 makes better sense than Q2. For instance, near the end of the play, when the parents have assembled and learned of the deaths of Romeo and Juliet, in Q2 the Prince says (5.3.208–9),

Come, *Montague;* for thou art early vp
To see thy sonne and heire, now earling downe.

The last three words of this speech surely do not make sense, and many editors turn to Q1, which instead of "now earling downe" has "more early downe." Some modern editors take only "early" from Q1, and print "now early down"; others take "more early," and print "more early down." Further, Q1 (though, again, quite clearly a garbled and abbreviated text) includes some stage directions that are not found in Q2, and today many editors who base their text on Q2 are glad to add these stage directions, because the directions help to give us a sense of what the play looked like on Shakespeare's stage. Thus, in 4.3.58, after Juliet drinks the potion, Q1 gives us this stage direction, not in Q2: *"She falls upon her bed within the curtains."*

In short, an editor's decisions do not end with the choice of a single copy text. First of all, editors must reckon with Elizabethan spelling. If they are not producing a facsimile, they probably modernize the spelling, but ought they to preserve the old forms of words that apparently were pronounced quite unlike their modern forms—*lanthorn, alablaster*? If they preserve these forms are they really preserving Shakespeare's forms or perhaps those of a compositor in the printing house? What is one to do when one finds *lanthorn* and *lantern* in adjacent lines? (The editors of this series in general, but not invariably, assume that words should be spelled in their modern form, unless, for instance, a rhyme is involved.) Elizabethan punctuation, too, presents problems. For example, in the First Folio, the only text for the play, Macbeth rejects his wife's idea that he can wash the blood from his hand (2.2.60–62):

> No: this my Hand will rather
> The multitudinous Seas incarnardine,
> Making the Greene one, Red.

Obviously an editor will remove the superfluous capitals, and will probably alter the spelling to "incarnadine," but what about the comma before "Red"? If we retain the comma, Macbeth is calling the sea "the green one." If we drop the comma, Macbeth is saying that his bloody hand will make the sea ("the Green") *uniformly* red.

An editor will sometimes have to change more than spelling and punctuation. Macbeth says to his wife (1.7.46–47):

> I dare do all that may become a man,
> Who dares no more, is none.

For two centuries editors have agreed that the second line is unsatisfactory, and have emended "no" to "do": "Who dares do more is none." But when in the same play (4.2.21–22) Ross says that fearful persons

> Floate vpon a wilde and violent Sea
> Each way, and moue,

need we emend the passage? On the assumption that the compositor misread the manuscript, some editors emend "each way, and move" to "and move each way"; others emend "move" to "none" (i.e., "Each way and none"). Other editors, however, let the passage stand as in the original. The editors of the Signet Classic Shakespeare have restrained themselves from making abundant emendations. In their minds they hear Samuel Johnson on the dangers of emendation: "I have adopted the Roman sentiment, that it is more honorable to save a citizen than to kill an enemy." Some departures (in addition to spelling, punctuation, and lineation) from the copy text have of course been made, but the original readings are listed in a note following the play, so that readers can evaluate the changes for themselves.

Following tradition, the editors of the Signet Classic Shakespeare have prefaced each play with a list of characters, and throughout the play have regularized the names of the speakers. Thus, in our text of *Romeo and Juliet*, all speeches by Juliet's mother are prefixed "Lady Capulet," although the 1599 Quarto of the play, which provides our copy text, uses at various points seven speech tags for this one character: *Capu. Wi.* (i.e., Capulet's wife), *Ca. Wi., Wi., Wife, Old La.* (i.e., Old Lady), *La.,* and *Mo.* (i.e., Mother). Similarly, in *All's Well That Ends Well*, the character whom we regularly call "Countess" is in the Folio (the copy text) variously identified as *Mother, Countess, Old Countess, Lady,* and *Old Lady.* Admittedly there is some loss in regularizing, since the various prefixes may give us a hint of the way Shakespeare (or a scribe who copied Shakespeare's manuscript) was thinking of the character in a particular scene—for instance, as a mother, or as an old lady. But too much can be made of these differing prefixes, since the social relationships implied are *not* always relevant to the given scene.

We have also added line numbers and in many cases act and scene divisions as well as indications of locale at the beginning of scenes. The Folio divided most of the plays into acts and some into scenes. Early eighteenth-century editors increased the divisions. These divisions, which provide a convenient way of referring to passages in the plays, have been retained, but when not in the text chosen as the basis for the Signet Classic text they are enclosed within square brackets, [ ], to indicate that they are editorial additions. Similarly, though no play of Shakespeare's was equipped with indications of the locale at the heads of scene divisions, locales have here been added in square brackets for the convenience of readers, who lack the information that costumes, properties, gestures, and scenery afford to spectators. Spectators can tell at a glance they are in the throne room, but without an editorial indication the reader may be puzzled for a while. It should be mentioned, incidentally, that there are a few authentic stage directions—perhaps Shakespeare's, perhaps a prompter's—that suggest locales, such as *"Enter Brutus in his orchard,"* and *"They go up into the Senate house."* It is hoped that the bracketed additions in the Signet text will provide readers with the sort of help provided by these two authentic directions, but it is equally hoped that the reader will remember that the stage was not loaded with scenery.

Shakespeare on the Stage

Each volume in the Signet Classic Shakespeare includes a brief stage (and sometimes film) history of the play. When we read about earlier productions, we are likely to find them eccentric, obviously wrongheaded—for instance, Nahum Tate's version of *King Lear*, with a happy ending, which held the stage for about a century and a half, from the late seventeenth century until the end of the first quarter of the nineteenth. We see engravings of David Garrick, the greatest actor of the eighteenth century, in eighteenth-century garb as King Lear, and we smile, thinking how absurd the production must have been. If we are more thoughtful, we say, with the English novelist L. P. Hartley, "The past is a foreign country: they do things differently there." But if the eighteenth-century staging is a foreign country, what of the plays of the late sixteenth and seventeenth centuries? A foreign language, a foreign theater, a foreign audience.

Probably all viewers of Shakespeare's plays, beginning with Shakespeare himself, at times have been unhappy with the plays on the stage. Consider three comments about production that we find in the plays themselves, which suggest Shakespeare's concerns. The Chorus in *Henry V* complains that the heroic story cannot possibly be adequately staged:

> But pardon, gentles all,
> The flat unraisèd spirits that hath dared
> On this unworthy scaffold to bring forth
> So great an object. Can this cockpit hold
> The vasty fields of France? Or may we cram
> Within this wooden *O* the very casques
> That did affright the air at Agincourt?
>
> . . . .
>
> Piece out our imperfections with your thoughts.
>
> (Prologue 1.8–14,23)

Second, here are a few sentences (which may or may not represent Shakespeare's own views) from Hamlet's longish lecture to the players:

> Speak the speech, I pray you, as I pronounced it to you, trippingly on the tongue. But if you mouth it, as many of our players do, I had as lief the town crier spoke my lines. . . . O, it offends me to the soul to hear a robustious periwig-pated fellow tear a passion to tatters, to very rags, to split the ears of the groundlings. . . . And let those that play your clowns speak no more than is set down for them, for there be of them that will themselves laugh, to set on some quantity of barren spectators to laugh too, though in the meantime some necessary question of the play be then to be considered. That's villainous and shows a most pitiful ambition in the fool that uses it. (3.2.1–47)

Finally, we can quote again from the passage cited earlier in this introduction, concerning the boy actors who played the female roles. Cleopatra imagines with horror a theatrical version of her activities with Antony:

> The quick comedians
> Extemporally will stage us, and present
> Our Alexandrian revels: Antony
> Shall be brought drunken forth, and I shall see
> Some squeaking Cleopatra boy my greatness
> I' th' posture of a whore.   (5.2.216–21)

It is impossible to know how much weight to put on such passages—perhaps Shakespeare was just being modest about his theater's abilities—but it is easy enough to think that he was unhappy with some aspects of Elizabethan production. Probably no production can fully satisfy a playwright, and for that matter, few productions can fully satisfy *us;* we regret this or that cut, this or that way of costuming the play, this or that bit of business.

One's first thought may be this: Why don't they just do "authentic" Shakespeare, "straight" Shakespeare, the play as Shakespeare wrote it? But as we read the plays—words written to be performed—it sometimes becomes clear that we do not know *how* to perform them. For instance, in *Antony and Cleopatra* Antony, the Roman general who has succumbed to Cleopatra and to Egyptian ways, says, "The nobleness of life / Is to do thus" (1.1.36–37). But what is "thus"? Does Antony at this point embrace Cleopatra? Does he embrace and kiss her? (There are, by the way, very few scenes of kissing on Shakespeare's stage, possibly because boys played the female roles.) Or does he make a sweeping gesture, indicating the Egyptian way of life?

This is not an isolated example; the plays are filled with lines that call for gestures, but we are not sure what the gestures should be. *Interpretation* is inevitable. Consider a passage in *Hamlet*. In 3.1, Polonius persuades his daughter, Ophelia, to talk to Hamlet while Polonius and Claudius eavesdrop. The two men conceal themselves, and Hamlet encounters Ophelia. At 3.1.131 Hamlet suddenly says to her, "Where's your father?" Why does Hamlet, apparently out of nowhere—they have not been talking about Polonius—ask this question? Is this an example of the "antic disposition" (fantastic behavior) that Hamlet earlier (1.5.172) had told Horatio and others—including us—he would display? That is, is the question about the whereabouts of her father a seemingly irrational one, like his earlier question (3.1.103) to Ophelia, "Ha, ha! Are you honest?" Or, on the other hand, has Hamlet (as in many productions) suddenly glimpsed Polonius's foot protruding from beneath a drapery at the rear? That is, does Hamlet ask the question because he has suddenly seen something suspicious and now is testing Ophelia? (By the way, in productions that do give Hamlet a physical cue, it is almost always Polonius rather than Claudius who provides the clue. This itself is an act of interpretation on the part of the director.) Or (a third possibility) does Hamlet get a clue from Ophelia, who inadvertently betrays the spies by nervously glancing at their place of hiding? This is the interpretation used in the BBC television version, where Ophelia glances in fear toward the hiding place just after Hamlet says "Why wouldst thou be a breeder of sinners?" (121–22). Hamlet, realizing that he is being observed, glances here and there *before* he asks "Where's your father?" The question thus is a climax to what he has been doing while speaking the preceding lines. Or (a fourth interpretation) does Hamlet suddenly, without the aid of any clue whatsoever, intuitively (insightfully, mysteriously, wonderfully) sense that someone is spying? Directors must decide, of course—and so must readers.

Recall, too, the preceding discussion of the texts of the plays, which argued that the texts—though they seem to be before us in permanent black on white—are unstable. The Signet text of *Hamlet*, which draws on the Second Quarto (1604) and the First Folio (1623) is considerably longer than any version staged in Shakespeare's time. Our version, even if spoken very briskly and played without any intermission, would take close to four hours, far beyond "the two hours' traffic of our stage" mentioned in the Prologue to *Romeo and Juliet*. (There are a few contemporary references to the duration of a play, but none mentions more than three hours.) Of Shakespeare's plays, only *The Comedy of Errors*, *Macbeth*, and *The Tempest* can be done in less than three hours without cutting. And even if we take a play that exists only in a short text, *Macbeth*, we cannot claim that we are experiencing the very play that Shakespeare conceived, partly because some of the Witches' songs almost surely are non-Shakespearean additions, and partly because we are not willing to watch the play performed without an intermission and with boys in the female roles.

Further, as the earlier discussion of costumes mentioned, the plays apparently were given chiefly in contemporary, that is, in Elizabethan dress. If today we give them in the costumes that Shakespeare probably saw, the plays seem not contemporary but curiously dated. Yet if we use our own dress, we find lines of dialogue that are at odds with what we see; we may feel that the language, so clearly not our own, is inappropriate coming out of people in today's dress. A common solution, incidentally, has been to set the plays in the nineteenth century, on the grounds that this attractively distances the plays (gives them a degree of foreignness, allowing for interesting costumes) and yet doesn't put them into a museum world of Elizabethan England.

Inevitably our productions are adaptations, *our* adaptations, and inevitably they will look dated, not in a century but in twenty years, or perhaps even in a decade. Still, we cannot escape from our own conceptions. As the director Peter Brook has said, in *The Empty Space* (1968):

> It is not only the hair-styles, costumes and make-ups that look dated. All the different elements of staging—the shorthands of behavior that stand for emotions; gestures, gesticulations and tones of voice—are all fluctuating on an invisible stock exchange all the time. . . . A living theatre that thinks it can stand aloof from anything as trivial as fashion will wilt. (p. 16)

As Brook indicates, it is through today's hairstyles, costumes, makeup, gestures, gesticulations, tones of voice—this includes our *conception* of earlier hairstyles, costumes, and so forth if we stage the play in a period other than our own—that we inevitably stage the plays.

It is a truism that every age invents its own Shakespeare, just as, for instance, every age has invented its own classical world. Our view of ancient Greece, a slave-holding society

in which even free Athenian women were severely circum-
scribed, does not much resemble the Victorians' view of
ancient Greece as a glorious democracy, just as, perhaps, our
view of Victorianism itself does not much resemble theirs.
We cannot claim that the Shakespeare on our stage is the
true Shakespeare, but in our stage productions we find a
Shakespeare that speaks to us, a Shakespeare that our ances-
tors doubtless did not know but one that seems to us to be the
true Shakespeare—at least for a while.

Our age is remarkable for the wide variety of kinds of
staging that it uses for Shakespeare, but one development
deserves special mention. This is the now common practice
of race-blind or color-blind or nontraditional casting, which
allows persons who are not white to play in Shakespeare.
Previously blacks performing in Shakespeare were limited
to a mere three roles, Othello, Aaron (in *Titus Andronicus*),
and the Prince of Morocco (in *The Merchant of Venice*),
and there were no roles at all for Asians. Indeed, African-
Americans rarely could play even one of these three roles,
since they were not welcome in white companies. Ira
Aldridge (c.1806–1867), a black actor of undoubted talent,
was forced to make his living by performing Shakespeare
in England and in Europe, where he could play not only
Othello but also—in whiteface—other tragic roles such as
King Lear. Paul Robeson (1898–1976) made theatrical history when he played Othello in London in 1930, and there
was some talk about bringing the production to the United
States, but there was more talk about whether American
audiences would tolerate the sight of a black man—a real
black man, not a white man in blackface—kissing and then
killing a white woman. The idea was tried out in summer
stock in 1942, the reviews were enthusiastic, and in the following year Robeson opened on Broadway in a production
that ran an astounding 296 performances. An occasional all-
black company sometimes performed Shakespeare's plays,
but otherwise blacks (and other minority members) were in
effect shut out from performing Shakespeare. Only since
about 1970 has it been common for nonwhites to play major
roles along with whites. Thus, in a 1996–97 production of
Antony and Cleopatra, a white Cleopatra, Vanessa Redgrave, played opposite a black Antony, David Harewood.

Multiracial casting is now especially common at the New York Shakespeare Festival, founded in 1954 by Joseph Papp, and in England, where even siblings such as Claudio and Isabella in *Measure for Measure* or Lear's three daughters may be of different races. Probably most viewers today soon stop worrying about the lack of realism, and move beyond the color of the performers' skin to the quality of the performance.

Nontraditional casting is not only a matter of color or race; it includes sex. In the past, occasionally a distinguished woman of the theater has taken on a male role—Sarah Bernhardt (1844–1923) as Hamlet is perhaps the most famous example—but such performances were widely regarded as eccentric. Although today there have been some performances involving cross-dressing (a drag *As You Like It* staged by the National Theatre in England in 1966 and in the United States in 1974 has achieved considerable fame in the annals of stage history), what is more interesting is the casting of women in roles that traditionally are male but that need not be. Thus, a 1993–94 English production of *Henry V* used a woman—*not* cross-dressed—in the role of the governor of Harfleur. According to Peter Holland, who reviewed the production in *Shakespeare Survey* 48 (1995), "having a female Governor of Harfleur feminized the city and provided a direct response to the horrendous threat of rape and murder that Henry had offered, his language and her body in direct connection and opposition" (p. 210). Ten years from now the device may not play so effectively, but today it speaks to us. Shakespeare, born in the Elizabethan Age, has been dead nearly four hundred years, yet he is, as Ben Jonson said, "not of an age but for all time." We must understand, however, that he is "for all time" precisely because each age finds in his abundance something for itself and something of itself.

And here we come back to two issues discussed earlier in this introduction—the instability of the text and, curiously, the Bacon/Oxford heresy concerning the authorship of the plays. *Of course* Shakespeare wrote the plays, and we should daily fall on our knees to thank him for them—and yet there is something to the idea that he is not their only author. Every editor, every director and actor, and every reader to some degree shapes them, too, for when we edit, direct, act, or read, we inevitably become Shakespeare's collaborator and re-create the plays. The plays, one might say, are so cunningly contrived that they guide our responses, tell us how we ought to feel, and make a mark on us, but (for better or for worse) we also make a mark on them.

—SYLVAN BARNET
Tufts University

Introduction

Samuel Johnson found the story of *As You Like It* "wild and pleasing," the dialogue "sprightly," but regretted Shakespeare's "hastening to the end of his work," especially because it meant suppressing the "dialogue between the usurper and the hermit" and thereby losing "an opportunity of exhibiting a moral lesson." From the eighteenth century on, critics have often said that Shakespeare's craftsmanship in *As You Like It* is poor. G. B. Shaw, perhaps with tongue in cheek, in *The Dark Lady of the Sonnets* has Will Shakespear say to Queen Elizabeth: "I have also stole from a book of idle wanton tales two of the most damnable foolishnesses in the world, in the one of which a woman goeth in man's attire and maketh impudent love to her swain, who pleaseth the groundlings by overthrowing a wrestler.... I have writ these to save my friends from penury, yet shewing my scorn for such follies and for them that praise them by calling the one As You Like It, meaning that it is not as *I* like it."

Some critics have complained of inconsistencies in the plotting. From several speeches in the play, it would appear that Duke Senior has been banished to the Forest of Arden for a long time, but other speeches suggest that his banishment is recent. In the first scene of the play Shakespeare gives the name Jaques to the middle son of Sir Rowland de Boys, but this Jaques does not appear until the close of the play and his speeches are simply marked "Second Brother." In the meantime we have heard much from another Jaques, the melancholy Jaques, who is one of Duke Senior's retainers. Two characters called by the same name can make for some confusion. These bits of carelessness, if that is what they are, are not unusual in Shakespeare and not peculiar to this play. What is unusual is the extraordinary dispatch with which the plot unfolds. Almost everything that is to happen, happens in the first act; murders are attempted, ribs are cracked, and several major characters are packed off to the Forest of Arden. In the ensuing acts Shakespeare scarcely concerns himself with the troubles that were introduced in the first act. Except for three short scenes we are always in Arden, where the dangers we are chiefly aware of are falling in love or being worsted in a discussion. So that the audience may go home, the two villains are reported to have been converted and four pairs of lovers are lined up to be wed.

Shakespeare has certainly handled the narrative expeditiously. It is very much as if he were eager to be in Arden to "fleet the time carelessly as they did in the golden world." We cannot regret that he missed the "opportunity of exhibiting a moral lesson." Nor can we regret that he gave himself a holiday from the intricate plotting that marks what seems to be the play anterior to *As You Like It*, *Much Ado About Nothing*. Who has not looked at his or her watch during the last act of a well-made plot and sighed to think of the knots still to be untied? We had rather be in Arden where the wicked are converted by fiat and lovers marry in half-dozen lots.

The plot moves swiftly in the beginning of *As You Like It* (and then stands almost still until the fifth act) because the interest of the play is not intended to arise out of the action or situation. And, as William Hazlitt has remarked, it does not. The play is chiefly concerned with two enduring human illusions—the pastoral ideal, or the dream of a simple life, and the ideal of romantic love. These are given an extremely complex representation through dialogue and contrasting relationships. The plot creates the conditions for this representation. The characters are given reason to wander in the woodland, the proper setting in which to develop the theme of pastoralism. Four diverse pairs are caused to fall in love and their contrasting romances will exemplify the varieties of love. Rosalind, given a double identity, can spoof love and yet be a lover. The plot does very well what it is designed to do.

The motives of the chief characters in *As You Like It* are as simple and abrupt as the action of the play, and they could surely be put in evidence by those who think the play a piece of indifferent craftsmanship. Oliver would see an end to his brother Orlando. Why? "For my soul, yet I know not why, hates nothing more than he" (1.1.157–59). Duke Frederick, the usurper who has banished Duke Senior, would now banish Rosalind. The reason? "Grounded upon no other argument / But that the people praise her for her virtues" (1.2. 269–70). In her scenes with Orlando, Rosalind is in no danger; thus her original reason for pretending to be a man does not apply. Yet she does pretend, and it is only her disguise that prevents their immediate marriage. How is so crucial a decision motivated? "I will speak to him like a saucy lackey, and under that habit play the knave with him" (3.2.292–93). Which is to say that she did it because she would do it.

In *As You Like It* each action follows directly from the uncomplicated nature of the person acting. It is his natural wickedness that impels Oliver to hate Orlando, and it is wickedness that causes Frederick to banish Rosalind. Antonio, in Shakespeare's *The Tempest*, is another younger brother who banishes his elder brother (Prospero) and usurps the dukedom. But Antonio's case is more complex than Frederick's, since, while the usurpation is not justified, there is the excuse that Prospero had neglected his duties as a ruler, and Antonio, Prospero's delegate, through the exercise of ducal power, came to believe (as a liar may come to believe his lie) that he was in fact the Duke. But neither Rosalind nor Duke Senior is culpable, and Duke Frederick's usurpation is not said to result from any such interesting state of mind as Antonio's. Duke Frederick's crimes derive from his nature alone. In *As You Like It* a good nature is as unfailingly manifest as a bad one. Because their hearts are blithe, Celia and Rosalind are able to go into exile saying: "Now go in we content / To liberty, and not to banishment" (1.3.135–36). Because his nature is noble, Duke Senior can say "Sweet are the uses of adversity" and can find "good in everything" (2.1.12, 17). The good in this play will be good

lxvi INTRODUCTION

whatever the occasion seems to warrant and the evil, at first, will be evil. Of Shakespeare's comedies only *The Comedy of Errors* makes so simple a connection between temperament and action. *The Comedy of Errors* is a farce, but *As You Like It* is not.

Englishmen in the Renaissance liked to construe life as an interaction of Fortune and Nature, and in *As You Like It* there is some talk of these two goddesses. Rosalind, for instance, instructs Celia: "Fortune reigns in gifts of the world, not in the lineaments of Nature" (1.2.40–41). The only tension in the plot of *As You Like It*, set up in the first act, derives from Fortune's unjust distribution of the gifts of the world. The nobler natures, Duke Senior, Rosalind, Celia, and Orlando, are made to suffer by Fortune while the wicked, Oliver and Duke Frederick, thrive. This imbalance between Fortune and Nature requires resolution. The resolution provided is exceptionally good-humored, far more so than in either *Much Ado About Nothing* or *Twelfth Night*, the two plays with which *As You Like It* is conventionally grouped. The wicked are not punished or left rancorous but are converted and, now as virtuous men, Frederick and Oliver bring the fortunes of Duke Senior, Rosalind, and Orlando into harmony with their natures. Frederick's conversion is accomplished by contact with an old religious man, Oliver's by Orlando's generosity in saving his life. Fortunes are adjusted and dark natures are brightened by the simple impact of virtue. All of this makes a tidy package if Fortune and Nature are conceived as the major forces in life and if these forces are thought to work toward human happiness. Shakespeare's world view was ordinarily more complex.

It is, after all, a kind of innocence to believe that evil is certain men and that goodness is certain other men. And it is the sunniest optimism to believe that the evil are converted by contact with the good. In other plays of Shakespeare, even in the other comedies, temperaments are not so consistently agreeable or disagreeable and resolutions are not so sweet. Orsino, in *Twelfth Night*, is as romantic as Orlando but, where Orlando is vigorous and sensible, Orsino is passive and self-indulgent. Orsino is a generally sympathetic character, but there is something in him which dissatisfies us. Beatrice, in *Much Ado About Nothing*, is as witty as Rosalind but lacks her self-knowledge and is sometimes near to shrewishness. Beatrice is an attractive figure, but she has traits that threaten her happiness. The unsympathetic Malvolio, in *Twelfth Night*, is not transformed by contact with goodness—his last line is: "I'll be revenged on the whole pack of you" (5.1.380). Shakespeare's characters ordinarily mix good with evil. His dramatic tension often derives from irreconcilable desires within each nature rather than from an easily corrected malallocation of Fortune's gifts. The exercise of virtue in some of his plays only stimulates the wicked to further wickedness. Why are these darker principles suspended in *As You Like It*?

The play is intended to suggest that human life can be harmoniously lived; that good sense, love, humor, and a generous disposition will produce happiness. Such a view requires not suppression of, but inattention to, those aspects of motivation and of human relationship that, in life, continually postpone a general harmony. A world that includes irreconcilable personal conflict and unrepenting evil can achieve justice, but not universal happiness.

As You Like It causes us to entertain seriously an illusion—a view of life in which a human wish plays a greater role than reality. Yet the play is far from being continuously idyllic. It is filled with sharp comment and disillusioning fact, particularly in connection with its chief subjects—the simple life and romantic love. These subjects are themselves illusions, conventional illusions, sentimental and foolish. Shakespeare laughs at their conventional treatment, threatens them with contrary views and conflicting facts, but in the end preserves them. The play reconciles the ideal with the actual. But not all of the actual. Shakespeare has looked away from the uglier facts, the ultimate ironies that cannot be integrated into a vision of harmony and happiness. Perhaps it is only *The Tempest* and *The Winter's Tale*, plays written after the great tragedies, that make happiness seem to be generally possible and yet also offer powerful representations of evil and suffering.

If *As You Like It* offered a completely one-sided presentation of harmony, we might be armed against it. But it does not. It presents numerous contrary arguments, and the tension they bring to the debate in Arden lends credence to the resolution. For as long as the play lasts we do not notice that the case against the ideal has not been as strong as it could be; that matters that cannot be reconciled with the ideal have been passed over. It is an illusion that *As You Like It* creates, but an illusion that admits so much of life as to seem possible.

What is the nature of the contrarieties that are reconciled with the pastoral ideal and the ideal of romantic love? Arrived in Arden, Touchstone is asked how he likes the shepherd's life and he replies:

> In respect that it is solitary, I like it very well; but in respect that it is private, it is a very vile life. Now in respect it is in the fields, it pleaseth me well; but in respect it is not in the court, it is tedious. As it is a spare life, look you, it fits my humor well; but as there is no more plenty in it, it goes much against my stomach.   (3.2.15–21)

The expression of one idea stimulates Touchstone to the expression of its contrary. But the ideas are not contraries of objective fact. To be solitary is to be private; to be in the fields is to be not in the court; to lead a spare life is to lead a life that has no more plenty in it. The objective facts are the same and the opposition is one of sentiment. A life spent apart from others can be agreeable or it can be disagreeable. When it is agreeable Touchstone would call it solitary and when it is disagreeable he would call it private. What can cause the same objective condition to change its nature?

Rosalind, who stands in the center of all things in this play, answers our question, but with reference to time rather than life in the forest. "Time," she says, "travels in divers paces with divers persons" (304–5). She goes on to particularize. For a young maid "between the contract of her marriage and the day it is solemnized" time trots too slowly. For a rich man who "hath not the gout" time ambles most agreeably. For a thief on his way to the gallows time goes too swiftly. To generalize Rosalind's remarks: time and life in the forest are apprehended differently by different persons and differently by one person according to his condition of life and state of appetite. Life in the forest and romantic love are ideal in their season but they are not for all seasons. Like a holiday, the Greenwood and true love offer refreshment and regeneration. Prolonged beyond their season they become absurd and distasteful.

Touchstone concludes the speech quoted above by asking Corin: "Hast any philosophy in thee, shepherd?" Corin's response begins: "No more, but that I know the more one sickens, the worse at ease he is" (23–24). At first this reply seems a simple extension of Touchstone's list of on-the-one-hand-this, but-on-the-other-hand-that. Then one realizes that the contrast between Corin's two terms, "the more one sickens" and "the worse at ease," does not follow Touchstone's principle. Corin's terms are objective synonyms as are Touchstone's, but Corin's are also subjective synonyms; to be sick and to be ill at ease are both disagreeable. It seems then that simple Corin has missed the point. Except that sickness is one of the things in life that is not psychologically relative, we never have an appetite for it. It is an absolute evil. Without knowing just how much philosophy the old shepherd had in him, we can take his line as the text for another proposition about *As You Like It*. The relativism of the play's discourse is bounded by a set of moral absolutes that cannot be taken as you like it.

Touchstone's speech concerns the pastoral life and this is a major subject of the conversations in Arden through Act 3, Scene 2. Pastoralism is a place and time apart. It is the restorative Greenwood, where men live in the simplicity of nature. It is a remote Golden Age of harmony and innocence. The modern time and the corrupt court are its antithesis.

Duke Senior realizes the pastoral dream in Arden, finding "books in the running brooks" and "sermons in stones" (2.1.16–17). Amiens sings sweetly of pastoralism in "Under the greenwood tree'" (2.5). But Jaques, who is of another humor, adds a jaundiced verse calling that man a fool who leaves wealth and ease for the wilderness. In course of time it develops that the winds are cold in Arden and the ground is hard, that the deer, "native burghers of this desert city," can be as indifferent to the misery of one of their kind as human beings can be, and that at least one lion and one snake are among the animal life. Life in the forest is not a fixed reality. It is able to produce happiness and able to produce misery. Love has potentialities that are more complex.

Love is revealed directly in the romance of Rosalind and Orlando and, by contrast, in the matching of Silvius with Phebe, and the mating of Audrey with Touchstone. The former pair disenchants us with certain aspects of both pastoralism and love. Silvius at first appears as the lovelorn shepherd of pastoral romance and Phebe as his pouting shepherdess. The sighing and spurning that are so graceful in the classical picture are distasteful when we see a little more of them. Silvius is an abject figure with his "Sweet Phebe, pity me." He shows what love can descend to when it is not combined with good sense. Phebe shows the response such love will inspire in a petulant nature:

> But since that thou canst talk of love so well,
> Thy company, which erst was irksome to me,
> I will endure; and I'll employ thee too.
> But do not look for further recompense
> Than thine own gladness that thou art employed.　(3.5.94–98)

We delight in Rosalind's pungent advice to Phebe: "Sell when you can, you are not for all markets" (60).

For Touchstone love is a ubiquitous human need that seeks an object; it is very like a need that in animals is seasonal. Audrey, falling within his tolerance limits, is taken as an object. Romantic love does not have an object; it has an incomparable inspiration. Orlando, with Rosalind for inspiration, hangs love poems on trees and cries her name throughout the forest. Rosalind, hearing that Celia has seen Orlando, excitedly asks: "What did he when thou saw'st him? What said he? How looked he? Wherein went he? What makes he here?" (3.2.218–20)

The several aspects of love are revealed by the three unlike love affairs. They are revealed also in the running discourse in Arden. There is no scene in which the nature of love is debated. No one keeps to the subject for long; Rosalind ends her catechism of love, in which Orlando and Phebe echo Silvius's exalted sentiments, with: "Pray you, no more of this; 'tis like the howling of Irish wolves against the moon" (5.2.107–8). The discourse is composed of an ironic remark from Touchstone in one scene, something extravagantly amorous from Orlando in another, a joke from Celia in still another. The touches of color, the shading, the points of light, are distributed in time, but they come together to make a rather complex representation.

The disillusioned remarks on love, as on pastoralism, come chiefly from Jaques and Touchstone. Jaques is a man who has traveled and come back a weary malcontent; he stands somewhat detached from life. He is a variation on a familiar kind of stage figure in Shakespeare's day, a type first found in the snarling verse satires written by John Marston and Joseph Hall in the 1590s. After 1599 the type appears in the drama: the bitter critic who defends his railing and abusive language by saying that such attacks as his are the only way to purge the world of its vices. In Act 2, Scene 7, Duke Senior attacks Jaques as if he were a perfect instance of this type, and Jaques responds with the critic's familiar defense. In fact, however, Shakespeare has departed from the type.

Jaques ridicules human ideals, but his attacks are not corrosive and they are entertainingly expressed. Seeing Touchstone and Audrey press in among the country copulatives, Jaques remarks: "There is, sure, another flood toward, and these couples are coming to the ark" (5.4.35–36). That he enjoys hearing Amiens sing argues a certain sweetness of nature, sweeter at any rate than the nature of Shylock, to whom music is the "vile squeaking of the wry-necked fife." The other characters appear to enjoy the company of Jaques as they would not the company of so vicious a satirist as Thersites in *Troilus and Cressida*. Duke Senior loves to be with him in his "sullen fits," for then Jaques is "full of matter" (2.1.67–68), and at the end the Duke urges Jaques to return with him to the court.

The darker potentialities of Jaques are hinted at, but on the whole he is an entertaining fellow and much that he says about love is true—when one is not in love. However, those who are most in love do not envy Jaques' detachment and knowledge of life. Rosalind gives her opinion that those who are either too sad or too merry are "abominable fellows," but between the two she would rather "have a fool to make me merry than experience to make me sad" (4.1.6, 25–27).

In Touchstone we have the fool Rosalind asks for. He sees as little in life to make one sad as Jaques sees to make one merry. Jaques is perhaps a disappointed idealist; but Touchstone is a realist who believes that happiness derives from the satisfactions of the body and from a wit that is quick to see the absurdity and folly in life. As Miss Gardner points out, Touchstone is the great parodist of the play (see, for instance, his love poem to Rosalind following those of Orlando). Touchstone's marriage to Audrey, the simple-minded shepherdess, who in fact is a goatherd, is itself a parody, but one of Shakespeare's making rather than Touchstone's. It is a parody on romance and pastoralism; but it is also the author's comment on the limitations of Touchstone's view of life.

Touchstone and Jaques are alike in their rejection of the ideal and alike therefore in their incompleteness. They show us the ideal as absurdity and sentimentality. Orlando and Rosalind show us romantic love as the best part of life so long as it is understood to be only a part, something that is here and now and should be enjoyed in its time. The play as a whole presents this view, but it is fully articulated by Rosalind alone.

Many romantic lines come from Orlando and Rosalind, and if they were to follow one upon another it would be "to have honey a sauce to sugar" (3.3.29–30). Between sweets, however, there is always something sharp to taste. Sometimes it is provided by Jaques or Touchstone or Celia but most often perhaps by Rosalind as Ganymede. The contrast preserves the flavor. When Orlando swears that he will die of love if he cannot have Rosalind, she gives him her answer: "Men have died from time to time, and worms have eaten them, but not for love" (4.1.101–2).

To speak of contrast is to suggest that one aspect is subordinate to the others; in the extreme case, that it exists only to set off the others. This is not the case with Rosalind's statements about love. Rosalind's line is comically matter-of-fact, very flat, but, after all, true. It checks Orlando just as he is about to move into absurdity. He loves her and it seems to him now that he cannot live without her, but if, in fact, he could not have her he would find reason to live.

Romantic love strains toward eternity. Memory and observation and the foresight they give are its enemies. When Orlando swears that he will love forever and a day, Rosalind responds: "Say 'a day' without the 'ever.' No, no, Orlando. Men are April when they woo, December when they wed. Maids are May when they are maids, but the sky changes when they are wives" (139–42).

On another occasion Rosalind as Ganymede teases Orlando by insisting that he has not the look of the distracted lover. "You are rather point-device in your accouterments, as loving yourself than seeming the lover of any other" (3.2.374–76). Here again she is ridiculing the extremities of romantic love. At times she makes jokes that are bawdy and so reveal a facet of love. Orlando brings his destiny with him, she says. "What's that?" he asks. "Why horns; which such as you are fain to be beholding to your wives for" (4.1.55–57). And when Orlando asks if she will love him—"Ay, and twenty such" (112).

Yet Rosalind is unquestionably in love. To Celia she confides "that thou didst know how many fathom deep I am in love. But it cannot be sounded. My affection hath an unknown bottom, like the Bay of Portugal" (4.2.196–99). Rosalind's disguise as Ganymede and her game with Orlando in which she is supposed to try to cure him of love provide an excuse for the expression of her many unromantic sentiments. But they are not to be understood as ideas invented for Ganymede with no validity for Rosalind. While in love she is able to realize what love may become in time and how it can appear to those who are not in love. She sees all around her subject, combining perspectives in the manner of certain Picasso portraits. In Rosalind's conversation we see love's two eyes and also its profile and the back of its neck.

Rosalind integrates the ideal and the working-day world; love is a good time of life, it is youth and springtime. It is not everything, but in its season it would be folly not to enjoy it. "Come, woo me, woo me," she says, "for now I am in a holiday humor and like enough to consent" (4.1.64–65). Rosalind, whose nature unites ardor and intelligence, synthesizes the ideas of the play.

When so much has been said about cuckoldry and about April turning to December, it may be a little difficult to accept the four marriages of the last scene as a happy ending. But the jokes and the irony and the mockery have been directed primarily at love, not at marriage. Marriage belongs to the institutions of a stable society, and these are never questioned in the play. The responsibility of an elder brother for a younger is the institutional frame that immediately establishes Oliver's villainy. The respect a younger brother owes an elder is the standard that marks Frederick a scoundrel. And the last words about love, the words that assign it to its proper place in an orderly society and prepare for the festive dance at the end, are delivered by Hymen:

> Wedding is great Juno's crown,
>   O blessed bond of board and bed!
> 'Tis Hymen peoples every town;
>   High wedlock then be honorèd.   (5.4.141–44)

Note on the Date

On 4 August 1600, the Lord Chamberlain's Men entered *As You Like It* and three other plays in the Stationers' Register "to be staied" as a way of preventing their unauthorized publication. This entry sets the later limit for the date of *As You Like It*. An earlier limit is set by its absence from the list of Shakespeare's plays given by Francis Meres in *Palladis Tamia* (1598). In one of her speeches Celia says: "Since the little wit that fools have was silenced, the little foolery that wise men have makes a great show" (1.2.85–87). This remark may be a reference to an official order of 1 June 1599, whereby the published writings of a number of satirists were burnt and the future printing of satires prohibited. In view of this possibility and the two limiting dates, the best supposition is that the play was written in the latter half of 1599 or early in 1600.

—ALBERT GILMAN
Boston University

As You Like It

[*Dramatis Personae*

Duke Senior, in banishment in
   the Forest of Arden
Duke Frederick, his brother,
   usurper of the Dukedom
Amiens } lords attending on Duke Senior
Jaques
Le Beau, a courtierp
Charles, a wrestler
Oliver
Jaques } sons of Sir Rowland de Boys
Orlando
Adam } servants to Oliver
Dennis
Touchstone, a clown
Sir Oliver Mar-text, a vicar
Corin } shepherds
Silvius
William, a country fellow
Hymen
Rosalind, daughter to Duke Senior
Celia, daughter to Duke Frederick
Phebe, a shepherdess
Audrey, a country girl
Lords, Pages, Foresters, and Attendants

   Scene: Oliver's house; the court;
      the Forest of Arden]

As You Like It

ACT 1

Scene 1. [*Orchard of Oliver's house.*]

Enter Orlando and Adam.

Orlando. As I remember, Adam, it was upon this fashion
bequeathed me by will but poor a°¹ thousand crowns,
and, as thou say'st, charged my brother on his blessing
to breed me well; and there begins my sadness. My
brother Jaques he keeps at school, and report speaks   5
goldenly of his profit.° For my part, he keeps me
rustically° at home or, to speak more properly, stays
me here at home unkept;° for call you that keeping
for a gentleman of my birth that differs not from the
stalling of an ox? His horses are bred better, for,   10
besides that they are fair° with their feeding, they are
taught their manage,° and to that end riders dearly
hired; but I, his brother, gain nothing under him but
growth, for the which his animals on his dunghills
are as much bound to him as I. Besides this nothing   15
that he so plentifully gives me, the something that

---

¹The degree sign (°) indicates a footnote, which is keyed to the
text by line number. Text references are printed in **boldface** type; the
annotation follows in roman type.
1.1.2 **poor a** a mere   6 **goldenly of his profit** glowingly of his progress
6–7 **keeps me rustically** supports me like a peasant   8 **unkept** uncared
for   11 **fair** handsome   12 **manage** paces

nature gave me his countenance° seems to take from
me. He lets me feed with his hinds,° bars me the place
of a brother, and, as much as in him lies, mines my
20 gentility° with my education. This is it, Adam, that
grieves me; and the spirit of my father, which I think
is within me, begins to mutiny against this servitude.
I will no longer endure it, though yet I know no wise
remedy how to avoid it.

Enter Oliver.

25 *Adam.* Yonder comes my master, your brother.

Orlando. Go apart, Adam, and thou shalt hear how he
will shake me up.°

Oliver. Now, sir, what make you° here?

Orlando. Nothing. I am not taught to make anything.

30 *Oliver.* What mar you then, sir?

Orlando. Marry,° sir, I am helping you to mar that
which God made, a poor unworthy brother of yours,
with idleness.

Oliver. Marry, sir, be better employed, and be naught
35 awhile.°

Orlando. Shall I keep your hogs and eat husks with
them? What prodigal portion have I spent° that I
should come to such penury?

Oliver. Know you where° you are, sir?

40 *Orlando.* O, sir, very well. Here in your orchard.

Oliver. Know you before whom, sir?

Orlando. Ay, better than him I am before knows me. I

---

17 **countenance** behavior   18 **hinds** farm hands   19–20 **mines my gen-
tility** undermines my good birth   27 **shake me up** berate me   28 **make
you** are you doing (in the next line Orlando pretends to take the phrase
to mean "accomplish")   31 **Marry** (an expletive, from "By the Virgin
Mary")   34–35 **be naught awhile** i.e., don't bother me   36–37 **Shall I
. . . spent** (an allusion to the story of the Prodigal Son. See Luke
15:11–32)   39 **where** i.e., in whose presence (Orlando pretends to take it
literally)

know you are my eldest brother, and in the gentle
condition of blood° you should so know me. The
courtesy of nations° allows you my better in that you   45
are the first born, but the same tradition takes not
away my blood were there twenty brothers betwixt
us. I have as much of my father in me as you, albeit
I confess your coming before me is nearer to his
reverence.°   50

Oliver. What, boy!   [*Strikes him.*]

Orlando. Come, come, elder brother, you are too young
in this.   [*Seizes him.*]

Oliver. Wilt thou lay hands on me, villain?°

Orlando. I am no villain. I am the youngest son of Sir   55
Rowland de Boys; he was my father, and he is thrice
a villain that says such a father begot villains. Wert
thou not my brother, I would not take this hand from
thy throat till this other had pulled out thy tongue
for saying so. Thou hast railed on thyself.   60

Adam. Sweet masters, be patient. For your father's
remembrance, be at accord.

Oliver. Let me go, I say.

Orlando. I will not till I please. You shall hear me. My
father charged you in his will to give me good educa-   65
tion. You have trained me like a peasant, obscuring
and hiding from me all gentlemanlike qualities.° The
spirit of my father grows strong in me, and I will no
longer endure it. Therefore allow me such exercises°
as may become a gentleman, or give me the poor   70
allottery° my father left me by testament; with that I
will go buy my fortunes.

43–44 **in the gentle condition of blood** i.e., of the same good blood
45 **courtesy of nations** i.e., sanctioned custom of primogeniture 49–50 **your
coming . . . reverence** i.e., as the eldest son you are head of the family and
therefore entitled to respect   54 **villain** (Oliver uses it in the sense of
"wicked person," but Orlando plays on its other meaning, "low-born
person")   67 **qualities** accomplishments   69 **exercises** occupations   71 **al-
lottery** share

Oliver. And what wilt thou do? Beg when that is spent?
Well, sir, get you in. I will not long be troubled with
75   you. You shall have some part of your will. I pray
you leave me.

Orlando. I will no further offend you than becomes me
for my good.

Oliver. Get you with him, you old dog.

80   *Adam.* Is "old dog" my reward? Most true, I have lost
my teeth in your service. God be with my old master;
he would not have spoke such a word.

                          Exeunt Orlando, Adam.

Oliver. Is it even so? Begin you to grow upon me?° I
will physic your rankness° and yet give no thousand
85   crowns neither. Holla, Dennis!

                          Enter Dennis.

Dennis. Calls your worship?

Oliver. Was not Charles, the Duke's wrestler, here to
speak with me?

Dennis. So please you, he is here at the door and impor-
90   tunes access to you.

Oliver. Call him in. [*Exit Dennis.*] 'Twill be a good way;
and tomorrow the wrestling is.

                          Enter Charles.

Charles. Good morrow to your worship.

Oliver. Good Monsieur Charles, what's the new news
95   at the new court?

Charles. There's no news at the court, sir, but the old
news. That is, the old Duke° is banished by his
younger brother the new Duke, and three or four
loving lords have put themselves into voluntary exile
100   with him, whose lands and revenues enrich the new

---

83 **grow upon me** i.e., usurp my place   84 **physic your rankness** purge
your overgrowth   97 **old Duke** i.e., Duke Senior

Duke; therefore he gives them good leave to wander.

Oliver. Can you tell if Rosalind, the Duke's daughter, be banished with her father?

Charles. O, no; for the Duke's daughter, her cousin, so loves her, being ever from their cradles bred together, *105* that she would have followed her exile, or have died to stay behind her. She is at the court, and no less beloved of her uncle than his own daughter, and never two ladies loved as they do.

Oliver. Where will the old Duke live?   *110*

Charles. They say he is already in the Forest of Arden,° and a many merry men with him; and there they live like the old Robin Hood of England. They say many young gentlemen flock to him every day, and fleet the time carelessly° as they did in the golden world.° *115*

Oliver. What, you wrestle tomorrow before the new Duke?

Charles. Marry, do I, sir; and I came to acquaint you with a matter. I am given, sir, secretly to understand that your younger brother, Orlando, hath a disposi- *120* tion to come in disguised against me to try a fall.° Tomorrow, sir, I wrestle for my credit, and he that escapes me without some broken limb shall acquit him well. Your brother is but young and tender, and for your love I would be loath to foil° him, as I must *125* for my own honor if he come in. Therefore, out of my love to you, I came hither to acquaint you withal, that either you might stay him from his intendment, or brook° such disgrace well as he shall run into, in that it is a thing of his own search and altogether *130* against my will.

---

111 **Forest of Arden** Ardennes (in France; though Shakespeare may also have had in mind the Forest of Arden near his birthplace)   114–115 **fleet the time carelessly** pass the time at ease   115 **golden world** (the Golden Age of classical mythology, when men were free of sin, want, and care)   121 **fall** bout   125 **foil** throw, defeat   129 **brook** endure

Oliver. Charles, I thank thee for thy love to me, which
thou shalt find I will most kindly requite. I had myself notice of my brother's purpose herein and have
135   by underhand means° labored to dissuade him from
it; but he is resolute. I'll tell thee, Charles, it is the
stubbornest young fellow of France; full of ambition,
an envious emulator° of every man's good parts,° a
secret and villainous contriver against me his natural°
140   brother. Therefore use thy discretion. I had as lief°
thou didst break his neck as his finger. And thou
wert best look to't; for if thou dost him any slight
disgrace, or if he do not mightily grace himself on
thee,° he will practice° against thee by poison, entrap
145   thee by some treacherous device, and never leave thee
till he hath ta'en thy life by some indirect means or
other; for, I assure thee, and almost with tears I
speak it, there is not one so young and so villainous
this day living. I speak but brotherly of him, but
150   should I anatomize° him to thee as he is, I must
blush and weep, and thou must look pale and wonder.

Charles. I am heartily glad I came hither to you. If he
come tomorrow, I'll give him his payment. If ever he
go alone° again, I'll never wrestle for prize more. And
155   so God keep your worship.   *Exit.*

Oliver. Farewell, good Charles. Now will I stir this
gamester.° I hope I shall see an end of him; for my
soul, yet I know not why, hates nothing more than
he. Yet he's gentle,° never schooled and yet learned,
160   full of noble device,° of all sorts° enchantingly beloved; and indeed so much in the heart of the world,
and especially of my own people, who best know him,
that I am altogether misprized.° But it shall not be so

---

135 **by underhand means** indirectly   138 **envious emulator** malicious
rival   138 **parts** abilities   139 **natural** blood   140 **lief** soon   143–
144 **grace himself on thee** gain credit at your expense   144 **practice**
plot   150 **anatomize** fully describe   154 **go alone** i.e., walk without
crutches   157 **gamester** athlete, sportsman   159 **gentle** endowed with
the qualities of a gentleman   160 **noble device** gentlemanlike purposes
160 **all sorts** all kinds of people   163 **misprized** scorned

long; this wrestler shall clear all.° Nothing remains
but that I kindle the boy thither, which now I'll go   *165*
about.   *Exit.*

Scene 2. [*The Duke's palace.*]

Enter Rosalind and Celia.

Celia. I pray thee, Rosalind, sweet my coz,° be merry.

Rosalind. Dear Celia, I show more mirth than I am
mistress of, and would you yet I were merrier? Unless
you could teach me to forget a banished father, you
must not learn° me how to remember any extraordi-   *5*
nary pleasure.

Celia. Herein I see thou lov'st me not with the full
weight that I love thee. If my uncle, thy banished
father, had banished thy uncle, the Duke my father,
so° thou hadst been still with me, I could have taught   *10*
my love to take thy father for mine. So wouldst thou,
if the truth of thy love to me were so righteously
tempered° as mine is to thee.

Rosalind. Well, I will forget the condition of my estate°
to rejoice in yours.   *15*

Celia. You know my father hath no child but I, nor
none is like to have; and truly, when he dies, thou
shalt be his heir; for what he hath taken away from
thy father perforce,° I will render thee again in affection. By mine honor, I will, and when I break that   *20*
oath, let me turn monster. Therefore, my sweet Rose,
my dear Rose, be merry.

---

164 **clear all** settle matters   1.2.1 **sweet my coz** my sweet cousin
5 **learn** teach   10 **so** provided that   12–13 **righteously tempered** perfectly composed   14 **estate** fortune   19 **perforce** forcibly

Rosalind. From henceforth I will, coz, and devise sports.
Let me see, what think you of falling in love?

25 *Celia.* Marry, I prithee, do, to make sport withal; but
love no man in good earnest, nor no further in sport
neither than with safety of a pure° blush thou mayst
in honor come off° again.

Rosalind. What shall be our sport then?

30 *Celia.* Let us sit and mock the good housewife° Fortune
from her wheel,° that her gifts may henceforth be
bestowed equally.

Rosalind. I would we could do so, for her benefits are
mightily misplaced, and the bountiful blind woman
35 doth most mistake in her gifts to women.

Celia. 'Tis true, for those that she makes fair,° she scarce
makes honest,° and those that she makes honest, she
makes very ill-favoredly.°

Rosalind. Nay, now thou goest from Fortune's office°
40 to Nature's. Fortune reigns in gifts of the world,° not
in the lineaments of Nature.°

                 Enter [*Touchstone, the*] *Clown.*

Celia. No; when Nature hath made a fair creature, may
she not by Fortune fall into the fire? Though Nature
hath given us wit to flout at Fortune, hath not For-
45 tune sent in this fool to cut off the argument?

Rosalind. Indeed, there is Fortune too hard for Nature
when Fortune makes Nature's natural° the cutter-off
of Nature's wit.

Celia. Peradventure° this is not Fortune's work neither,
50 but Nature's, who perceiveth our natural wits too

---

27 **pure** mere   28 **come off** get away   30 **housewife** (1) woman of the
house (with a spinning wheel) (2) inconstant hussy   31 **wheel** (the wheel
turned by Fortune, blind goddess who distributed her favors at ran-
dom, elevated some men and hurled others down)   36 **fair** beautiful
37 **honest** chaste   38 **ill-favoredly** ugly   39 **office** function   40 **gifts of
the world** e.g., wealth, power   41 **lineaments of Nature** e.g., virtue,
intelligence   47 **natural** born fool, halfwit   49 **Peradventure** perhaps

dull to reason of such goddesses and hath sent this
natural for our whetstone. For always the dullness of
the fool is the whetstone of the wits. How now, wit;
whither wander you?

Touchstone. Mistress, you must come away to your   *55*
father.

Celia. Were you made the messenger?

Touchstone. No, by mine honor, but I was bid to come
for you.

Rosalind. Where learned you that oath, fool?   *60*

Touchstone. Of a certain knight that swore by his honor
they were good pancakes, and swore by his honor the
mustard was naught.° Now I'll stand to it,° the pancakes were naught, and the mustard was good, and
yet was not the knight forsworn.°   *65*

Celia. How prove you that in the great heap of your
knowledge?

Rosalind. Ay, marry, now unmuzzle your wisdom.

Touchstone. Stand you both forth now. Stroke your
chins, and swear by your beards that I am a knave.   *70*

Celia. By our beards, if we had them, thou art.

Touchstone. By my knavery, if I had it, then I were;
but if you swear by that that is not, you are not forsworn; no more was this knight, swearing by his
honor, for he never had any; or if he had, he had   *75*
sworn it away before ever he saw those pancakes or
that mustard.

Celia. Prithee, who is't that thou mean'st?

Touchstone. One that old Frederick, your father, loves.

Celia. My father's love is enough to honor him enough.   *80*

---

63 **naught** worthless   63 **stand to it** swear   65 **forsworn** perjured

Speak no more of him; you'll be whipped for taxa-
tion° one of these days.

Touchstone. The more pity that fools may not speak
wisely what wise men do foolishly.

85 *Celia.* By my troth,° thou sayest true, for since the little
wit that fools have was silenced, the little foolery that
wise men have makes a great show. Here comes
Monsieur Le Beau.

Enter Le Beau.

Rosalind. With his mouth full of news.

90 *Celia.* Which he will put° on us as pigeons feed their
young.

Rosalind. Then shall we be news-crammed.

Celia. All the better; we shall be the more marketable.
Bon jour, Monsieur Le Beau, what's the news?

95 *Le Beau.* Fair princess, you have lost much good sport.

Celia. Sport? Of what color?°

Le Beau. What color, madam? How shall I answer you?

Rosalind. As wit and fortune° will.

Touchstone. Or as the Destinies decrees.°

100 *Celia.* Well said; that was laid on with a trowel.

Touchstone. Nay, if I keep not my rank—

Rosalind. Thou losest thy old smell.

Le Beau. You amaze° me, ladies. I would have told you
of good wrestling, which you have lost the sight of.°

105 *Rosalind.* Yet tell us the manner of the wrestling.

Le Beau. I will tell you the beginning; and if it please
your ladyships, you may see the end, for the best is

82 **taxation** slander   85 **troth** faith   90 **put** force   96 **color** sort   98 **fortune** good luck   99 **decrees** (the ending s was a common variant in the
third person plural)   103 **amaze** confuse   104 **lost the sight of** missed

yet to do,° and here, where you are, they are coming to perform it.

Celia. Well, the beginning that is dead and buried.   *110*

Le Beau. There comes an old man and his three sons—

Celia. I could match this beginning with an old tale.°

Le Beau. Three proper° young men, of excellent growth and presence.

Rosalind. With bills° on their necks, "Be it known unto *115* all men by these presents."°

Le Beau. The eldest of the three wrestled with Charles, the Duke's wrestler; which Charles in a moment threw him and broke three of his ribs, that there is little hope of life in him. So he served the second, and *120* so the third. Yonder they lie, the poor old man, their father, making such pitiful dole° over them that all the beholders take his part with weeping.

Rosalind. Alas!

Touchstone. But what is the sport, monsieur, that the *125* ladies have lost?

Le Beau. Why, this that I speak of.

Touchstone. Thus men may grow wiser every day. It is the first time that ever I heard breaking of ribs was sport for ladies.   *130*

Celia. Or I, I promise thee.

Rosalind. But is there any° else longs to see this broken music° in his sides? Is there yet another dotes upon rib-breaking? Shall we see this wrestling, cousin?

Le Beau. You must, if you stay here, for here is the *135*

---

108 **do** be done   112 **old tale** (Le Beau's story has a "Once upon a time" beginning)   113 **proper** fine   115 **bills** notices   116 **by these presents** (part of the opening formula of many legal documents. Rosalind puns on Le Beau's use of "presence," meaning "bearing")   122 **dole** lamentation 132 **any** anyone   132–133 **broken music** music arranged in parts for different instruments

place appointed for the wrestling, and they are ready to perform it.

Celia. Yonder sure they are coming. Let us now stay and see it.

Flourish.° *Enter Duke [Frederick], Lords, Orlando, Charles, and Attendants.*

140 *Duke Frederick.* Come on. Since the youth will not be entreated, his own peril on his forwardness.

Rosalind. Is yonder the man?

Le Beau. Even he, madam.

Celia. Alas, he is too young; yet he looks successfully.°

145 *Duke Frederick.* How now, daughter and cousin; are you crept hither to see the wrestling?

Rosalind. Ay, my liege, so please you give us leave.

Duke Frederick. You will take little delight in it, I can tell you, there is such odds in the man.° In pity of the
150 challenger's youth I would fain° dissuade him, but he will not be entreated. Speak to him, ladies; see if you can move him.

Celia. Call him hither, good Monsieur Le Beau.

Duke Frederick. Do so. I'll not be by.

155 *Le Beau.* Monsieur the challenger, the princess calls for you.

Orlando. I attend them with all respect and duty.

Rosalind. Young man, have you challenged Charles the wrestler?

160 *Orlando.* No, fair princess. He is the general challenger; I come but in as others do, to try with him the strength of my youth.

Celia. Young gentleman, your spirits are too bold for

---

139 **s.d. Flourish** trumpet fanfare   144 **successfully** able to succeed
149 **such odds in the man** i.e., the odds are all in Charles' favor   150 **fain**
like to

your years. You have seen cruel proof of this man's
strength; if you saw yourself with your eyes or knew　165
yourself with your judgment, the fear of your adventure would counsel you to a more equal enterprise.
We pray you for your own sake to embrace your own
safety and give over this attempt.

Rosalind. Do, young sir. Your reputation shall not　170
therefore be misprized;° we will make it our suit to
the Duke that the wrestling might not go forward.

Orlando. I beseech you, punish me not with your hard
thoughts, wherein I confess me much guilty to deny
so fair and excellent ladies anything. But let your fair　175
eyes and gentle wishes go with me to my trial; wherein
if I be foiled,° there is but one shamed that was never
gracious;° if killed, but one dead that is willing to be
so. I shall do my friends no wrong, for I have none
to lament me; the world no injury, for in it I have　180
nothing. Only in the world I° fill up a place, which
may be better supplied when I have made it empty.

Rosalind. The little strength that I have, I would it were
with you.

Celia. And mine to eke° out hers.　　　　　185

Rosalind. Fare you well. Pray heaven I be deceived in
you!°

Celia. Your heart's desires be with you!

Charles. Come, where is this young gallant that is so
desirous to lie with his mother earth?　　　190

Orlando. Ready, sir; but his will hath in it a more
modest working.°

Duke Frederick. You shall try but one fall.

Charles. No, I warrant your Grace you shall not entreat

---

171 **misprized** despised 177 **foiled** thrown 178 **gracious** graced by
Fortune 181 **Only in the world I** in the world I only 185 **eke** stretch
186–187 **deceived in you** i.e., wrong in my estimation of your strength
192 **modest working** humble aim

195 him to a second that have so mightily persuaded him
     from a first.

Orlando. You mean to mock me after. You should not
have mocked me before. But come your ways.°

Rosalind. Now Hercules be thy speed,° young man!

200 *Celia.* I would I were invisible, to catch the strong
     fellow by the leg.   *Wrestle.*

Rosalind. O excellent young man!

Celia. If I had a thunderbolt in mine eye, I can tell who
should down.   [*Charles is thrown.*] *Shout.*

205 *Duke Frederick.* No more, no more.

Orlando. Yes, I beseech your Grace; I am not yet well
breathed.°

Duke Frederick. How dost thou, Charles?

Le Beau. He cannot speak, my lord.

210 *Duke Frederick.* Bear him away. What is thy name,
     young man?

Orlando. Orlando, my liege, the youngest son of Sir
Rowland de Boys.

Duke Frederick. I would thou hadst been son to some
man else.
215 The world esteemed thy father honorable,
     But I did find him still° mine enemy.
     Thou shouldst have better pleased me with this deed
     Hadst thou descended from another house.
     But fare thee well; thou art a gallant youth;
220 I would thou hadst told me of another father.
                                   Exit Duke, [*with Train*].

Celia. Were I my father, coz, would I do this?

Orlando. I am more proud to be Sir Rowland's son,

---

198 **come your ways** i.e., let's get started   199 **Hercules be thy speed**
may Hercules help you   206–207 **well breathed** fully warmed up
216 **still** always

His youngest son, and would not change that calling°
To be adopted heir to Frederick.

Rosalind. My father loved Sir Rowland as his soul,   225
And all the world was of my father's mind.
Had I before known this young man his son,
I should have given him tears unto° entreaties
Ere he should thus have ventured.

Celia.   Gentle cousin,
Let us go thank him and encourage him.   230
My father's rough and envious disposition
Sticks° me at heart. Sir, you have well deserved;
If you do keep your promises in love
But justly° as you have exceeded all promise,
Your mistress shall be happy.

Rosalind.   Gentleman, [*gives chain*]   235
Wear this for me, one out of suits° with fortune,
That could° give more but that her hand lacks means.
Shall we go, coz?

Celia.   Ay. Fare you well, fair gentleman.

Orlando. Can I not say "I thank you"? My better parts°
Are all thrown down, and that which here stands up   240
Is but a quintain,° a mere lifeless block.

Rosalind. He calls us back. My pride fell with my
    fortunes;
I'll ask him what he would. Did you call, sir?
Sir, you have wrestled well, and overthrown
More than your enemies.

Celia.   Will you go, coz?   245

Rosalind. Have with you.° Fare you well.
                          Exit [*with Celia*].

Orlando. What passion° hangs these weights upon my
    tongue?

223 **calling** name   228 **unto** as well as   232 **Sticks** pains   234 **justly**
exactly   236 **out of suits** in disfavor   237 **could** would   239 **parts** qualities   241 **quintain** wooden post (used for tilting practice)   246 **Have with
you** I'm coming   247 **passion** strong feeling

I cannot speak to her, yet she urged conference.°

Enter Le Beau.

O poor Orlando, thou art overthrown!
250   Or Charles or something weaker masters thee.

Le Beau. Good sir, I do in friendship counsel you
    To leave this place. Albeit you have deserved
    High commendation, true applause, and love,
    Yet such is now the Duke's condition
255   That he misconsters° all that you have done.
    The Duke is humorous.° What he is, indeed,
    More suits you to conceive° than I to speak of.

Orlando. I thank you, sir; and pray you, tell me this:
    Which of the two was daughter of the Duke,
260   That here was at the wrestling?

Le Beau. Neither his daughter, if we judge by manners,
    But yet indeed the taller° is his daughter,
    The other is daughter to the banished Duke,
    And here detained by her usurping uncle
265   To keep his daughter company, whose loves
    Are dearer than the natural bond of sisters.
    But I can tell you that of late this Duke
    Hath ta'en displeasure 'gainst his gentle niece,
    Grounded upon no other argument°
270   But that the people praise her for her virtues
    And pity her for her good father's sake;
    And, on my life, his malice 'gainst the lady
    Will suddenly break forth. Sir, fare you well.
    Hereafter, in a better world° than this,
275   I shall desire more love and knowledge of you.

Orlando. I rest much bounden° to you. Fare you well.
                                              [*Exit Le Beau.*]
    Thus must I from the smoke into the smother,°

---

248 **conference** conversation   255 **misconsters** misinterprets   256 **humorous** moody   257 **conceive** understand   262 **taller** (unless "taller"
is a printer's slip for "smaller," Shakespeare here erred. Rosalind is later
said to be taller)   269 **argument** basis   274 **a better world** better
times   276 **bounden** indebted   277 **smother** smothering smoke (the
idea is: "Out of the frying pan into the fire")

From tyrant Duke unto a tyrant brother.
But heavenly Rosalind! *Exit.*

Scene 3. [*The palace.*]

Enter Celia and Rosalind.

Celia. Why, cousin, why, Rosalind! Cupid have mercy, not a word?

Rosalind. Not one to throw at a dog.

Celia. No, thy words are too precious to be cast away upon curs; throw some of them at me; come, lame 5
me with reasons.

Rosalind. Then there were two cousins laid up, when the one should be lamed with reasons and the other mad° without any.

Celia. But is all this for your father? 10

Rosalind. No, some of it is for my child's father.° O, how full of briers is this working-day world!

Celia. They are but burrs, cousin, thrown upon thee in holiday foolery; if we walk not in the trodden paths, our very petticoats will catch them. 15

Rosalind. I could shake them off my coat; these burrs are in my heart.

Celia. Hem° them away.

Rosalind. I would try, if I could cry "hem,"° and have him. 20

Celia. Come, come, wrestle with thy affections.°

1.3.9 **mad** melancholy   11 **child's father** i.e., future husband, Orlando
18 **Hem** (1) cough (2) tuck   19 **cry "Hem"** clear my throat (with a pun on "him")   21 **affections** feelings

Rosalind. O, they take the part of a better wrestler than
    myself!

Celia. O, a good wish upon you! You will try° in time,
25   in despite of a fall. But turning these jests out of
    service,° let us talk in good earnest. Is it possible on
    such a sudden you should fall into so strong a liking
    with old Sir Rowland's youngest son?

Rosalind. The Duke my father loved his father dearly.

30 *Celia.* Doth it therefore ensue that you should love his
    son dearly? By this kind of chase,° I should hate him,
    for my father hated his father dearly; yet I hate not
    Orlando.

Rosalind. No, faith, hate him not, for my sake.

35 *Celia.* Why should I not? Doth he not deserve well?°

       Enter Duke [Frederick], with Lords.

Rosalind. Let me love him for that,° and do you love
    him because I do. Look, here comes the Duke.

Celia. With his eyes full of anger.

Duke Frederick. Mistress, dispatch you with your safest
    haste
    And get you from our court.

Rosalind.   Me, uncle?

40 *Duke Frederick.*   You, cousin.°
    Within these ten days if that thou beest found
    So near our public court as twenty miles,
    Thou diest for it.

Rosalind.   I do beseech your Grace
    Let me the knowledge of my fault bear with me.
45   If with myself I hold intelligence°

---

24 **try** i.e., chance a bout   25–26 **turning ... service** to stop joking
31 **chase** pursuit (of the argument)   35 **deserve well** i.e., deserve to be
hated (if Rosalind's reasoning is valid, it follows that Celia should hate
Orlando)   36 **for that** i.e., for his virtues (Rosalind takes "deserve well" in
its usual sense)   40 **cousin** kinsman   45 **hold intelligence** communicate

Or have acquaintance with mine own desires,
If that I do not dream or be not frantic,°
As I do trust I am not; then, dear uncle,
Never so much as in a thought unborn
Did I offend your Highness.

Duke Frederick.   Thus do all traitors. 50
If their purgation° did consist in words,
They are as innocent as grace° itself.
Let it suffice thee that I trust thee not.

Rosalind. Yet your mistrust cannot make me a traitor.
Tell me whereon the likelihoods° depends. 55

Duke Frederick. Thou art thy father's daughter, there's
enough.

Rosalind. So was I when your Highness took his duke-
dom;
So was I when your Highness banished him.
Treason is not inherited, my lord,
Or if we did derive it from our friends,° 60
What's that to me? My father was no traitor.
Then, good my liege, mistake me not so much
To think my poverty is treacherous.

Celia. Dear sovereign, hear me speak.

Duke Frederick. Ay, Celia. We stayed° her for your sake, 65
Else had she with her father ranged° along.

Celia. I did not then entreat to have her stay;
It was your pleasure and your own remorse.°
I was too young that time to value her,
But now I know her. If she be a traitor, 70
Why, so am I. We still° have slept together,
Rose at an instant, learned, played, eat° together;
And wheresoe'er we went, like Juno's swans,
Still we went coupled and inseparable.

---

47 **frantic** insane   51 **purgation** clearance   52 **grace** virtue   55 **likeli-**
hoods possibilities   60 **friends** relatives   65 **stayed** kept   66 **ranged**
wandered   68 **remorse** pity   71 **still** always   72 **eat** eaten

Duke Frederick. She is too subtile° for thee; and her
75   smoothness,
        Her very silence and her patience,
        Speak to the people, and they pity her.
        Thou art a fool. She robs thee of thy name,
        And thou wilt show more bright and seem more
            virtuous°
80   When she is gone. Then open not thy lips.
        Firm and irrevocable is my doom°
        Which I have passed upon her; she is banished.

Celia. Pronounce that sentence then on me, my liege;
        I cannot live out of her company.

Duke Frederick. You are a fool. You, niece, provide
85   yourself;
        If you outstay the time, upon mine honor,
        And in the greatness° of my word, you die.
                                        Exit Duke, &c.

Celia. O my poor Rosalind, whither wilt thou go?
        Wilt thou change fathers? I will give thee mine.
90   I charge thee be not thou more grieved than I am.

Rosalind. I have more cause.

Celia.   Thou hast not, cousin.
        Prithee be cheerful. Know'st thou not the Duke
        Hath banished me, his daughter?

Rosalind.   That he hath not.

Celia. No? Hath not? Rosalind lacks then the love
95   Which teacheth thee that thou and I am one.
        Shall we be sund'red, shall we part, sweet girl?
        No, let my father seek another heir.
        Therefore devise with me how we may fly,
        Whither to go, and what to bear with us;
100   And do not seek to take your change° upon you,
        To bear your griefs yourself and leave me out;

---

75 **subtile** crafty   79 **virtuous** full of good qualities   81 **doom** sentence
87 **greatness** power   100 **change** i.e., change of fortune

For, by this heaven, now at our sorrows pale,°
Say what thou canst, I'll go along with thee.

Rosalind. Why, whither shall we go?

Celia. To seek my uncle in the Forest of Arden.   *105*

Rosalind. Alas, what danger will it be to us,
    Maids as we are, to travel forth so far!
    Beauty provoketh thieves sooner than gold.

Celia. I'll put myself in poor and mean° attire
    And with a kind of umber° smirch my face;   *110*
    The like do you; so shall we pass along
    And never stir assailants.

Rosalind.   Were it not better,
    Because that I am more than common° tall,
    That I did suit me all points° like a man?
    A gallant curtle-ax° upon my thigh,   *115*
    A boar-spear in my hand, and, in my heart
    Lie there what hidden woman's fear there will,
    We'll have a swashing° and a martial outside,
    As many other mannish cowards have
    That do outface° it with their semblances.°   *120*

Celia. What shall I call thee when thou art a man?

Rosalind. I'll have no worse a name than Jove's own
    page,
    And therefore look you call me Ganymede.
    But what will you be called?

Celia. Something that hath a reference to my state: *125*
    No longer Celia, but Aliena.°

Rosalind. But, cousin, what if we assayed° to steal
    The clownish fool out of your father's court;
    Would he not be a comfort to our travel?

---

102 **now at our sorrows pale** now pale at our sorrows   109 **mean** lowly
110 **umber** reddish-brown color   113 **common** usually   114 **suit me at
all points** dress myself entirely   115 **curtle-ax** cutlass   118 **swashing**
blustering   120 **outface** bluff   120 **semblances** appearances (of bravery)
126 **Aliena** (Latin: the estranged one)   127 **assayed** attempted

130   *Celia.* He'll go along o'er the wide world with me;
        Leave me alone to woo° him. Let's away
        And get our jewels and our wealth together,
        Devise the fittest time and safest way
        To hide us from pursuit that will be made
135   After my flight. Now go in we content
        To liberty, and not to banishment.   *Exeunt.*

131 **woo** coax

ACT 2

Scene 1. [*The Forest of Arden.*]

Enter Duke Senior, Amiens, and two or three Lords, like Foresters.

Duke Senior. Now, my co-mates and brothers in exile,°
    Hath not old custom made this life more sweet
    Than that of painted pomp? Are not these woods
    More free from peril than the envious court?
    Here feel we not° the penalty of Adam;°   *5*
    The seasons' difference, as° the icy fang
    And churlish° chiding of the winter's wind,
    Which, when it bites and blows upon my body
    Even till I shrink with cold, I smile and say
    "This is no flattery; these are counselors   *10*
    That feelingly° persuade me what I am."
    Sweet are the uses of adversity,
    Which, like the toad, ugly and venomous,
    Wears yet a precious jewel° in his head;
    And this our life, exempt from public haunt,°   *15*
    Finds tongues in trees, books in the running brooks,
    Sermons in stones, and good in everything.

2.1.1 **exile** (accent on second syllable)   5 **feel we not** we do not feel (some editors emend "not" to "but")   5 **penalty of Adam** loss of Eden 6 **as** for example   7 **churlish** harsh   11 **feelingly** (1) through the senses (2) with intensity   14 **a precious jewel** (the fabled toadstone)   15 **public haunt** society

Amiens. I would not change it; happy is your Grace
    That can translate the stubbornness° of fortune
20   Into so quiet and so sweet a style.

Duke Senior. Come, shall we go and kill us venison?
    And yet it irks me the poor dappled fools,°
    Being native burghers° of this desert° city,
    Should, in their own confines, with forkèd heads°
    Have their round haunches gored.

25 *First Lord.*   Indeed, my lord,
    The melancholy Jaques° grieves at that,
    And in that kind° swears you do more usurp
    Than doth your brother that hath banished you.
    Today my Lord of Amiens and myself
30   Did steal behind him as he lay along°
    Under an oak, whose antique root peeps out
    Upon the brook that brawls° along this wood;
    To the which place a poor sequest'red° stag
    That from the hunter's aim had ta'en a hurt
35   Did come to languish; and indeed, my lord,
    The wretched animal heaved forth such groans
    That their discharge did stretch his leathern coat
    Almost to bursting, and the big round tears
    Coursed one another down his innocent nose
40   In piteous chase; and thus the hairy fool,
    Much markèd of° the melancholy Jaques,
    Stood on th' extremest verge of the swift brook,
    Augmenting it with tears.

Duke Senior.   But what said Jaques?
    Did he not moralize° this spectacle?

45 *First Lord.* O, yes, into a thousand similes.
    First, for his weeping into the needless° stream:
    "Poor deer," quoth he, "thou mak'st a testament
    As worldlings do, giving thy sum of more

19 **stubbornness** hardness 22 **fools** simple creatures 23 **burghers** citizens 23 **desert** deserted 24 **forkèd heads** arrows 26 **Jaques** (dissylabic, pronounced "Jā′ kis") 27 **kind** way 30 **along** stretched out 32 **brawls** makes noise 33 **sequest'red** separated 41 **markèd of** noted by 44 **moralize** sermonize 46 **needless** i.e., needing no more water

To that which had too much." Then, being there alone,
Left and abandoned of his velvet° friend: 50
" 'Tis right," quoth he, "thus misery doth part
The flux° of company." Anon a careless° herd,
Full of the pasture, jumps along by him
And never stays to greet him: "Ay," quoth Jaques,
"Sweep on, you fat and greasy citizens, 55
'Tis just the fashion: wherefore do you look°
Upon that poor and broken bankrupt there?"
Thus most invectively he pierceth through
The body of the country, city, court,
Yea, and of this our life, swearing that we 60
Are mere usurpers, tyrants, and what's worse,
To fright the animals and to kill them up
In their assigned° and native dwelling place.

Duke Senior. And did you leave him in this contemplation?

Second Lord. We did, my lord, weeping and commenting 65
Upon the sobbing deer.

Duke Senior.   Show me the place.
I love to cope° him in these sullen fits,
For then he's full of matter.

First Lord. I'll bring you to him straight.°   *Exeunt.*

50 **velvet** i.e., courtierlike (the furry skin on the antlers, or the sleek hide, makes the deer resemble a velvet-clad courtier) 52 **flux** stream 52 **Anon a careless** soon an untroubled 56 **wherefore do you look** why should you bother looking 63 **assigned** allotted (by nature) 67 **cope** encounter 69 **straight** at once

Scene 2. [*The palace.*]

Enter Duke [Frederick], with Lords.

Duke Frederick. Can it be possible that no man saw
      them?
    It cannot be; some villains of my court
    Are of consent and sufferance° in this.

First Lord. I cannot hear of any that did see her.
5   The ladies, her attendants of her chamber,
    Saw her abed, and in the morning early
    They found the bed untreasured of their mistress.

Second Lord. My lord, the roynish° clown at whom so
      oft
    Your Grace was wont to laugh is also missing.
10   Hisperia, the princess' gentlewoman,
    Confesses that she secretly o'erheard
    Your daughter and her cousin much commend
    The parts and graces° of the wrestler
    That did but lately foil the sinewy Charles,
15   And she believes, wherever they are gone,
    That youth is surely in their company.

Duke Frederick. Send to his brother, fetch that gallant
      hither;
    If he be absent, bring his brother to me;
    I'll make him find him. Do this suddenly,°
20   And let not search and inquisition quail°
    To bring again these foolish runaways.   *Exeunt.*

2.2.3 **Are of consent and sufferance** approved and helped 8 **roynish**
scurvy 13 **parts and graces** good qualities and manner 19 **suddenly**
immediately 20 **quail** fail.

Scene 3. [*Oliver's house.*]

Enter Orlando and Adam.

Orlando. Who's there?

Adam. What, my young master, O my gentle master,
    O my sweet master, O you memory
    Of old Sir Rowland, why, what make you° here?
    Why are you virtuous? Why do people love you?   *5*
    And wherefore are you gentle, strong, and valiant?
    Why would you be so fond° to overcome
    The bonny prizer° of the humorous° Duke?
    Your praise is come too swiftly home before you.
    Know you not, master, to some kind of men   *10*
    Their graces serve them but as enemies?
    No more° do yours. Your virtues, gentle master,
    Are sanctified and holy traitors to you.°
    O, what a world is this, when what is comely
    Envenoms him that bears it!   *15*

Orlando. Why, what's the matter?

Adam.   O unhappy youth,
    Come not within these doors; within this roof
    The enemy of all your graces lives.
    Your brother—no, no brother, yet the son—
    Yet not the son, I will not call him son,   *20*
    Of him I was about to call his father—
    Hath heard your praises, and this night he means
    To burn the lodging where you use° to lie.
    And you within it. If he fail of that,

2.3.4 **make you** are you doing   7 **fond** foolish   8 **bonny prizer** stout fighter   8 **humorous** moody, temperamental   12 **No more** no better   12–13 **Your virtues . . . traitors to you** i.e., Orlando's blessed virtues have worked against him   23 **use** are accustomed.

25 He will have other means to cut you off.
I overheard him, and his practices;°
This is no place, this house is but a butchery;°
Abhor it, fear it, do not enter it!

Orlando. Why, whither, Adam, wouldst thou have me
   go?

30 *Adam.* No matter whither, so you come not here.

Orlando. What, wouldst thou have me go and beg my
   food,
Or with a base and boist'rous° sword enforce
A thievish living on the common road?°
This I must do, or know not what to do;
35 Yet this I will not do, do how I can.
I rather will subject me to the malice
Of a diverted° blood and bloody brother.

Adam. But do not so. I have five hundred crowns,
The thrifty hire I saved° under your father,
40 Which I did store to be my foster nurse
When service should in my old limbs lie lame
And unregarded age in corners thrown.
Take that, and he that doth the ravens feed,
Yea, providently caters for the sparrow,°
45 Be comfort to my age. Here is the gold;
All this I give you. Let me be your servant;
Though I look old, yet I am strong and lusty,
For in my youth I never did apply
Hot and rebellious° liquors in my blood,
50 Nor did not with unbashful forehead° woo
The means of weakness and debility;
Therefore my age is as a lusty winter,
Frosty, but kindly. Let me go with you;
I'll do the service of a younger man
55 In all your business and necessities.

---

26 **practices** plots   27 **butchery** slaughterhouse   32 **base and boist'rous**
low and swaggering   33 **common road** highway   37 **diverted** estranged
39 **thrifty hire I saved** wages I carefully saved   43–44 **he that ... the
sparrow** (see Psalms 147:9, Luke 12:6)   49 **rebellious** i.e., causing the
flesh to rebel   50 **unbashful forehead** bold face

Orlando. O good old man, how well in thee appears
   The constant° service of the antique world,°
   When service sweat for duty, not for meed!°
   Thou art not for the fashion of these times,
   Where none will sweat but for promotion,   60
   And having that, do choke their service up
   Even with the having; it is not so with thee.
   But, poor old man, thou prun'st a rotten tree
   That cannot so much as a blossom yield
   In lieu of° all thy pains and husbandry.   65
   But come thy ways, we'll go along together,
   And ere we have thy youthful wages spent,
   We'll light upon some settled low content.°

Adam. Master, go on, and I will follow thee
   To the last gasp with truth and loyalty.   70
   From seventeen years till now almost fourscore
   Here livèd I, but now live here no more;
   At seventeen years many their fortunes seek,
   But at fourscore it is too late a week;°
   Yet fortune cannot recompense me better   75
   Than to die well and not my master's debtor. *Exeunt.*

Scene 4. [*The Forest of Arden.*]

*Enter Rosalind for Ganymede, Celia for Aliena, and
Clown, alias Touchstone.*

Rosalind. O Jupiter, how weary are my spirits!

Touchstone. I care not for my spirits if my legs were
   not weary.

Rosalind. I could find in my heart to disgrace my man's

57 **constant** faithful   57 **the antique world** the past   58 **meed** reward
65 **In lieu of** in return for   68 **low content** humble way of life   74 **week**
time

5   apparel and to cry like a woman; but I must comfort
the weaker vessel, as doublet and hose° ought to
show itself courageous to petticoat. Therefore, courage, good Aliena!

Celia. I pray you bear with me; I cannot go no further.

10   *Touchstone.* For my part, I had rather bear with you
than bear you; yet I should bear no cross° if I did
bear you, for I think you have no money in your
purse.

Rosalind. Well, this is the Forest of Arden.

15   *Touchstone.* Ay, now am I in Arden, the more fool I.
When I was at home, I was in a better place, but
travelers must be content.

Enter Corin and Silvius.

Rosalind. Ay, be so, good Touchstone. Look you, who
comes here, a young man and an old in solemn talk.

20   *Corin.* That is the way to make her scorn you still.

Silvius. O Corin, that thou knew'st how I do love her!

Corin. I partly guess, for I have loved ere now.

Silvius. No, Corin, being old, thou canst not guess,
Though in thy youth thou wast as true a lover
25   As ever sighed upon a midnight pillow.
But if thy love were ever like to mine,
As sure I think did never man love so,
How many actions most ridiculous
Hast thou been drawn to by thy fantasy?°

30   *Corin.* Into a thousand that I have forgotten.

Silvius. O, thou didst then never love so heartily!
If thou rememb'rest not the slightest folly
That ever love did make thee run into,
Thou hast not loved.

2.4.6 **doublet and hose** jacket and breeches   11 **cross** (1) trouble (2)
coin stamped with a cross   29 **fantasy** love (and all its fancies)

Or if thou hast not sat as I do now,   *35*
Wearing° thy hearer in thy mistress's praise,
Thou hast not loved.
Or if thou hast not broke from company
Abruptly, as my passion now makes me,
Thou has not loved.   *40*
O Phebe, Phebe, Phebe!   *Exit.*

Rosalind. Alas, poor shepherd! Searching of° thy wound,
I have by hard adventure° found mine own.

Touchstone. And I mine. I remember, when I was in love
I broke my sword upon a stone and bid him take that   *45*
for coming a-night to Jane Smile; and I remember
the kissing of her batler,° and the cow's dugs that her
pretty chopt° hands had milked; and I remember the
wooing of a peascod° instead of her, from whom I
took two cods, and giving her them again, said with   *50*
weeping tears, "Wear these for my sake." We that
are true lovers run into strange capers; but as all is
mortal in nature, so is all nature in love mortal in
folly.°

Rosalind. Thou speak'st wiser than thou art ware° of.   *55*

Touchstone. Nay, I shall ne'er be ware of mine own wit°
till I break my shins against it.

Rosalind. Jove, Jove! This shepherd's passion
Is much upon my fashion.

Touchstone. And mine, but it grows something stale   *60*
with me.

Celia. I pray you, one of you question yond man
If he for gold will give us any food.
I faint almost to death.

Touchstone. Holla, you clown!°   *65*

---

36 **Wearing** exhausting   42 **Searching of** probing   43 **hard adventure**
bad luck   47 **batler** wooden paddle (used in washing clothes)   48 **chopt**
chapped   49 **peascod** peapod   52–54 **as all is mortal ... folly** just as
everything that lives must die, so all who love inevitably do foolish
things   55 **art ware** know   56 **wit** wisdom   65 **clown** (1) rustic (2) fool

Rosalind. Peace, fool! He's not thy kinsman.

Corin. Who calls?

Touchstone. Your betters, sir.

Corin.   Else are they very wretched.

Rosalind. Peace, I say! Good even to you, friend.

70 *Corin.* And to you, gentle sir, and to you all.

Rosalind. I prithee, shepherd, if that love or gold
      Can in this desert place buy entertainment,°
      Bring us where we may rest ourselves and feed.
      Here's a young maid with travel much oppressed,
      And faints for succor.

75 *Corin.*   Fair sir, I pity her
      And wish, for her sake more than for mine own,
      My fortunes were more able to relieve her;
      But I am shepherd to another man
      And do not shear the fleeces that I graze.
80   My master is of churlish° disposition
      And little recks° to find the way to heaven
      By doing deeds of hospitality.
      Besides, his cote,° his flocks, and bounds of feed°
      Are now on sale, and at our sheepcote now,
85   By reason of his absence, there is nothing
      That you will feed on; but what is, come see,
      And in my voice° most welcome shall you be.

Rosalind. What is he that shall buy his flock and pasture?

Corin. That young swain that you saw here but ere-
      while,°
90   That little cares for buying anything.

Rosalind. I pray thee, if it stand° with honesty,
      Buy thou the cottage, pasture, and the flock,
      And thou shalt have° to pay for it of us.

---

72 **entertainment** food and shelter   80 **churlish** miserly   81 **recks** thinks
83 **cote** cottage   83 **bounds of feed** pastures   87 **in my voice** as far as my
position allows   89 **erewhile** a short while ago   91 **stand** be consistent
93 **have** i.e., have the money

Celia. And we will mend° thy wages. I like this place
   And willingly could waste° my time in it.   95

Corin. Assuredly the thing is to be sold.
   Go with me; if you like upon report
   The soil, the profit, and this kind of life,
   I will your very faithful feeder° be
   And buy it with your gold right suddenly.   *Exeunt.*   100

Scene 5. [*The forest.*]

Enter Amiens, Jaques, and others.

Song.

Amiens.   Under the greenwood tree
                  Who loves to lie with me,
               And turn° his merry note
                  Unto the sweet bird's throat,
            Come hither, come hither, come hither.   5
                  Here shall he see no enemy
               But winter and rough weather.

Jaques. More, more, I prithee more!

Amiens. It will make you melancholy, Monsieur Jaques.

Jaques. I thank it. More, I prithee more! I can suck   10
   melancholy out of a song as a weasel sucks eggs.
   More, I prithee more!

Amiens. My voice is ragged. I know I cannot please you.

Jaques. I do not desire you to please me; I do desire you
   to sing. Come, more, another stanzo! Call you 'em   15
   stanzos?

---

94 **mend** improve   95 **waste** spend   99 **feeder** servant   2.5.3 **turn** at-
tune, adapt

Amiens. What you will, Monsieur Jaques.

Jaques. Nay, I care not for their names; they owe me
nothing.° Will you sing?

20 *Amiens.* More at your request than to please myself.

Jaques. Well then, if ever I thank any man, I'll thank
you. But that they call compliment° is like th' encounter of two dog-apes,° and when a man thanks
me heartily, methinks I have given him a penny and
25   he renders me the beggarly thanks.° Come, sing; and
you that will not, hold your tongues.

Amiens. Well, I'll end the song. Sirs, cover the while;°
the Duke will drink under this tree. He hath been all
this day to look you.

30 *Jaques.* And I have been all this day to avoid him. He
is too disputable for my company. I think of as many
matters as he, but I give heaven thanks and make no
boast of them. Come, warble, come.

Song.

All together here.

Who doth ambition shun
35   And loves to live i' th' sun,
Seeking the food he eats,
     And pleased with what he gets,
Come hither, come hither, come hither.
     Here shall he see no enemy
40   But winter and rough weather.

Jaques. I'll give you a verse to this note° that I made
yesterday in despite of my invention.°

18–19 **names ... nothing** (Jaques plays on the word "name," a term for
the borrower's signature on a loan)   22 **compliment** politeness   23 **dog-
apes** baboons   23–25 **and when ... beggarly thanks** i.e., the hearty
thanks of polite society are no more sincere than the extravagant gratitude
of a beggar given a small coin   27 **cover the while** lay the table in the
meantime   41 **note** tune   42 **in despite of my invention** without using
my imagination

Amiens. And I'll sing it.

Jaques. Thus it goes.
        If it do come to pass   *45*
        That any man turn ass,
        Leaving his wealth and ease
        A stubborn will to please,
        Ducdame,° ducdame, ducdame.
        Here shall he see gross fools as he,   *50*
        An if° he will come to me.

Amiens. What's that "ducdame"?

Jaques. 'Tis a Greek° invocation to call fools into a
circle. I'll go sleep, if I can; if I cannot, I'll rail against
all the first-born of Egypt.°   *55*

Amiens. And I'll go seek the Duke. His banquet° is
prepared.   *Exeunt.*

Scene 6. [*The forest.*]

Enter Orlando and Adam.

Adam. Dear master, I can go no further. O, I die for
food. Here lie I down and measure out my grave.
Farewell, kind master.

Orlando. Why, how now, Adam? No greater heart in
thee? Live a little, comfort° a little, cheer thyself a   *5*

---

49 **Ducdame** (various derivations have been suggested: Romany *dukră
mē* ["I tell fortunes"]; Welsh *dewch 'da mi* ["come with me"]; Latin *duc
ad me* ["bring (him) to me"]; Italian *Duc' da mè* ["duke by myself" or
"duke without a dukedom"]. Probably the word is nonsense) 51 **An if**
if only 53 **Greek** unintelligible 55 **first-born of Egypt** (perhaps "persons of high rank," but perhaps an allusion to life in the Forest of Arden.
Exodus 11,12 reports that when the first-born of Egypt died, the Israelites
were sent into the wilderness) 56 **banquet** light meal 2.6.5 **comfort**
take comfort

little. If this uncouth° forest yield anything savage, I
will either be food for it or bring it for food to thee.
Thy conceit° is nearer death than thy powers. For my
sake be comfortable, hold death awhile at the arm's
10 end. I will here be with thee presently,° and if I bring
thee not something to eat, I will give thee leave to
die; but if thou diest before I come, thou art a mocker
of my labor. Well said; thou look'st cheerly, and I'll
be with thee quickly. Yet thou liest in the bleak air.
15 Come, I will bear thee to some shelter, and thou
shalt not die for lack of a dinner if there live anything
in this desert. Cheerly, good Adam.   *Exeunt.*

Scene 7. [*The forest.*]

Enter Duke Senior, and Lords, like Outlaws.

Duke Senior. I think he be transformed into a beast,
For I can nowhere find him like a man.

First Lord. My lord, he is but even now gone hence;
Here was he merry, hearing of a song.

5 *Duke Senior.* If he, compact of jars,° grow musical,
We shall have shortly discord in the spheres.°
Go seek him; tell him I would speak with him.

Enter Jaques.

First Lord. He saves my labor by his own approach.

Duke Senior. Why, how now, monsieur, what a life is
this,
10 That your poor friends must woo your company?
What, you look merrily.

6 **uncouth** wild   8 **conceit** thought   10 **presently** at once   2.7.5 **compact of jars** made up of discord   6 **discord in the spheres** (Ptolemaic astronomy taught that the planetary spheres produced a ravishing harmony as they revolved)

Jaques. A fool, a fool! I met a fool i' th' forest,
A motley° fool! A miserable world!
As I do live by food, I met a fool
Who laid him down and basked him in the sun   15
And railed on Lady Fortune in good terms,
In good set terms,° and yet a motley fool.
"Good morrow, fool," quoth I. "No, sir," quoth he,
"Call me not fool till heaven hath sent me fortune."°
And then he drew a dial from his poke,°   20
And looking on it with lack-luster eye,
Says very wisely, "It is ten o'clock.
Thus we may see," quoth he, "how the world wags.°
'Tis but an hour ago since it was nine,
And after one hour more 'twill be eleven;   25
And so, from hour to hour,° we ripe and ripe,
And then, from hour to hour, we rot and rot;
And thereby hangs a tale." When I did hear
The motley fool thus moral° on the time,
My lungs began to crow like chanticleer°   30
That fools should be so deep contemplative;
And I did laugh sans intermission°
An hour by his dial. O noble fool,
A worthy fool! Motley's the only wear.

Duke Senior. What fool is this?   35

Jaques. O worthy fool! One that hath been a courtier,
And says, if ladies be but young and fair,
They have the gift to know it. And in his brain,
Which is as dry as the remainder biscuit°
After a voyage, he hath strange places crammed   40
With observation, the which he vents°

---

13 **motley** garbed in the multicolored costume of the court fool (a motley costume is commonly thought to be checkered or patched; Leslie Hotson, in *Shakespeare's Motley,* argues it was of varicolored threads but drab, like a tweed)   17 **set terms** precise phrases   19 **Call me ... fortune** (fortune proverbially favors fools)   20 **dial from his poke** sundial from his pocket   23 **wags** goes   26 **hour to hour** (perhaps with a pun on "whore")   29 **moral** moralize   30 **chanticleer** (traditional name for a rooster)   32 **sans intermission** without stop   39 **remainder biscuit** leftover hardtack   41 **vents** gives forth

In mangled forms. O that I were a fool!
I am ambitious for a motley coat.

Duke Senior. Thou shalt have one.

Jaques.   It is my only suit,°
45   Provided that you weed your better judgments
        Of all opinion that grows rank° in them
        That I am wise. I must have liberty
        Withal, as large a charter° as the wind,
        To blow on whom I please, for so fools have.
50   And they that are most gallèd° with my folly,
        They most must laugh. And why, sir, must they so?
        The why is plain as way to parish church:
        He that a fool doth very wisely hit
        Doth very foolishly, although he smart,
55   Not to seem senseless of the bob.° If not,
        The wise man's folly is anatomized°
        Even by the squand'ring glances° of the fool.
        Invest° me in my motley, give me leave
        To speak my mind, and I will through and through
60   Cleanse the foul body of th' infected world,
        If they will patiently receive my medicine.

Duke Senior. Fie on thee! I can tell what thou wouldst
        do.

Jaques. What, for a counter,° would I do but good?

Duke Senior. Most mischievous foul sin, in chiding sin.
65   For thou thyself hast been a libertine,
        As sensual as the brutish sting° itself;
        And all th' embossèd° sores and headed evils
        That thou with license of free foot° hast caught,
        Wouldst thou disgorge into the general world.

70 *Jaques.* Why, who cries out on pride

---

44 **suit** (1) garment (2) petition   46 **rank** luxuriant   48 **large a charter**
liberal license   50 **gallèd** chafed   55 **senseless of the bob** unaware of
the hit   56 **anatomized** revealed   57 **squand'ring glances** chance hits
58 **Invest** clothe   63 **counter** worthless coin   66 **the brutish sting** lust
67 **embossèd** swollen   68 **license of free foot** complete freedom

That can therein tax any private party?°
Doth it not flow as hugely as the sea
Till that the weary very means do ebb?°
What woman in the city do I name
When that I say the city woman bears   75
The cost° of princes on unworthy shoulders?
Who can come in and say that I mean her,
When such a one as she, such is her neighbor?
Or what is he of basest function°
That says his bravery is not on my cost,°   80
Thinking that I mean him, but therein suits
His folly to the mettle of my speech?°
There then, how then, what then? Let me see wherein
My tongue hath wronged him. If it do him right,
Then he hath wronged himself. If he be free,°   85
Why, then my taxing like a wild goose flies
Unclaimed of any man. But who comes here?

    Enter Orlando [with his sword drawn].

Orlando. Forbear, and eat no more!

Jaques.   Why, I have eat none yet.

Orlando. Nor shalt not, till necessity be served.

Jaques. Of what kind° should this cock come of?   90

Duke Senior. Art thou thus boldened, man, by thy
        distress,
    Or else a rude despiser of good manners,
    That in civility thou seem'st so empty?

Orlando. You touched my vein at first.° The thorny
        point
    Of bare distress hath ta'en from me the show   95

---

71 **tax any private party** criticize any particular person   73 **weary very
means do ebb** (perhaps: "ostentation eventually exhausts the wealth that
makes it possible." Some editors emend "weary" to "wearer's")   76 **cost**
wealth   79 **function** position   80 **his bravery . . . cost** his fine dress is
not paid for by me (and therefore is not my business)   81–82 **suits . . .
my speech** matches his folly to the substance of my words   85 **free** innocent   90 **kind** breed   94 **You touched . . . first** i.e., the Duke's first supposition is correct

Of smooth civility; yet am I inland bred°
And know some nurture.° But forbear, I say!
He dies that touches any of this fruit
Till I and my affairs are answerèd.°

100   *Jaques.* An° you will not be answered with reason,° I
must die.

Duke Senior. What would you have? Your gentleness
shall force
More than your force move us to gentleness.

Orlando. I almost die for food, and let me have it!

Duke Senior. Sit down and feed, and welcome to our
105   table.

Orlando. Speak you so gently? Pardon me, I pray you.
I thought that all things had been savage here,
And therefore put I on the countenance
Of stern commandment. But whate'er you are
110   That in this desert inaccessible,
Under the shade of melancholy boughs,
Lose and neglect the creeping hours of time;
If ever you have looked on better days,
If ever been where bells have knolled° to church,
115   If ever sat at any good man's feast,
If ever from your eyelids wiped a tear
And know what 'tis to pity and be pitied,
Let gentleness my strong enforcement° be;
In the which hope I blush, and hide my sword.

120   *Duke Senior.* True is it that we have seen better days,
And have with holy bell been knolled to church,
And sat at good men's feasts, and wiped our eyes
Of drops that sacred pity hath engend'red;
And therefore sit you down in gentleness,
125   And take upon command° what help we have
That to your wanting° may be minist'red.

96 **inland bred** brought up in civilized society   97 **nurture** good breeding
99 **answerèd** provided for   100 **An** if   100 **reason** (perhaps Jaques puns,
eating a raisin [grape]).   114 **knolled** rung   118 **enforcement** support
125 **upon command** as you wish   126 **wanting** need

Orlando. Then but forbear your food a little while,
　Whiles, like a doe, I go to find my fawn
　And give it food. There is an old poor man
　Who after me hath many a weary step   *130*
　Limped in pure love. Till he be first sufficed,
　Oppressed with two weak evils,° age and hunger,
　I will not touch a bit.

Duke Senior   Go find him out,
　And we will nothing waste° till you return.

Orlando. I thank ye, and be blest for your good comfort! *135*
　　　　　　　　　　　　　　　　　　　[*Exit.*]

Duke Senior. Thou seest we are not all alone unhappy:
　This wide and universal theater
　Presents more woeful pageants° than the scene
　Wherein we play in.

Jaques.   All the world's a stage,
　And all the men and women merely players;   *140*
　They have their exits and their entrances,
　And one man in his time plays many parts,
　His acts being seven ages.° At first, the infant,
　Mewling° and puking in the nurse's arms.
· Then the whining schoolboy, with his satchel   *145*
　And shining morning face, creeping like snail
　Unwillingly to school. And then the lover,
　Sighing like furnace, with a woeful ballad
　Made to his mistress' eyebrow. Then a soldier,
　Full of strange oaths and bearded like the pard,°   *150*
　Jealous° in honor, sudden° and quick in quarrel,
　Seeking the bubble reputation
　Even in the cannon's mouth. And then the justice,
　In fair round belly with good capon lined,°

---

132 **weak evils** evils causing weakness 134 **waste** consume 138 **pageants** scenes 143 **seven ages** (for a survey in art and literature of the image of man's life divided into ages, see Samuel C. Chew, " 'This Strange Eventful History,' " in *Joseph Quincy Adams Memorial Studies,* ed. James G. McManaway *et al.*) 144 **Mewling** bawling 150 **pard** leopard 151 **Jealous** touchy 151 **sudden** rash 154 **capon lined** (perhaps an allusion to the practice of bribing a judge with a capon)

155 With eyes severe and beard of formal cut,
Full of wise saws° and modern instances;°
And so he plays his part. The sixth age shifts
Into the lean and slippered pantaloon,°
With spectacles on nose and pouch on side;
160 His youthful hose,° well saved, a world too wide
For his shrunk shank, and his big manly voice,
Turning again toward childish treble, pipes
And whistles in his° sound. Last scene of all,
That ends this strange eventful history,
165 Is second childishness and mere° oblivion,
Sans teeth, sans eyes, sans taste, sans everything.

Enter Orlando, with Adam.

Duke Senior. Welcome. Set down your venerable burden
And let him feed.

Orlando. I thank you most for him.

Adam.   So had you need.
170 I scarce can speak to thank you for myself.

Duke Senior. Welcome, fall to. I will not trouble you
As yet to question you about your fortunes.
Give us some music; and, good cousin, sing.

Song.

Amiens.
Blow, blow, thou winter wind,
175   Thou art not so unkind°
As man's ingratitude:
Thy tooth is not so keen,
Because thou art not seen,
Although thy breath be rude.
180 Heigh-ho, sing heigh-ho, unto the green holly.
Most friendship is faining,° most loving mere folly:

156 **saws** sayings 156 **modern instances** commonplace examples
158 **pantaloon** ridiculous old man (from Pantalone, a stock figure in
Italian comedy) 160 **hose** breeches 163 **his** its 165 **mere** utter 175
unkind unnatural 181 **faining** longing (perhaps with a pun on
"feigning" [pretending])

Then, heigh-ho, the holly.
This life is most jolly.

Freeze, freeze, thou bitter sky
That dost not bite so nigh   *185*
    As benefits forgot:
Though thou the waters warp,°
Thy sting is not so sharp
    As friend rememb'red not.
Heigh-ho, sing, &c.   *190*

Duke Senior. If that you were the good Sir Rowland's
    son,
As you have whispered faithfully you were,
And as mine eye doth his effigies° witness
Most truly limned° and living in your face,
Be truly welcome hither. I am the Duke   *195*
That loved your father. The residue of your fortune
Go to my cave and tell me. Good old man,
Thou art right welcome, as thy master is.
Support him by the arm. Give me your hand,
And let me all your fortunes understand.   *Exeunt.*   *200*

187 **warp** turn (into ice)   193 **effigies** likeness (accent on second syllable)   194 **limned** depicted

ACT 3

Scene 1. [*The palace.*]

Enter Duke [Frederick], Lords, and Oliver.

Duke Frederick. Not see him since? Sir, sir, that cannot
    be.
  But were I not the better part made mercy,°
  I should not seek an absent argument°
  Of my revenge, thou present. But look to it:
5 Find out thy brother, wheresoe'er he is;
  Seek him with candle; bring him dead or living
  Within this twelvemonth, or turn° thou no more
  To seek a living in our territory.
  Thy lands, and all things that thou dost call thine
10 Worth seizure, do we seize into our hands
  Till thou canst quit° thee by thy brother's mouth°
  Of what we think against thee.

Oliver. O that your Highness knew my heart in this!
  I never loved my brother in my life.

Duke Frederick. More villain thou. Well, push him out
15   of doors,
  And let my officers of such a nature°

3.1.2 **the better part made mercy** so merciful 3 **argument** object (i.e.,
Orlando) 7 **turn** return 11 **quit** acquit 11 **mouth** testimony 16 **of
such a nature** i.e., appropriate

46

Make an extent upon° his house and lands.
Do this expediently° and turn him going.   *Exeunt.*

Scene 2. [*The forest.*]

Enter Orlando, [with a paper].

Orlando. Hang there, my verse, in witness of my love;
   And thou, thrice-crownèd Queen of Night,° survey
With thy chaste eye, from thy pale sphere above,
   Thy huntress' name° that my full life doth sway.
O Rosalind! These trees shall be my books,   5
   And in their barks my thoughts I'll character,°
That every eye which in this forest looks
   Shall see thy virtue witnessed° everywhere.
Run, run, Orlando, carve on every tree
The fair, the chaste, and unexpressive she.°   *Exit.*   10

Enter Corin and [Touchstone, the] Clown.

Corin. And how like you this shepherd's life, Master
Touchstone?

Touchstone. Truly, shepherd, in respect of itself, it is a
good life; but in respect that it is a shepherd's life, it
is naught.° In respect that it is solitary, I like it very   15
well; but in respect that it is private,° it is a very vile
life. Now in respect it is in the fields, it pleaseth me
well; but in respect it is not in the court, it is tedious.
As it is a spare° life, look you, it fits my humor° well;
but as there is no more plenty in it, it goes much   20

17 **Make an extent upon** seize by writ   18 **expediently** speedily
3.2.2 **thrice-crownèd Queen of Night** Diana (goddess of the moon, the
hunt, and of chastity)   4 **Thy huntress' name** i.e., Rosalind, who, because she is chaste, serves Diana   6 **character** write   8 **virtue witnessed**
power attested to   10 **unexpressive she** i.e., woman beyond description
15 **naught** worthless   16 **private** lonely   19 **spare** frugal   19 **humor**
disposition

against my stomach. Hast any philosophy° in thee,
shepherd?

Corin. No more, but that I know the more one sickens,
the worse at ease he is; and that he that wants°
25 money, means, and content is without three good
friends; that the property of rain is to wet and fire
to burn; that good pasture makes fat sheep, and that
a great cause of the night is lack of the sun; that he
that hath learned no wit by nature nor art° may
30 complain° of good breeding, or comes of a very dull
kindred.

Touchstone. Such a one is a natural philosopher.° Wast
ever in court, shepherd?

Corin. No, truly.

35 *Touchstone.* Then thou art damned.

Corin. Nay, I hope.

Touchstone. Truly thou art damned, like an ill-roasted
egg, all on one side.

Corin. For not being at court? Your reason.

40 *Touchstone.* Why, if thou never wast at court, thou
never saw'st good manners;° if thou never saw'st
good manners, then thy manners must be wicked;
and wickedness is sin, and sin is damnation. Thou
art in a parlous° state, shepherd.

45 *Corin.* Not a whit, Touchstone. Those that are good
manners at the court are as ridiculous in the country
as the behavior of the country is most mockable at
the court. You told me you salute not at the court
but you kiss° your hands. That courtesy would be
50 uncleanly if courtiers were shepherds.

Touchstone. Instance,° briefly. Come, instance.

21 **philosophy** learning   24 **wants** lacks   29 **by nature nor art** by birth or
education   30 **complain** cry the lack   32 **a natural philosopher** (1) wise
by nature (2) a wise idiot   41 **manners** (1) behavior (2) morals   44 **par-
lous** dangerous   49 **but you kiss** without kissing   51 **Instance** proof

Corin. Why, we are still° handling our ewes, and their fells° you know are greasy.

Touchstone. Why, do not your courtier's hands sweat? And is not the grease of a mutton as wholesome as   55 the sweat of a man? Shallow, shallow. A better instance, I say. Come.

Corin. Besides, our hands are hard.

Touchstone. Your lips will feel them the sooner. Shallow again. A more sounder instance, come.   60

Corin. And they are often tarred over with the surgery° of our sheep, and would you have us kiss tar? The courtier's hands are perfumed with civet.°

Touchstone. Most shallow man! Thou worms' meat° in respect of° a good piece of flesh indeed! Learn of the   65 wise, and perpend.° Civet is of a baser birth than tar, the very uncleanly flux° of a cat. Mend the instance,° shepherd.

Corin. You have too courtly a wit for me; I'll rest.

Touchstone. Wilt thou rest damned? God help thee,   70 shallow man! God make incision in thee!° Thou art raw.°

Corin. Sir, I am a true laborer; I earn that° I eat, get that I wear, owe no man hate, envy no man's happiness, glad of other men's good, content with my   75 harm;° and the greatest of my pride is to see my ewes graze and my lambs suck.

Touchstone. That is another simple sin in you: to bring the ewes and the rams together and to offer to get your living by the copulation of cattle, to be bawd to   80

---

52 **still** always   53 **fells** fleeces   61 **tarred ... surgery** (shepherds used tar as an ointment)   63 **civet** perfume obtained from the civet cat   64 **worms' meat** food for worms   65 **respect of** comparison with   66 **perpend** consider   67 **flux** secretion   67 **Mend the instance** give a better example   71 **make incision in thee** let your blood (a common cure, here for folly)   72 **raw** (1) inexperienced (2) sore   73 **that** what   75–76 **content with my harm** bear with my troubles

a bell-wether° and to betray a she-lamb of a twelve-
month to a crookèd-pated° old cuckoldly° ram, out
of all reasonable match. If thou beest not damned for
this, the devil himself will have no shepherds; I can-
85   not see else how thou shouldst 'scape.

Corin. Here comes young Master Ganymede, my new
mistress' brother.

Enter Rosalind, [reading a paper].

Rosalind.
     "From the east to western Ind,
     No jewel is like Rosalind.
90   Her worth, being mounted on the wind,
     Through all the world bears Rosalind.
     All the pictures fairest lined°
     Are but black to Rosalind.
     Let no face be kept in mind
95   But the fair° of Rosalind."

Touchstone. I'll rhyme you so eight years together,
dinners and suppers and sleeping hours excepted. It
is the right butterwomen's rank to market.°

Rosalind. Out, fool!

100 *Touchstone.* For a taste:
     If a hart do lack a hind,
     Let him seek out Rosalind.
     If the cat will after kind,°
     So be sure will Rosalind.
105   Wintred° garments must be lined,°
     So must slender Rosalind.
     They that reap must sheaf and bind,
     Then to cart° with Rosalind.

81 **bell-wether** (the leading sheep of a flock carries a bell) 82 **crookèd-pated** i.e., with crooked horns 82 **cuckoldly** (because horned) 92 **lined** drawn 95 **fair** lovely face 98 **right butterwomen's rank to market** i.e., the verses jog along exactly like a procession of women riding to market 103 **kind** its own kind 105 **Wintred** i.e., prepared for winter 105 **lined** stuffed 108 **to cart** (perhaps an allusion not only to the harvest but to the custom of transporting prostitutes to jail in a cart)

　　　　Sweetest nut hath sourest rind,
　　　　Such a nut is Rosalind.　　　　　　　　　　*110*
　　　　He that sweetest rose will find
　　　　Must find love's prick, and Rosalind.
This is the very false gallop of verses. Why do you
infect yourself with them?

Rosalind. Peace, you dull fool! I found them on a tree.　*115*

Touchstone. Truly the tree yields bad fruit.

Rosalind. I'll graff° it with you and then I shall graff it
　with a medlar.° Then it will be the earliest fruit i' th'
　country; for you'll be rotten ere you be half ripe, and
　that's the right virtue° of the medlar.　　　　　　*120*

Touchstone. You have said; but whether wisely or no,
　let the forest judge.

　　　　　　Enter Celia, with a writing.

Rosalind. Peace! Here comes my sister reading; stand
　aside.

Celia. "Why should this a desert be?　　　　　　　*125*
　　　　For° it is unpeopled? No.
　　　Tongues I'll hang on every tree
　　　　That shall civil sayings° show:
　　　Some, how brief the life of man
　　　　Runs his erring pilgrimage,　　　　　　　*130*
　　　That the stretching of a span°
　　　　Buckles in° his sum of age;
　　　Some, of violated vows
　　　　'Twixt the souls of friend and friend;
　　　But upon the fairest boughs,　　　　　　　　*135*
　　　　Or at every sentence end,
　　　Will I 'Rosalinda' write,
　　　　Teaching all that read to know
　　　The quintessence of every sprite°

---

117 **graff** graft　118 **medlar** (1) an applelike fruit, not ready to eat until
it is almost rotten (2) interferer　120 **right virtue** true quality　126 **For**
because　128 **civil sayings** civilized maxims　131 **stretching of a span**
span of an open hand　132 **Buckles in** limits　139 **sprite** soul

140   Heaven would in little° show.
          Therefore heaven Nature charged
          That one body should be filled
          With all graces wide-enlarged.
          Nature presently° distilled
145   Helen's cheek, but not her heart,°
              Cleopatra's majesty,
          Atalanta's better part,°
              Sad° Lucretia's° modesty.
          Thus Rosalind of many parts
150   By heavenly synod° was devised,
          Of many faces, eyes, and hearts,
              To have the touches° dearest prized.
          Heaven would that she these gifts should have,
          And I to live and die her slave."

155 *Rosalind.* O most gentle pulpiter, what tedious homily
     of love have you wearied your parishioners withal,
     and never cried, "Have patience, good people"!

     Celia. How now? Back, friends. Shepherd, go off a
     little. Go with him, sirrah.

160 *Touchstone.* Come, shepherd, let us make an honorable
     retreat; though not with bag and baggage, yet with
     scrip and scrippage.°   *Exit [with Corin].*

     Celia. Didst thou hear these verses?

     Rosalind. O, yes, I heard them all, and more too; for
165 some of them had in them more feet° than the verses
     would bear.

     Celia. That's no matter. The feet might bear the verses.

     Rosalind. Ay, but the feet were lame, and could not

---

140 **in little** in miniature (i.e., the microcosm)   114 **presently** thereupon
145 **cheek . . . heart** i.e., Helen's beauty but not her false heart   147 **Atalanta's better part** i.e., Rosalind has the gracefulness but not the cruelty
of Atalanta, a huntress famed in Greek mythology for her fleetness
148 **Sad** dignified   148 **Lucretia** (a Roman matron who killed herself
rather than live dishonored)   150 **synod** council   152 **touches** features
162 **scrip and scrippage** shepherd's pouch and its contents   165 **feet**
metrical units

bear themselves without the verse, and therefore
stood lamely in the verse.   170

Celia. But didst thou hear without wondering how thy
name should be hanged and carved upon these trees?

Rosalind. I was seven of the nine days° out of the
wonder before you came; for look here what I found
on a palm tree. I was never so berhymed since   175
Pythagoras'° time that° I was an Irish rat,° which I
can hardly remember.

Celia. Trow° you who hath done this?

Rosalind. Is it a man?

Celia. And a chain that you once wore, about his neck.   180
Change you color?

Rosalind. I prithee who?

Celia. O Lord, Lord, it is a hard matter for friends to
meet; but mountains may be removed with earth-
quakes, and so encounter.   185

Rosalind. Nay, but who is it?

Celia. Is it possible?

Rosalind. Nay, I prithee now with most petitionary
vehemence,° tell me who it is.

Celia. O wonderful, wonderful, and most wonderful   190
wonderful, and yet again wonderful, and after that,
out of all hooping!°

Rosalind. Good my complexion!° Dost thou think,
though I am caparisoned° like a man, I have a doublet
and hose in my disposition? One inch of delay more   195

---

173 **seven of the nine days** (cf. the phrase "nine days' wonder")
176 **Pythagoras** (Greek philosopher who taught the doctrine of the trans-
migration of souls)   176 **that** when   176 **Irish rat** (it was believed that
Irish sorcerers could kill rats with rhymed spells)   178 **Trow** know
188–189 **with most petitionary vehemence** i.e., I beg you   192 **out of
all hooping** beyond all measure   193 **Good my complexion** (a mild
expletive)   194 **caparisoned** dressed

is a South Sea of discovery.° I prithee tell me who is
it quickly, and speak apace.° I would thou couldst
stammer, that thou mightst pour this concealed man
out of thy mouth as wine comes out of a narrow-
200   mouthed bottle; either too much at once, or none at
all. I prithee take the cork out of thy mouth, that I
may drink thy tidings.

Celia. So you may put a man in your belly.

Rosalind. Is he of God's making? What manner of man?
205   Is his head worth a hat? Or his chin worth a beard?

Celia. Nay, he hath but a little beard.

Rosalind. Why, God will send more, if the man will be
thankful. Let me stay° the growth of his beard, if
thou delay me not the knowledge of his chin.

210   *Celia.* It is young Orlando, that tripped up the wrestler's
heels and your heart both in an instant.

Rosalind. Nay, but the devil take mocking! Speak sad
brow and true maid.°

Celia. I' faith, coz, 'tis he.

215   *Rosalind.* Orlando?

Celia. Orlando.

Rosalind. Alas the day! What shall I do with my
doublet and hose? What did he when thou saw'st
him? What said he? How looked he? Wherein went
220   he?° What makes he here? Did he ask for me? Where
remains he? How parted he with thee? And when
shalt thou see him again? Answer me in one word.

Celia. You must borrow me Gargantua's° mouth first;
'tis a word too great for any mouth of this age's size.
225   To say "ay" and "no" to these particulars is more than
to answer in a catechism.

195–196 **One inch . . . discovery** i.e., another minute more will seem as
long as it takes to voyage to the South Seas   197 **apace** quickly
208 **stay** wait for   212–213 **sad brow and true maid** i.e., seriously and
truthfully   219–220 **Wherein went he** how was he dressed   223 **Gargantua** (a giant in Rabelais and other writers)

Rosalind. But doth he know that I am in this forest, and in man's apparel? Looks he as freshly° as he did the day he wrestled?

Celia. It is as easy to count atomies° as to resolve the propositions° of a lover; but take a taste of my finding him, and relish it with good observance.° I found him under a tree, like a dropped acorn.   230

Rosalind. It may well be called Jove's tree° when it drops forth fruit.   235

Celia. Give me audience,° good madam.

Rosalind. Proceed.

Celia. There lay he stretched along like a wounded knight.

Rosalind. Though it be pity to see such a sight, it well becomes the ground.   240

Celia. Cry "holla"° to the tongue, I prithee; it curvets° unseasonably. He was furnished° like a hunter.

Rosalind. O, ominous! He comes to kill my heart.°

Celia. I would sing my song without a burden.° Thou bring'st me out of tune.   245

Rosalind. Do you not know I am a woman? When I think, I must speak. Sweet, say on.

Enter Orlando and Jaques.

Celia. You bring me out. Soft. Comes he not here?

Rosalind. 'Tis he! Slink by, and note him.   250

Jaques. I thank you for your company; but, good faith, I had as lief have been myself alone.

Orlando. And so had I; but yet for fashion sake I thank you too for your society.

228 **freshly** handsome   230 **atomies** motes   230–231 **resolve the propositions** answer the questions   232 **good observance** close attention   234 **Jove's tree** (the oak, sacred to Jove)   236 **Give me audience** listen   242 **holla** whoa   242 **curvets** frolics   243 **furnished** dressed   244 **heart** (pun on "hart")   245 **burden** refrain

255 *Jaques.* God b' wi' you; let's meet as little as we can.

Orlando. I do desire we may be better strangers.

Jaques. I pray you mar no more trees with writing love songs in their barks.

Orlando. I pray you mar no moe° of my verses with
260 reading them ill-favoredly.°

Jaques. Rosalind is your love's name?

Orlando. Yes, that.

Jaques. I do not like her name.

Orlando. There was no thought of pleasing you when
265 she was christened.

Jaques. What stature is she of?

Orlando. Just as high as my heart.

Jaques. You are full of pretty answers. Have you not been acquainted with goldsmiths' wives, and conned
270 them out of rings?°

Orlando. Not so; but I answer you right painted cloth,° from whence you have studied your questions.

Jaques. You have a nimble wit; I think 'twas made of Atalanta's heels.° Will you sit down with me, and we
275 two will rail against our mistress the world and all our misery.

Orlando. I will chide no breather° in the world but myself, against whom I know most faults.

Jaques. The worst fault you have is to be in love.

280 *Orlando.* 'Tis a fault I will not change for your best virtue. I am weary of you.

259 **moe** more   260 **ill-favoredly** badly   269–270 **conned them out of rings** i.e., memorized the sentimental sayings inscribed in rings   271 **painted cloth** (cheap substitute for tapestry, on which were painted pictures with trite sayings)   274 **Atalanta's heels** (Atalanta was a symbol of speed)   277 **breather** creature

Jaques. By my troth, I was seeking for a fool when I found you.

Orlando. He is drowned in the brook. Look but in and you shall see him. 285

Jaques. There I shall see mine own figure.

Orlando. Which I take to be either a fool or a cipher.°

Jaques. I'll tarry no longer with you. Farewell, good Signior Love.

Orlando. I am glad of your departure. Adieu, good 290 Monsieur Melancholy.   *[Exit Jaques.]*

Rosalind. I will speak to him like a saucy lackey, and under that habit° play the knave with him. Do you hear, forester?

Orlando. Very well. What would you? 295

Rosalind. I pray you, what is't o'clock?

Orlando. You should ask me, what time o' day. There's no clock in the forest.

Rosalind. Then there is no true lover in the forest, else sighing every minute and groaning every hour would 300 detect° the lazy foot of Time as well as a clock.

Orlando. And why not the swift foot of Time? Had not that been as proper?

Rosalind. By no means, sir. Time travels in divers paces with divers persons. I'll tell you who Time 305 ambles withal, who Time trots withal, who Time gallops withal, and who he stands still withal.

Orlando. I prithee, who doth he trot withal?

Rosalind. Marry, he trots hard with a young maid between the contract of her marriage° and the day it 310

287 **cipher** zero   293 **habit** guise   301 **detect** show   310 **contract of her marriage** betrothal

is solemnized. If the interim be but a se'nnight,° Time's pace is so hard that it seems the length of seven year.

Orlando. Who ambles Time withal?

315 *Rosalind.* With a priest that lacks Latin and a rich man that hath not the gout; for the one sleeps easily because he cannot study, and the other lives merrily because he feels no pain; the one lacking the burden of lean and wasteful° learning, the other knowing no
320 burden of heavy tedious penury. These Time ambles withal.

Orlando. Who doth he gallop withal?

Rosalind. With a thief to the gallows; for though he go as softly° as foot can fall, he thinks himself too soon
325 there.

Orlando. Who stays it still withal?

Rosalind. With lawyers in the vacation; for they sleep between term° and term, and then they perceive not how time moves.

330 *Orlando.* Where dwell you, pretty youth?

Rosalind. With this shepherdess, my sister; here in the skirts of the forest, like fringe upon a petticoat.

Orlando. Are you native of this place?

Rosalind. As the cony° that you see dwell where she is
335 kindled.°

Orlando. Your accent is something finer than you could purchase° in so removed° a dwelling.

Rosalind. I have been told so of many. But indeed an old religious° uncle of mine taught me to speak, who
340 was in his youth an inland° man; one that knew

---

311 **a se'nnight** seven days, a week   319 **wasteful** i.e., causing one to waste away   324 **softly** slowly   328 **term** court session   334 **cony** rabbit   335 **kindled** born   337 **purchase** acquire   337 **removed** remote   339 **religious** i.e., a member of a religious order   340 **inland** city

courtship° too well, for there he fell in love. I have
heard him read many lectures against it; and I thank
God I am not a woman, to be touched° with so many
giddy° offenses as he hath generally taxed their whole
sex withal.   *345*

Orlando. Can you remember any of the principal evils
that he laid to the charge of women?

Rosalind. There were none principal. They were all like
one another as halfpence are, every one fault seeming
monstrous till his fellow fault came to match it.   *350*

Orlando. I prithee recount some of them.

Rosalind. No, I will not cast away my physic but on
those that are sick. There is a man haunts the forest
that abuses our young plants with carving "Rosalind"
on their barks, hangs odes upon hawthorns, and   *355*
elegies on brambles; all, forsooth, deifying the name
of Rosalind. If I could meet that fancy-monger,° I
would give him some good counsel, for he seems to
have the quotidian° of love upon him.

Orlando. I am he that is so love-shaked. I pray you tell   *360*
me your remedy.

Rosalind. There is none of my uncle's marks upon you.
He taught me how to know a man in love; in which
cage of rushes° I am sure you are not prisoner.

Orlando. What were his marks?   *365*

Rosalind. A lean cheek, which you have not; a blue eye°
and sunken, which you have not; an unquestionable°
spirit, which you have not; a beard neglected, which
you have not—but I pardon you for that, for simply
your having° in beard is a younger brother's revenue.°   *370*

---

341 **courtship** (1) court manners (2) wooing   343 **touched** tainted
344 **giddy** frivolous   357 **fancy-monger** dealer in love   359 **quotidian**
daily fever   364 **cage of rushes** i.e., prison easy to escape from   366 **a
blue eye** i.e., dark circles under the eyes   367 **unquestionable** averse to
conversation   369–370 **simply your having** truthfully what you have
370 **a younger brother's revenue** i.e., a small portion

Then your hose should be ungartered, your bonnet unbanded, your sleeve unbuttoned, your shoe untied, and everything about you demonstrating a careless desolation.° But you are no such man: you are rather
375   point-device in your accouterments,° as loving yourself than seeming the lover of any other.

Orlando. Fair youth, I would I could make thee believe I love.

Rosalind. Me believe it? You may as soon make her
380   that you love believe it, which I warrant she is apter to do than to confess she does; that is one of the points in the which women still give the lie to their consciences. But in good sooth, are you he that hangs the verses on the trees wherein Rosalind is so admired?

385 *Orlando.* I swear to thee, youth, by the white hand of Rosalind, I am that he, that unfortunate he.

Rosalind. But are you so much in love as your rhymes speak?

Orlando. Neither rhyme nor reason can express how
390   much.

Rosalind. Love is merely° a madness, and, I tell you, deserves as well a dark house and a whip° as madmen do; and the reason why they are not so punished and cured is that the lunacy is so ordinary that the
395   whippers are in love too. Yet I profess curing it by counsel.

Orlando. Did you ever cure any so?

Rosalind. Yes, one, and in this manner. He was to imagine me his love, his mistress; and I set him every
400   day to woo me. At which time would I, being but a moonish° youth, grieve, be effeminate, changeable, longing and liking, proud, fantastical,° apish, shallow,

---

373–374 **a careless desolation** indifferent despondency   375 **point-device in your accouterments** precise in your dress   391 **merely** completely   392 **a dark house and a whip** (the usual treatment of the insane in Shakespeare's day)   401 **moonish** changeable   402 **fantastical** capricious

inconstant, full of tears, full of smiles; for every
passion something and for no passion truly anything,
as boys and women are for the most part cattle of   405
this color; would now like him, now loathe him;
then entertain him, then forswear him; now weep
for him, then spit at him; that I drave my suitor from
his mad humor° of love to a living° humor of madness, which was, to forswear the full stream of the   410
world and to live in a nook merely monastic. And
thus I cured him; and this way will I take upon me
to wash your liver° as clean as a sound sheep's heart,
that there shall not be one spot of love in't.

Orlando. I would not be cured, youth.   415

Rosalind. I would cure you, if you would but call me
Rosalind and come every day to my cote and woo me.

Orlando. Now, by the faith of my love, I will. Tell me
where it is.

Rosalind. Go with me to it, and I'll show it you; and   420
by° the way you shall tell me where in the forest you
live. Will you go?

Orlando. With all my heart, good youth.

Rosalind. Nay, you must call me Rosalind. Come, sister,
will you go?   *Exeunt.*   425

Scene 3. [*The forest.*]

*Enter [Touchstone, the] Clown, Audrey; and Jaques
[apart].*

Touchstone. Come apace,° good Audrey. I will fetch up
your goats, Audrey. And how, Audrey, am I the man
yet? Doth my simple feature° content you?

409 **humor** condition   409 **living** real   413 **liver** (thought to be the seat
of love)   421 **by** along   3.3.1 **apace** swiftly   3 **feature** appearance

Audrey. Your features, Lord warrant° us! What features?

Touchstone. I am here with thee and thy goats, as the
most capricious poet, honest Ovid, was among the
Goths.°

Jaques. [*Aside*] O knowledge ill-inhabited,° worse than
Jove in a thatched house!

Touchstone. When a man's verses cannot be understood,
nor a man's good wit seconded with° the forward
child, understanding, it strikes a man more dead than
a great reckoning in a little room.° Truly, I would
the gods had made thee poetical.

Audrey. I do not know what poetical is. Is it honest in
deed and word? Is it a true thing?

Touchstone. No, truly; for the truest poetry is the most
feigning, and lovers are given to poetry, and what
they swear in poetry may be said as lovers they do
feign.°

Audrey. Do you wish then that the gods had made me
poetical?

Touchstone. I do truly; for thou swear'st to me thou
art honest. Now, if thou wert a poet, I might have
some hope thou didst feign.

Audrey. Would you not have me honest?

Touchstone. No, truly, unless thou wert hard-favored;°
for honesty coupled to beauty is to have honey a
sauce to sugar.

Jaques. [*Aside*] A material° fool.

---

4 **warrant** save   7–8 **capricious . . . Goths** (the Roman poet Ovid was
exiled among the Goths—pronounced in Elizabethan England the same as
"goats"—for the immorality of his verses. Touchstone plays on the words
"honest" [chaste] and "capricious" [derived from Latin *caper*, male
goat])   9 **ill-inhabited** ill-housed   12 **with** by   14 **great reckoning . . .
room** large bill for poor accommodations   21 **feign** (1) pretend (2) desire (a pun on "fain")   28 **hard-favored** ugly   31 **material** full of good
matter

Audrey. Well, I am not fair, and therefore I pray the gods make me honest.

Touchstone. Truly, and to cast away honesty upon a foul slut were to put good meat into an unclean dish. 35

Audrey. I am not a slut, though I thank the gods I am foul.

Touchstone. Well, praised be the gods for thy foulness! Sluttishness may come hereafter. But be it as it may be, I will marry thee; and to that end I have been 40 with Sir° Oliver Mar-text, the vicar of the next village, who hath promised to meet me in this place of the forest and to couple us.

Jaques. [*Aside*] I would fain see this meeting.

Audrey. Well, the gods give us joy! 45

Touchstone. Amen. A man may, if he were of a fearful heart, stagger° in this attempt; for here we have no temple but the wood, no assembly but horn-beasts.° But what though? Courage! As horns are odious, they are necessary.° It is said, "Many a man knows 50 no end of his goods." Right! Many a man has good horns and knows no end of them. Well, that is the dowry of his wife; 'tis none of his own getting. Horns! Even so, poor men alone. No, no; the noblest deer hath them as huge as the rascal.° Is the single man 55 therefore blessed? No; as a walled town is more worthier than a village, so is the forehead of a married man more honorable than the bare brow of a bachelor; and by how much defense° is better than no skill, by so much is a horn more precious than to 60 want.°

Enter Sir Oliver Mar-text.

Here comes Sir Oliver. Sir Oliver Mar-text, you are

---

41 **Sir** (an old form of address for a priest) 47 **stagger** tremble 48 **horn-beasts** (1) horned animals (2) cuckolds 50 **necessary** inevitable 55 **rascal** inferior deer 59 **defense** the art of defense 61 **want** i.e., lack horns

well met. Will you dispatch us° here under this tree,
or shall we go with you to your chapel?

65 *Oliver Mar-text.* Is there none here to give the woman?

Touchstone. I will not take her on gift of any man.

Oliver Mar-text. Truly, she must be given, or the marriage is not lawful.

Jaques. [*Comes forward*] Proceed, proceed; I'll give her.

70 *Touchstone.* Good even, good Master What-ye-call't.°
How do you, sir? You are very well met. God 'ield
you for your last company;° I am very glad to see
you. Even a toy° in hand here, sir. Nay, pray be
covered.°

75 *Jaques.* Will you be married, motley?

Touchstone. As the ox hath his bow,° sir, the horse his
curb, and the falcon her bells, so man hath his desires; and as pigeons bill, so wedlock would be
nibbling.

80 *Jaques.* And will you, being a man of your breeding, be
married under a bush like a beggar? Get you to
church, and have a good priest that can tell you what
marriage is. This fellow will but join you together as
they join wainscot;° then one of you will prove a
85 shrunk panel, and like green timber warp, warp.

Touchstone. [*Aside*] I am not in the mind but° I were
better to be married of him than of another; for he
is not like to marry me well; and not being well
married,° it will be a good excuse for me hereafter
90 to leave my wife.

63 **dispatch us** finish our business   70 **Master What-ye-call't** (Touchstone delicately avoids the name "Jaques," which could be pronounced
"jakes," a privy)   71–72 **God 'ield . . . company** God reward you for the
last time we met   73 **toy** trifle   73–74 **pray be covered** (Jaques has
removed his hat)   76 **bow** yoke   84 **wainscot** wood paneling   86 **I am
not in the mind but** I am not sure but that   88–89 **well married** (1)
legally married (2) happily married (3) married into wealth

Jaques. Go thou with me and let me counsel thee.

Touchstone. Come, sweet Audrey.
  We must be married, or we must live in bawdry.
  Farewell, good Master Oliver: not
      O sweet Oliver,   *95*
      O brave Oliver,
    Leave me not behind thee;
but
      Wind° away,
      Be gone, I say;   *100*
    I will not to wedding with thee.

Oliver Mar-text. 'Tis no matter. Ne'er a fantastical°
  knave of them all shall flout me out of my calling.
                          Exeunt.

Scene 4. [*The forest.*]

Enter Rosalind and Celia.

Rosalind. Never talk to me; I will weep.

Celia. Do, I prithee; but yet have the grace to consider
  that tears do not become a man.

Rosalind. But have I not cause to weep?

Celia. As good cause as one would desire; therefore   *5*
  weep.

Rosalind. His very hair is of the dissembling color.°

Celia. Something browner than Judas'. Marry, his kisses
  are Judas' own children.

Rosalind. I' faith, his hair is of a good color.   *10*

---

99 **Wind** turn   102 **fantastical** odd   3.4.7 **dissembling color** i.e., red
like the hair of Judas

Celia. An excellent color. Your chestnut was ever the only color.

Rosalind. And his kissing is as full of sanctity as the touch of holy bread.°

15 *Celia.* He hath bought a pair of cast° lips of Diana.° A nun of winter's sisterhood° kisses not more religiously; the very ice of chastity is in them.

Rosalind. But why did he swear he would come this morning, and comes not?

20 *Celia.* Nay, certainly there is no truth in him.

Rosalind. Do you think so?

Celia. Yes; I think he is not a pickpurse nor a horse-stealer, but for his verity in love, I do think him as concave° as a covered goblet or a worm-eaten nut.

25 *Rosalind.* Not true in love?

Celia. Yes, when he is in, but I think he is not in.

Rosalind. You have heard him swear downright he was.

Celia. "Was" is not "is." Besides, the oath of a lover is no stronger than the word of a tapster;° they are
30 both the confirmer of false reckonings. He attends here in the forest on the Duke your father.

Rosalind. I met the Duke yesterday and had much question° with him. He asked me of what parentage I was. I told him, of as good as he; so he laughed
35 and let me go. But what talk we of fathers when there is such a man as Orlando?

Celia. O, that's a brave° man; he writes brave verses, speaks brave words, swears brave oaths, and breaks them bravely, quite traverse,° athwart the heart of

---

14 **holy bread** (not the sacramental wafer, but bread brought to church to be blessed and then distributed to the poor)   15 **cast** (1) molded (2) castoff   15 **Diana** goddess of chastity   16 **winter's sisterhood** i.e., the most rigorous chastity   24 **concave** hollow   29 **tapster** waiter in a tavern   33 **question** talk   37 **brave** fine   39 **traverse** at an angle (instead of head-on)

his lover, as a puisny° tilter, that spurs his horse but   *40*
on one side, breaks his staff like a noble goose. But
all's brave that youth mounts and folly guides. Who
comes here?

Enter Corin.

Corin. Mistress and master, you have oft enquired
   After the shepherd that complained° of love,   *45*
   Who you saw sitting by me on the turf,
   Praising the proud disdainful shepherdess
   That was his mistress.

Celia.   Well, and what of him?

Corin. If you will see a pageant° truly played
   Between the pale complexion of true love   *50*
   And the red glow of scorn and proud disdain,
   Go hence a little, and I shall conduct you,
   If you will mark it.

Rosalind.   O, come, let us remove:
   The sight of lovers feedeth those in love.
   Bring us to this sight, and you shall say   *55*
   I'll prove a busy actor in their play.   . *Exeunt.*

Scene 5. [*The forest.*]

Enter Silvius and Phebe.

Silvius. Sweet Phebe, do not scorn me; do not, Phebe!
   Say that you love me not, but say not so
   In bitterness. The common executioner,
   Whose heart th' accustomed sight of death makes
      hard,
   Falls° not the ax upon the humbled neck   *5*

40 **puisny** inexperienced   45 **complained** lamented   49 **pageant** scene,
show   3.5.5 **Falls** lets fall

But first begs pardon. Will you sterner be
Than he that dies and lives° by bloody drops?

Enter [apart] Rosalind, Celia, and Corin.

Phebe. I would not be thy executioner.
   I fly thee, for I would not injure thee.
10   Thou tell'st me there is murder in mine eye:
   'Tis pretty, sure, and very probable
   That eyes, that are the frail'st and softest things,
   Who shut their coward gates on atomies,°
   Should be called tyrants, butchers, murderers.
15   Now I do frown on thee with all my heart,
   And if mine eyes can wound, now let them kill thee.
   Now counterfeit to swound;° why, now fall down;
   Or if thou canst not, O, for shame, for shame,
   Lie not, to say mine eyes are murderers.
20   Now show the wound mine eye hath made in thee;
   Scratch thee but with a pin, and there remains
   Some scar of it; lean upon a rush,
   The cicatrice and capable impressure°
   Thy palm some moment keeps; but now mine eyes,
25   Which I have darted at thee, hurt thee not,
   Nor I am sure there is no force in eyes
   That can do hurt.

Silvius.   O dear Phebe,
   If ever, as that ever may be near,°
   You meet in some fresh cheek the power of fancy,°
30   Then shall you know the wounds invisible
   That love's keen arrows make.

Phebe.   But till that time
   Come thou not near me; and when that time comes,
   Afflict me with thy mocks, pity me not,
   As till that time I shall not pity thee.

7 **dies and lives** earns his living   13 **atomies** motes   17 **counterfeit to swound** pretend to swoon   23 **cicatrice and capable impressure** mark and visible impression   28 **as that ever may be near** and may the time be soon   29 **fancy** love

Rosalind. And why, I pray you? Who might be your
    mother,   35
    That you insult, exult, and all at once,
    Over the wretched? What though you have no beauty
    (As, by my faith, I see no more in you
    Than without candle may go dark to bed°)
    Must you be therefore proud and pitiless?   40
    Why, what means this? Why do you look on me?
    I see no more in you than in the ordinary
    Of nature's sale-work.° 'Od's° my little life,
    I think she means to tangle my eyes too!
    No, faith, proud mistress, hope not after it;   45
    'Tis not your inky brows, your black silk hair,
    Your bugle° eyeballs, nor your cheek of cream
    That can entame my spirits to your worship.
    You foolish shepherd, wherefore do you follow her,
    Like foggy south,° puffing with wind and rain?   50
    You are a thousand times a properer° man
    Than she a woman. 'Tis such fools as you
    That makes the world full of ill-favored children.
    'Tis not her glass,° but you, that flatters her,
    And out of you she sees herself more proper   55
    Than any of her lineaments can show her.
    But mistress, know yourself. Down on your knees,
    And thank heaven, fasting, for a good man's love;
    For I must tell you friendly in your ear,
    Sell when you can, you are not for all markets.   60
    Cry the man mercy,° love him, take his offer;
    Foul° is most foul, being foul to be a scoffer;
    So take her to thee, shepherd. Fare you well.

Phebe. Sweet youth, I pray you chide a year together;
    I had rather hear you chide than this man woo.   65

Rosalind. [*Aside*] He's fall'n in love with your foulness,
    and she'll fall in love with my anger. If it be so, as

---

39 Than ... to bed i.e., your beauty is not so dazzling as to light up the
room   **42–43 ordinary/Of nature's sale-work** usual product of nature's
manufacture   **43 'Od's** God save   **47 bugle** black and glassy   **50 south**
south wind   **51 properer** more handsome   **54 glass** mirror   **61 Cry the
man mercy** ask the man's forgiveness   **62 Foul** (1) ugliness (2) wickedness

fast as she answers thee with frowning looks, I'll
sauce her with bitter words. [*To Phebe*] Why look
70 you so upon me?

Phebe. For no ill will I bear you.

Rosalind. I pray you do not fall in love with me,
For I am falser than vows made in wine.
Besides, I like you not. If you will know my house,
75 'Tis at the tuft of olives, here hard° by.
Will you go, sister? Shepherd, ply her hard.
Come, sister. Shepherdess, look on him better
And be not proud. Though all the world could see,
None could be so abused° in sight as he.
80 Come, to our flock.   *Exit [with Celia and Corin].*

Phebe. Dead shepherd, now I find thy saw° of might,
"Who ever loved that loved not at first sight?"°

Silvius. Sweet Phebe.

Phebe.   Ha! What say'st thou, Silvius?

Silvius. Sweet Phebe, pity me.

85 *Phebe.* Why, I am sorry for thee, gentle Silvius.

Silvius. Wherever sorrow is, relief would be.
If you do sorrow at my grief in love,
By giving love your sorrow and my grief
Were both extermined.°

90 *Phebe.* Thou hast my love. Is not that neighborly?°

Silvius. I would have you.

Phebe.   Why, that were covetousness.
Silvius, the time was that I hated thee;
And yet it is not that I bear thee love,
But since that thou canst talk of love so well,
95 Thy company, which erst° was irksome to me,

75 **hard** near   79 **abused** deceived   81 **saw** saying   82 **Who ever ...
sight** (a line from Christopher Marlowe's poem *Hero and Leander,* published in 1598. The "Dead shepherd" is Marlowe, who died in 1593)
89 **extermined** ended   90 **neighborly** friendly (perhaps alluding to the
commandment to love one's neighbor)   95 **erst** formerly

I will endure; and I'll employ thee too;
But do not look for further recompense
Than thine own gladness that thou art employed.

Silvius. So holy and so perfect is my love,
And I in such a poverty of grace,°   *100*
That I shall think it a most plenteous crop
To glean the broken ears after the man
That the main harvest reaps. Loose now and then
A scatt'red° smile, and that I'll live upon.

Phebe. Know'st thou the youth that spoke to me ere-
    while?°   *105*

Silvius. Not very well, but I have met him oft,
And he hath bought the cottage and the bounds
That the old carlot° once was master of.

Phebe. Think not I love him, though I ask for him;
'Tis but a peevish boy; yet he talks well.   *110*
But what care I for words? Yet words do well
When he that speaks them pleases those that hear.
It is a pretty youth. Not very pretty.
But sure he's proud. And yet his pride becomes him.
He'll make a proper man. The best thing in him   *115*
Is his complexion. And faster than his tongue
Did make offense, his eye did heal it up.
He is not very tall. Yet for his years he's tall.
His leg is but so so. And yet 'tis well.
There was a pretty redness in his lip,   *120*
A little riper and more lusty red
Than that mixed in his cheek. 'Twas just the difference
Betwixt the constant° red and mingled damask.°
There be some women, Silvius, had they marked him
In parcels° as I did, would have gone near   *125*
To fall in love with him; but, for my part,
I love him not nor hate him not. And yet
I have more cause to hate him than to love him;
For what had he to do to chide at me?

---

100 **a poverty of grace** small favor   104 **scatt'red** stray   150 **erewhile**
a short time ago   108 **carlot** countryman   123 **constant** uniform
123 **mingled damask** pink and white   125 **In parcels** piece by piece

130   He said mine eyes were black and my hair black;
        And, now I am rememb'red,° scorned at me.
        I marvel why I answered not again.
        But that's all one: omittance is no quittance.°
        I'll write to him a very taunting letter,
135   And thou shalt bear it. Wilt thou, Silvius?

Silvius. Phebe, with all my heart.

Phebe.   I'll write it straight;°
        The matter's in my head and in my heart;
        I will be bitter with him and passing short.°
        Go with me, Silvius.   *Exeunt.*

---

131 **rememb'red** reminded   133 **omittance is no quittance** i.e., the fact that I
did not reply does not mean I will not do so later   136 **straight** at once
138 **passing short** very curt

ACT 4

Scene 1. [*The forest.*]

Enter Rosalind and Celia and Jaques.

Jaques. I prithee, pretty youth, let me be better acquainted with thee.

Rosalind. They say you are a melancholy fellow.

Jaques. I am so; I do love it better than laughing.

Rosalind. Those that are in extremity of° either are   *5*
abominable fellows, and betray themselves to every
modern censure° worse than drunkards.

Jaques. Why, 'tis good to be sad and say nothing.

Rosalind. Why then, 'tis good to be a post.

Jaques. I have neither the scholar's melancholy, which   *10*
is emulation;° nor the musician's, which is fantastical;
nor the courtier's, which is proud; nor the soldier's,
which is ambitious; nor the lawyer's, which is politic;°
nor the lady's, which is nice;° nor the lover's, which
is all these: but it is a melancholy of mine own, com-   *15*
pounded of many simples,° extracted from many
objects, and indeed the sundry contemplation of my

4.1.5 **are in extremity of** go to extremes in   6–7 **every modern censure**
i.e., the average man's disapproval   11 **emulation** envy   13 **politic** i.e.,
put on to seem grave   14 **nice** fastidious   16 **simples** ingredients

travels, in which my often rumination° wraps me in
a most humorous sadness.

20 *Rosalind.* A traveler! By my faith, you have great reason
to be sad. I fear you have sold your own lands to see
other men's. Then to have seen much and to have
nothing is to have rich eyes and poor hands.

Jaques. Yes, I have gained my experience.

Enter Orlando.

25 *Rosalind.* And your experience makes you sad. I had
rather have a fool to make me merry than experience
to make me sad—and to travel° for it too.

Orlando. Good day and happiness, dear Rosalind.

Jaques. Nay then, God b'wi'you, an° you talk in
30 blank verse.   [*Exit.*]

Rosalind. Farewell, Monsieur Traveler. Look you lisp°
and wear strange suits, disable° all the benefits of
your own country, be out of love with your nativity,°
and almost chide God for making you that counte-
35 nance you are; or I will scarce think you have swam
in a gundello.° Why, how now, Orlando, where have
you been all this while? You a lover? An you serve
me such another trick, never come in my sight more.

Orlando. My fair Rosalind, I come within an hour of
40 my promise.

Rosalind. Break an hour's promise in love? He that
will divide a minute into a thousand parts and break
but a part of the thousand part of a minute in the
affairs of love, it may be said of him that Cupid hath
45 clapped° him o' th' shoulder, but I'll warrant him
heart-whole.

Orlando. Pardon me, dear Rosalind.

---

18 **often rumination** constant reflection   27 **travel** (pun on "travail")
29 **an** if   31 **lisp** speak affectedly   32 **disable** disparage   33 **nativity**
birthplace   36 **gundello** gondola   45 **clapped** touched

Rosalind. Nay, an you be so tardy, come no more in my sight. I had as lief be wooed of a snail.

Orlando. Of a snail? 50

Rosalind. Ay, of a snail; for though he comes slowly, he carries his house on his head; a better jointure,° I think, than you make a woman. Besides, he brings his destiny with him.

Orlando. What's that? 55

Rosalind. Why, horns; which such as you are fain to be beholding to your wives for; but he comes armed° in his fortune and prevents° the slander of his wife.

Orlando. Virtue is no horn-maker, and my Rosalind is virtuous. 60

Rosalind. And I am your Rosalind.

Celia. It pleases him to call you so; but he hath a Rosalind of a better leer° than you.

Rosalind. Come, woo me, woo me; for now I am in a holiday humor and like enough to consent. What 65 would you say to me now, an I were your very very Rosalind?

Orlando. I would kiss before I spoke.

Rosalind. Nay, you were better speak first, and when you were graveled for lack of matter,° you might take 70 occasion to kiss. Very good orators, when they are out,° they will spit; and for lovers, lacking—God warn° us!—matter, the cleanliest shift is to kiss.

Orlando. How if the kiss be denied?

Rosalind. Then she puts you to entreaty, and there 75 begins new matter.

---

52 **jointure** marriage settlement 57 **armed** i.e., with horns 58 **prevents** (1) forestalls (2) anticipates (?) 63 **leer** face 70 **graveled for lack of matter** hard put for something to say 72 **out** i.e., out of material 73 **warn** protect (warrant)

Orlando. Who could be out, being before his beloved mistress?

Rosalind. Marry, that should you, if I were your mis-
80   tress, or I should think my honesty ranker° than my wit.

Orlando. What, of my suit?

Rosalind. Not out of your apparel, and yet out of your suit.° Am not I your Rosalind?

85 *Orlando.* I take some joy to say you are, because I would be talking of her.

Rosalind. Well, in her person, I say I will not have you.

Orlando. Then, in mine own person, I die.

Rosalind. No, faith, die by attorney.° The poor world
90   is almost six thousand years old, and in all this time there was not any man died in his own person,° videlicet,° in a love cause. Troilus° had his brains dashed out with a Grecian club; yet he did what he could to die before, and he is one of the patterns of
95   love. Leander,° he would have lived many a fair year though Hero had turned nun, if it had not been for a hot midsummer night; for, good youth, he went but forth to wash him in the Hellespont, and being taken with the cramp, was drowned; and the foolish
100   chroniclers of that age found° it was "Hero of Sestos." But these are all lies. Men have died from time to time, and worms have eaten them, but not for love.

Orlando. I would not have my right Rosalind of this mind, for I protest her frown might kill me.

---

80 **honesty ranker** virtue fouler   84 **suit** (1) apparel (2) entreaty   89 **attorney** proxy   91 **in his own person** in real life (as opposed to fiction)   92 **videlicet** that is to say   92 **Troilus** (Priam's son, betrayed in love by Cressida and killed by the spear of Achilles. "As true as Troilus" became a proverbial expression)   95 **Leander** (a prototype of dedicated love, who swam the Hellespont nightly to see his mistress, Hero of Sestos)   100 **found** gave the verdict

Rosalind. By this hand, it will not kill a fly. But come, 105
now I will be your Rosalind in a more coming-on
disposition; and ask me what you will, I will grant it.

Orlando. Then love me, Rosalind.

Rosalind. Yes, faith, will I, Fridays and Saturdays and
all. 110

Orlando. And wilt thou have me?

Rosalind. Ay, and twenty such.

Orlando. What sayest thou?

Rosalind. Are you not good?

Orlando. I hope so. 115

Rosalind. Why then, can one desire too much of a good
thing? Come, sister, you shall be the priest and marry
us. Give me your hand, Orlando. What do you say,
sister?

Orlando. Pray thee marry us. 120

Celia. I cannot say the words.

Rosalind. You must begin, "Will you, Orlando—"

Celia. Go to.° Will you, Orlando, have to wife this
Rosalind?

Orlando. I will. 125

Rosalind. Ay, but when?

Orlando. Why now, as fast as she can marry us.

Rosalind. Then you must say, "I take thee, Rosalind,
for wife."

Orlando. I take thee, Rosalind, for wife. 130

Rosalind. I might ask you for your commission;° but I
do take thee, Orlando, for my husband. There's a

---

123 **Go to** that's enough   131 **commission** license

girl goes before° the priest, and certainly a woman's
thought runs before her actions.

135   *Orlando.* So do all thoughts; they are winged.

Rosalind. Now tell me how long you would have her
after you have possessed her.

Orlando. For ever and a day.

Rosalind. Say "a day," without the "ever." No, no,
140   Orlando. Men are April when they woo, December
when they wed. Maids are May when they are maids,
but the sky changes when they are wives. I will be
more jealous of thee than a Barbary cock-pigeon°
over his hen, more clamorous than a parrot against°
145   rain, more newfangled° than an ape, more giddy° in
my desires than a monkey. I will weep for nothing,
like Diana in the fountain,° and I will do that when
you are disposed to be merry; I will laugh like a hyen,
and that when thou art inclined to sleep.

150   *Orlando.* But will my Rosalind do so?

Rosalind. By my life, she will do as I do.

Orlando. O, but she is wise.

Rosalind. Or else she could not have the wit to do this;
the wiser, the waywarder. Make° the doors upon a
155   woman's wit, and it will out at the casement; shut
that, and 'twill out at the keyhole; stop that, 'twill fly
with the smoke out at the chimney.

Orlando. A man that had a wife with such a wit, he
might say, "Wit, whither wilt?"°

160   *Rosalind.* Nay, you might keep that check° for it till you
met your wife's wit going to your neighbor's bed.

133 **goes before** runs ahead (Rosalind has not waited for Celia to say, "Will
you, Rosalind, have to husband")   143 **Barbary cock-pigeon** Barb pigeon
("Barbary" suggests jealousy)   144 **against** before   145 **newfangled**
given to novelty   145 **giddy** changeable   147 **like Diana in the fountain**
i.e., steadily (Diana was a popular subject for fountain statuary)
154 **Make** shut   159 **Wit, whither wilt** i.e., where are your senses
160 **check** rebuke

Orlando. And what wit could wit have to excuse that?

Rosalind. Marry, to say she came to seek you there. You shall never take her without her answer unless you take her without her tongue. O, that woman that cannot make her fault her husband's occasion,° let her never nurse her child herself, for she will breed it like a fool. 165

Orlando. For these two hours, Rosalind, I will leave thee.

Rosalind. Alas, dear love, I cannot lack thee two hours! 170

Orlando. I must attend the Duke at dinner. By two o'clock I will be with thee again.

Rosalind. Ay, go your ways, go your ways; I knew what you would prove. My friends told me as much, and I thought no less. That flattering tongue of yours won me. 'Tis but one cast away,° and so, come death! Two o'clock is your hour? 175

Orlando. Ay, sweet Rosalind.

Rosalind. By my troth, and in good earnest, and so God mend me, and by all pretty oaths that are not dangerous, if you break one jot of your promise or come one minute behind your hour, I will think you the most pathetical° break-promise, and the most hollow lover, and the most unworthy of her you call Rosalind, that may be chosen out of the gross° band of the unfaithful. Therefore beware my censure and keep your promise. 180 185

Orlando. With no less religion° than if thou wert indeed my Rosalind. So adieu.

Rosalind. Well, Time is the old justice that examines all such offenders, and let Time try. Adieu. 190

Exit [Orlando].

---

166 **make . . . occasion** i.e., turn defense of her own actions into an accusation of her husband's   176 **one cast away** i.e., one girl deserted   183 **pathetical** (1) pitiful (2) passionate (?)   185 **gross** large   188 **religion** faith

Celia. You have simply misused° our sex in your love-prate. We must have your doublet and hose plucked over your head, and show the world what the bird
195 hath done to her own nest.

Rosalind. O coz, coz, coz, my pretty little coz, that thou didst know how many fathom deep I am in love! But it cannot be sounded. My affection hath an unknown bottom, like the Bay of Portugal.

200 *Celia.* Or rather, bottomless, that as fast as you pour affection in, it runs out.

Rosalind. No, that same wicked bastard of Venus° that was begot of thought,° conceived of spleen,° and born of madness, that blind rascally boy that abuses every
205 one's eyes because his own are out, let him be judge how deep I am in love. I'll tell thee, Aliena, I cannot be out of the sight of Orlando. I'll go find a shadow, and sigh till he come.

Celia. And I'll sleep.   *Exeunt.*

Scene 2. [*The forest.*]

Enter Jaques; and Lords, [*like*] *Foresters.*

Jaques. Which is he that killed the deer?

Lord. Sir, it was I.

Jaques. Let's present him to the Duke like a Roman conqueror; and it would do well to set the deer's
5 horns upon his head for a branch of victory. Have you no song, forester, for this purpose?

Another Lord. Yes, sir.

192 **simply misused** completely abused   202 **bastard of Venus** Cupid
203 **thought** despondency   203 **spleen** sheer impulse

Jaques. Sing it. 'Tis no matter how it be in tune, so it
make noise enough. *Music.*

• *Song.*

What shall he have that killed the deer? 10
His leather skin and horns to wear:
 Then sing him home. The rest shall bear
  This burden.°

Take thou no scorn° to wear the horn,
It was a crest ere thou wast born, 15
 Thy father's father wore it,
 And thy father bore it.
The horn, the horn, the lusty horn,
Is not a thing to laugh to scorn.° *Exeunt.*

Scene 3. [*The forest.*]

Enter Rosalind and Celia.

Rosalind. How say you now, is it not past two o'clock?
And here much° Orlando!

Celia. I warrant you, with pure love and troubled brain,
he hath ta'en his bow and arrows and is gone forth
to sleep. 5

4.2.12–13 **The rest shall bear This burden** i.e., not only the forester who
killed the deer but all men will wear the horns of cuckoldry (many editors
read the line as a stage direction: the other foresters ["the rest"] are to join
in the refrain ["burden"] after one forester has sung the first three lines
of the song. If the Folio version—here followed—is correct, it is likely that
all sing the song from the beginning) 14 **Take thou no scorn** do not be
ashamed 19 **laugh to scorn** ridicule 4.3.2 **much** i.e., not much

Enter Silvius.

Look who comes here.

Silvius. My errand is to you, fair youth.
My gentle Phebe bid me give you this.
I know not the contents, but, as I guess
10   By the stern brow and waspish action
Which she did use as she was writing of it,
It bears an angry tenor. Pardon me;
I am but as a guiltless messenger.

Rosalind. Patience herself would startle at this letter
15   And play the swaggerer. Bear this, bear all!
She says I am not fair, that I lack manners;
She calls me proud, and that she could not love me,
Were man as rare as phoenix.° 'Od's my will!
Her love is not the hare that I do hunt.
20   Why writes she so to me? Well, shepherd, well,
This is a letter of your own device.

Silvius. No, I protest, I know not the contents.
   Phebe did write it.

Rosalind.   Come, come, you are a fool,
And turned into the extremity° of love.
25   I saw her hand. She has a leathern hand,
A freestone-colored° hand. I verily did think
That her old gloves were on, but 'twas her hands.
She has a housewife's hand; but that's no matter:
I say she never did invent° this letter;
30   This is a man's invention and his hand.

Silvius. Sure it is hers.

Rosalind. Why, 'tis a boisterous and a cruel style,
A style for challengers. Why, she defies me
Like Turk to Christian. Women's gentle brain
35   Could not drop forth such giant-rude° invention,

18 **phoenix** (a legendary bird, of which there was only one in the world at any time)   24 **turned into the extremity** became the very essence   26 **freestone-colored** i.e., yellowish-brown   29 **invent** compose   35 **giant-rude** incredibly rude

    Such Ethiop words, blacker in their effect
    Than in their countenance. Will you hear the letter?

Silvius. So please you, for I never heard it yet;
    Yet heard too much of Phebe's cruelty.

Rosalind. She Phebes me.° Mark how the tyrant writes.   *40*
    (*Read.*) "Art thou god, to shepherd turned,
           That a maiden's heart hath burned?"
    Can a woman rail thus?

Silvius. Call you this railing?

Rosalind.
    (*Read.*) "Why, thy godhead laid apart,°   *45*
           Warr'st thou with a woman's heart?"
    Did you ever hear such railing?
         "Whiles the eye of man did woo me,
           That could do no vengeance° to me."
    Meaning me a beast.   *50*
         "If the scorn of your bright eyne°
         Have power to raise such love in mine,
         Alack, in me what strange effect
         Would they work in mild aspect!°
         Whiles you chid me, I did love;   *55*
         How then might your prayers move!
         He that brings this love to thee
         Little knows this love in me;
         And by him seal up thy mind,°
         Whether that thy youth and kind°   *60*
         Will the faithful offer take
         Of me and all that I can make,°
         Or else by him my love deny,
         And then I'll study how to die."

Silvius. Call you this chiding?   *65*

Celia. Alas, poor shepherd!

---

40 **She Phebes me** i.e., she writes with her customary disdain   45 **thy god-head laid apart** i.e., having assumed human form   49 **vengeance** harm
51 **eyne** eyes   54 **aspect** (1) look (2) planetary influence   59 **seal up thy mind** i.e., tell your feelings in a letter   60 **youth and kind** youthful nature
62 **make** give

Rosalind. Do you pity him? No, he deserves no pity.
Wilt thou love such a woman? What, to make thee
an instrument,° and play false strains upon thee? Not
70   to be endured! Well, go your way to her, for I see
love hath made thee a tame snake,° and say this to
her: that if she love me, I charge her to love thee; if
she will not, I will never have her unless thou entreat
for her. If you be a true lover, hence, and not a word;
75   for here comes more company.   *Exit Silvius.*

            Enter Oliver.

Oliver. Good morrow, fair ones. Pray you, if you know,
Where in the purlieus° of this forest stands
A sheepcote, fenced about with olive trees?

Celia. West of this place, down in the neighbor bottom.°
80   The rank of osiers° by the murmuring stream
Left on your right hand brings you to the place.
But at this hour the house doth keep itself;
There's none within.

Oliver. If that an eye may profit by a tongue,
85   Then should I know you by description,
Such garments and such years: "The boy is fair,
Of female favor,° and bestows° himself
Like a ripe sister;° the woman low,°
And browner than her brother." Are not you
90   The owner of the house I did enquire for?

Celia. It is no boast, being asked, to say we are.

Oliver. Orlando doth commend him to you both,
And to that youth he calls his Rosalind
He sends this bloody napkin.° Are you he?

95   *Rosalind.* I am. What must we understand by this?

Oliver. Some of my shame, if you will know of me

68–69 **make thee an instrument** use you   71 **tame snake** poor worm
77 **purlieus** borders   79 **neighbor bottom** nearby valley   80 **rank of
osiers** row of willows   87 **favor** features   87 **bestows** carries   88 **ripe
sister** grown-up woman (some editors emend "sister" to "forester")
88 **low** short   94 **napkin** handkerchief

What man I am, and how and why and where
This handkercher was stained.

Celia.   I pray you tell it.

Oliver. When last the young Orlando parted from you,
He left a promise to return again   *100*
Within an hour; and pacing through the forest,
Chewing the food of sweet and bitter fancy,°
Lo, what befell. He threw his eye aside,
And mark what object did present itself:
Under an old oak, whose boughs were mossed with
   age   *105*
And high top bald with dry antiquity,
A wretched ragged man, o'ergrown with hair,
Lay sleeping on his back; about his neck
A green and gilded snake had wreathed itself,
Who with her head, nimble in threats, approached   *110*
The opening of his mouth; but suddenly,
Seeing Orlando, it unlinked itself
And with indented° glides did slip away
Into a bush, under which bush's shade
A lioness, with udders all drawn dry,   *115*
Lay couching,° head on ground, with catlike watch
When that the sleeping man should stir; for 'tis
The royal disposition of that beast
To prey on nothing that doth seem as dead.
This seen, Orlando did approach the man   *120*
And found it was his brother, his elder brother.

Celia. O, I have heard him speak of that same brother,
And he did render° him the most unnatural
That lived amongst men.

Oliver.   And well he might so do,
For well I know he was unnatural.   *125*

Rosalind. But, to Orlando: did he leave him there,
Food to the sucked and hungry lioness?

Oliver. Twice did he turn his back and purposed so;

102 **fancy** love   113 **indented** serpentine   116 **couching** crouching
123 **render** describe

But kindness,° nobler ever than revenge,
130 And nature, stronger than his just occasion,°
Made him give battle to the lioness,
Who quickly fell before him; in which hurtling
From miserable slumber I awaked.

Celia. Are you his brother?

Rosalind.   Was't you he rescued?

135 *Celia.* Was't you that did so oft contrive° to kill him?

Oliver. 'Twas I. But 'tis not I. I do not shame
To tell you what I was, since my conversion
So sweetly tastes, being the thing I am.

Rosalind. But, for the bloody napkin?

Oliver.   By and by.°
140 When from the first to last, betwixt us two,
Tears our recountments° had most kindly bathed,
As how I came into that desert place:
In brief, he led me to the gentle Duke,
Who gave me fresh array and entertainment,°
145 Committing me unto my brother's love,
Who led me instantly unto his cave,
There stripped himself, and here upon his arm
The lioness had torn some flesh away,
Which all this while had bled; and now he fainted,
150 And cried, in fainting, upon Rosalind.
Brief, I recovered° him, bound up his wound;
And after some small space, being strong at heart,
He sent me hither, stranger as I am,
To tell this story, that you might excuse
155 His broken promise, and to give this napkin,
Dyed in his blood, unto the shepherd youth
That he in sport doth call his Rosalind.
                    [*Rosalind swoons.*]

Celia. Why, how now, Ganymede, sweet Ganymede!

---

129 **kindness** familial affection   130 **occasion** opportunity   135 **contrive** plot   139 **By and by** soon   141 **recountments** recital (of our adventures since we last met)   144 **entertainment** hospitality   151 **recovered** revived

Oliver. Many will swoon when they do look on blood.

Celia. There is more in it. Cousin Ganymede!   160

Oliver. Look, he recovers.

Rosalind. I would I were at home.

Celia.   We'll lead you thither.
I pray you, will you take him by the arm?

Oliver. Be of good cheer, youth. You a man! You lack
a man's heart.   165

Rosalind. I do so, I confess it. Ah, sirrah, a body would
think this was well counterfeited.° I pray you tell
your brother how well I counterfeited. Heigh-ho!

Oliver. This was not counterfeit. There is too great
testimony in your complexion that it was a passion   170
of earnest.°

Rosalind. Counterfeit, I assure you.

Oliver. Well then, take a good heart and counterfeit to
be a man.

Rosalind. So I do; but, i' faith, I should have been a   175
woman by right.

Celia. Come, you look paler and paler. Pray you draw
homewards. Good sir, go with us.

Oliver. That will I, for I must bear answer back
How you excuse my brother, Rosalind.   180

Rosalind. I shall devise something. But I pray you
commend my counterfeiting to him. Will you go?
                                        Exeunt.

---

167 **counterfeited** pretended   170–171 **passion of earnest** real emotion

ACT 5

Scene 1. [*The forest.*]

Enter [Touchstone, the] Clown and Audrey.

Touchstone. We shall find a time, Audrey. Patience, gentle Audrey.

Audrey. Faith, the priest was good enough, for all the old gentleman's saying.

5 *Touchstone.* A most wicked Sir Oliver, Audrey, a most vile Mar-text. But, Audrey, there is a youth here in the forest lays claim to you.

Audrey. Ay, I know who 'tis. He hath no interest in me in the world. Here comes the man you mean.

Enter William.

10 *Touchstone.* It is meat and drink to me to see a clown° by my troth, we that have good wits have much to answer for. We shall be flouting;° we cannot hold.°

William. Good ev'n, Audrey.

Audrey. God ye° good ev'n, William.

15 *William.* And good ev'n to you, sir.

5.1.10 **clown** yokel 12 **flouting** mocking 12 **hold** i.e., keep from mocking 14 **God ye** God give you

Touchstone. Good ev'n, gentle friend. Cover thy head,°
cover thy head. Nay, prithee be covered. How old
are you, friend?

William. Five-and-twenty, sir.

Touchstone. A ripe° age. Is thy name William?   20

William. William, sir.

Touchstone. A fair name. Wast born i' th' forest here?

William. Ay, sir, I thank God.

Touchstone. "Thank God." A good answer. Art rich?

William. Faith, sir, so so.   25

Touchstone. "So so" is good, very good, very excellent
good; and yet it is not, it is but so so. Art thou wise?

William. Ay, sir, I have a pretty wit.

Touchstone. Why, thou say'st well. I do now remember a
saying, "The fool doth think he is wise, but the wise   30
man knows himself to be a fool." The heathen philosopher, when he had a desire to eat a grape, would
open his lips when he put it into his mouth, meaning
thereby that grapes were made to eat and lips to open.
You do love this maid?   35

William. I do, sir.

Touchstone. Give me your hand. Art thou learned?

William. No, sir.

Touchstone. Then learn this of me: to have is to have;
for it is a figure° in rhetoric that drink, being poured   40
out of a cup into a glass, by filling the one doth
empty the other; for all your writers do consent that
ipse° is he. Now, you are not *ipse,* for I am he.

William. Which he, sir?

Touchstone. He, sir, that must marry this woman. There-   45

16 **Cover thy head** (William has removed his hat)   20 **ripe** fine
40 **figure** figure of speech   43 **ipse** he himself (Latin)

fore, you clown, abandon—which is in the vulgar,
leave—the society—which in the boorish is, company
—of this female—which in the common is, woman.
Which together is, abandon the society of this female,
50   or, clown, thou perishest; or, to thy better understanding, diest; or, to wit, I kill thee, make thee away,
translate thy life into death, thy liberty into bondage.
I will deal in poison with thee, or in bastinado,° or
in steel; I will bandy with thee in faction;° I will
55   o'errun thee with policy;° I will kill thee a hundred
and fifty ways. Therefore tremble and depart.

Audrey. Do, good William.

William. God rest you merry, sir.   *Exit.*

Enter Corin.

Corin. Our master and mistress seeks you. Come away,
60   away!

Touchstone. Trip, Audrey, trip, Audrey. I attend,° I
attend.   *Exeunt.*

Scene 2. [*The forest.*]

Enter Orlando and Oliver.

Orlando. Is't possible that on so little acquaintance you
should like her? That but seeing, you should love
her? And loving, woo? And wooing, she should
grant? And will you persever to enjoy her?

5   *Oliver.* Neither call the giddiness° of it in question, the
poverty of her, the small acquaintance, my sudden
wooing, nor her sudden consenting; but say with me,

---

53 **bastinado** cudgeling   54 **bandy with thee in faction** i.e., argue with
you as do politicians   55 **o'errun thee with policy** overwhelm you with
craft   61 **attend** come   5.2.5 **giddiness** suddenness

I love Aliena; say with her that she loves me; consent
with both that we may enjoy each other. It shall be
to your good; for my father's house, and all the   10
revenue that was old Sir Rowland's, will I estate°
upon you, and here live and die a shepherd.

Enter Rosalind.

Orlando. You have my consent. Let your wedding be
tomorrow: thither will I invite the Duke and all's
contented followers. Go you and prepare Aliena; for   15
look you, here comes my Rosalind.

Rosalind. God save you, brother.

Oliver. And you, fair sister.   [*Exit.*]

Rosalind. O my dear Orlando, how it grieves me to see
thee wear thy heart in a scarf!°   20

Orlando. It is my arm.

Rosalind. I thought thy heart had been wounded with
the claws of a lion.

Orlando. Wounded it is, but with the eyes of a lady.

Rosalind. Did your brother tell you how I counterfeited   25
to sound° when he showed me your handkercher?

Orlando. Ay, and greater wonders than that.

Rosalind. O, I know where you are! Nay, 'tis true.
There was never anything so sudden but the fight of
two rams and Caesar's thrasonical° brag of "I came,   30
saw, and overcame"; for your brother and my sister
no sooner met but they looked; no sooner looked
but they loved; no sooner loved but they sighed; no
sooner sighed but they asked one another the reason;
no sooner knew the reason but they sought the   35
remedy: and in these degrees° have they made a pair
of stairs to marriage, which they will climb incon-

---

11 **estate** settle   20 **scarf** sling   26 **sound** swoon   30 **thrasonical**
boastful (after the braggart soldier Thraso in Terence's comedy
Eunuchus)   36 **degrees** (a pun on the literal meaning, "steps")

tinent, or else be incontinent° before marriage: they
are in the very wrath of love, and they will together;
40   clubs cannot part them.

Orlando. They shall be married tomorrow, and I will
bid the Duke to the nuptial. But, O, how bitter a
thing it is to look into happiness through another
man's eyes! By so much the more shall I tomorrow
45   be at the height of heart-heaviness, by how much I
shall think my brother happy in having what he
wishes for.

Rosalind. Why then, tomorrow I cannot serve your
turn for Rosalind?

50   *Orlando.* I can live no longer by thinking.

Rosalind. I will weary you then no longer with idle
talking. Know of me then, for now I speak to some
purpose, that I know you are a gentleman of good
conceit.° I speak not this that you should bear a good
55   opinion of my knowledge, insomuch I say I know
you are; neither do I labor for a greater esteem than
may in some little measure draw a belief from you,
to do yourself good, and not to grace me.° Believe
then, if you please, that I can do strange things. I
60   have, since I was three year old, conversed° with a
magician, most profound in his art and yet not
damnable.° If you do love Rosalind so near the heart
as your gesture° cries it out, when your brother
marries Aliena shall you marry her. I know into what
65   straits of fortune she is driven; and it is not impossible to me, if it appear not inconvenient° to you, to
set her before your eyes tomorrow, human as she is,°
and without any danger.

Orlando. Speak'st thou in sober meanings?

37–38 **incontinent . . . incontinent** with all haste . . . unchaste   54 **conceit** understanding   58 **to grace me** to do credit to myself   60 **con-
versed** spent time   61–62 **and yet not damnable** (because he practices
white, not black, magic)   63 **gesture** conduct   66 **inconvenient** unfit-
ting   67 **human as she is** i.e., Rosalind herself, not a spirit

Rosalind. By my life, I do, which I tender dearly,°   70
though I say I am a magician.° Therefore put you in
your best array, bid your friends; for if you will be
married tomorrow, you shall; and to Rosalind, if
you will.

Enter Silvius and Phebe.

Look, here comes a lover of mine and a lover of hers.   75

Phebe. Youth, you have done me much ungentleness
To show the letter that I writ to you.

Rosalind. I care not if I have. It is my study°
To seem despiteful° and ungentle to you.
You are there followed by a faithful shepherd: 80
Look upon him, love him; he worships you.

Phebe. Good shepherd, tell this youth what 'tis to love.

Silvius. It is to be all made of sighs and tears;
And so am I for Phebe.

Phebe. And I for Ganymede.   85

Orlando. And I for Rosalind.

Rosalind. And I for no woman.

Silvius. It is to be all made of faith and service;
And so am I for Phebe.

Phebe. And I for Ganymede.   90

Orlando. And I for Rosalind.

Rosalind. And I for no woman.

Silvius. It is to be all made of fantasy,°
All made of passion, and all made of wishes,
All adoration, duty, and observance,°   95
All humbleness, all patience, and impatience,

---

70 **tender dearly** hold precious   71 **though ... magician** (a magician
could be punished with death)   78 **study** intention   79 **despiteful** scornful
93 **fantasy** fancy   95 **observance** devoted attention

All purity, all trial, all observance;°
And so am I for Phebe.

Phebe. And so am I for Ganymede.

100 *Orlando.* And so am I for Rosalind.

Rosalind. And so am I for no woman.

Phebe. If this be so, why blame you me to love you?

Silvius. If this be so, why blame you me to love you?

Orlando. If this be so, why blame you me to love you?

Rosalind. Why do you speak too,° "Why blame you me
105   to love you?"

Orlando. To her that is not here, nor doth not hear.

Rosalind. Pray you, no more of this; 'tis like the howling
of Irish wolves against the moon. [*To Silvius*] I will
help you if I can. [*To Phebe*] I would love you if I
110   could. Tomorrow meet me all together. [*To Phebe*] I
will marry you if ever I marry woman, and I'll be
married tomorrow. [*To Orlando*] I will satisfy you if
ever I satisfied man, and you shall be married tomorrow. [*To Silvius*] I will content you if what pleases
115   you contents you, and you shall be married tomorrow. [*To Orlando*] As you love Rosalind, meet. [*To
Silvius*] As you love Phebe, meet. And as I love no
woman, I'll meet. So fare you well. I have left you
commands.

120 *Silvius.* I'll not fail if I live.

Phebe. Nor I.

Orlando. Nor I.   *Exeunt.*

---

97 **observance** (some editors emend to "obedience")   105 **Why do you
speak too** (some editors emend to "Who do you speak to")

Scene 3. [*The forest.*]

Enter [Touchstone, the] Clown and Audrey.

Touchstone. Tomorrow is the joyful day, Audrey; tomorrow will we be married.

Audrey. I do desire it with all my heart; and I hope it is no dishonest desire to desire to be a woman of the world.° Here come two of the banished Duke's pages.   5

Enter two Pages.

First Page. Well met, honest° gentleman.

Touchstone. By my troth, well met. Come, sit, sit, and a song!

Second Page. We are for you. Sit i'th'middle.

First Page. Shall we clap into't roundly,° without hawk-   10
ing or spitting or saying we are hoarse, which are the only° prologues to a bad voice?

Second Page. I'faith, i'faith! and both in a tune,° like two gypsies on a horse.

Song.

It was a lover and his lass,   15
    With a hey, and a ho, and a hey nonino,
That o'er the green cornfield° did pass
    In springtime, the only pretty ringtime,°

5.3.4–5 **a woman of the world** i.e., (1) married (2) fashionable 6 **honest** honorable 10 **clap into't roundly** begin directly 11–12 **the only** merely the 13 **in a tune** in unison 17 **cornfield** wheatfield 18 **ring-time** i.e., the time for giving marriage rings

When birds do sing, hey ding a ding, ding.
20   Sweet lovers love the spring.

Between the acres° of the rye,
    With a hey, and a ho, and a hey nonino,
These pretty country folks would lie
    In springtime, &c.

25   This carol they began that hour,
    With a hey, and a ho, and a hey nonino,
How that a life was but a flower
    In springtime, &c.

And therefore take° the present time,
30   With a hey, and a ho, and a hey nonino,
For love is crowned with the prime°
    In springtime, &c.

Touchstone. Truly, young gentlemen, though there was
    no great matter in the ditty,° yet the note° was very
35   untuneable.

First Page. You are deceived, sir. We kept time, we lost
    not our time.

Touchstone. By my troth, yes; I count it but time lost to
    hear such a foolish song. God b' wi' you, and God
40   mend your voices. Come, Audrey.   *Exeunt.*

Scene 4. [*The forest.*]

*Enter Duke Senior, Amiens, Jaques, Orlando, Oliver,
    Celia.*

Duke Senior. Dost thou believe, Orlando, that the boy
    Can do all this that he hath promised?

21 **Between the acres** i.e., in the strips of unploughed land   29 **take**
seize   31 **prime** spring   34 **ditty** words of the song   34 **note** melody

Orlando. I sometimes do believe, and sometimes do not,
　As those that fear they hope,° and know they fear.

　　　Enter Rosalind, Silvius, and Phebe.

Rosalind. Patience once more, whiles our compact is
　urged.°   5
　You say, if I bring in your Rosalind,
　You will bestow her on Orlando here?

Duke Senior. That would I, had I kingdoms to give
　with her.

Rosalind. And you say you will have her when I bring
　her?

Orlando. That would I, were I of all kingdoms king.   10

Rosalind. You say you'll marry me, if I be willing?

Phebe. That will I, should I die the hour after.

Rosalind. But if you do refuse to marry me,
　You'll give yourself to this most faithful shepherd?

Phebe. So is the bargain.   15

Rosalind. You say that you'll have Phebe, if she will?

Silvius. Though to have her and death were both one
　thing.

Rosalind. I have promised to make all this matter even.°
　Keep you your word, O Duke, to give your daughter;
　You yours, Orlando, to receive his daughter;   20
　Keep you your word, Phebe, that you'll marry me,
　Or else, refusing me, to wed this shepherd;
　Keep your word, Silvius, that you'll marry her
　If she refuse me; and from hence I go,
　To make these doubts all even.   25
　　　　　　　　　Exit Rosalind and Celia.

Duke Senior. I do remember in this shepherd boy
　Some lively° touches of my daughter's favor.°

─────────────────────────────

5.4.4 **hope** i.e., hope in vain 5 **compact is urged** agreement is
restated 18 **make all this matter even** straighten out everything 27
lively living 27 **favor** features

Orlando. My lord, the first time that I ever saw him
    Methought he was a brother to your daughter.
30   But, my good lord, this boy is forest-born,
    And hath been tutored in the rudiments
    Of many desperate° studies by his uncle,
    Whom he reports to be a great magician,
    Obscurèd° in the circle of this forest.

    Enter [Touchstone, the] Clown and Audrey.

35 *Jaques.* There is, sure, another flood toward,° and
    these couples are coming to the ark.° Here comes a
    pair of very strange beasts, which in all tongues are
    called fools.

  Touchstone. Salutation and greeting to you all!

40 *Jaques.* Good my lord, bid him welcome. This is the
    motley-minded gentleman that I have so often met
    in the forest. He hath been a courtier, he swears.

  Touchstone. If any man doubt that, let him put me to
    my purgation.° I have trod a measure;° I have flat-
45   tered a lady; I have been politic° with my friend,
    smooth with mine enemy; I have undone° three tail-
    ors; I have had four quarrels, and like to have fought
    one.°

  Jaques. And how was that ta'en up?°

50 *Touchstone.* Faith, we met, and found the quarrel was
    upon the seventh cause.

  Jaques. How seventh cause? Good my lord, like this
    fellow.

  Duke Senior. I like him very well.

55 *Touchstone.* God 'ield° you, sir; I desire you of the like.°

32 **desperate** dangerous   34 **Obscurèd** hidden   35 **toward** approaching
36 **couples are coming to the ark** (cf. Genesis 7:2, "and of beasts that are
not clean by two, the male and his female")   43–44 **put me to my purgation** test me   44 **measure** stately dance   45 **politic** crafty   46 **undone**
ruined (by not paying his bills)   47–48 **like to have fought one** almost
fought over one   49 **ta'en up** settled   55 **God 'ield** God reward   55 **I
desire you of the like** may I return the compliment

I press in here, sir, amongst the rest of the country copulatives,° to swear and to forswear, according as marriage binds and blood breaks.° A poor virgin, sir, an ill-favored thing, sir, but mine own; a poor humor° of mine, sir, to take that that no man else will. Rich honesty° dwells like a miser, sir, in a poor house, as your pearl in your foul oyster. 60

Duke Senior. By my faith, he is very swift and sententious.°

Touchstone. According to the fool's bolt,° sir, and such dulcet diseases.° 65

Jaques. But, for the seventh cause. How did you find the quarrel on the seventh cause?

Touchstone. Upon a lie seven times removed—bear your body more seeming,° Audrey—as thus, sir. I did dislike the cut of a certain courtier's beard. He sent me word, if I said his beard was not cut well, he was in the mind it was: this is called the Retort Courteous. If I sent him word again it was not well cut, he would send me word he cut it to please himself: this is called the Quip Modest.° If again, it was not well cut, he disabled° my judgment: this is called the Reply Churlish. If again, it was not well cut, he would answer I spake not true: this is called the Reproof Valiant. If again, it was not well cut, he would say I lie: this is called the Countercheck° Quarrelsome: and so to the Lie Circumstantial° and the Lie Direct. 70 75 80

Jaques. And how oft did you say his beard was not well cut?

Touchstone. I durst go no further than the Lie Circum- 85

57 **copulatives** couples soon to be wed   58 **blood breaks** sexual interest wanes   59 **humor** whim   61 **honesty** virtue   63–64 **swift and sententious** quick-witted and pithy   65 **According to the fool's bolt** (cf. the proverb "A fool's bolt [arrow] is soon shot")   66 **dulcet diseases** pleasing weaknesses   70 **seeming** becomingly   76 **Modest** moderate   77 **disabled** did not value   81 **Countercheck** contradiction   82 **Circumstantial** indirect

stantial, nor he durst not give me the Lie Direct; and
so we measured swords° and parted.

Jaques. Can you nominate° in order now the degrees
of the lie?

90 *Touchstone.* O sir, we quarrel in print, by the book,° as
you have books for good manners. I will name you
the degrees. The first, the Retort Courteous; the
second, the Quip Modest; the third, the Reply Churlish; the fourth, the Reproof Valiant; the fifth, the
95 Countercheck Quarrelsome; the sixth, the Lie with
Circumstance; the seventh, the Lie Direct. All these
you may avoid but the Lie Direct, and you may avoid
that too, with an If. I knew when seven justices could
not take up° a quarrel, but when the parties were
100 met themselves, one of them thought but of an If:
as, "If you said so then I said so"; and they shook
hands and swore brothers. Your If is the only peace-
maker. Much virtue in If.

Jaques. Is not this a rare fellow, my lord? He's as good
105 at anything, and yet a fool.

Duke Senior. He uses his folly like a stalking horse,°
and under the presentation° of that he shoots his wit.

Enter Hymen,° Rosalind, and Celia. Still° music.

Hymen. Then is there mirth in heaven
            When earthly things made even°
110   Atone together.°
        Good Duke, receive thy daughter;
        Hymen from heaven brought her,
            Yea, brought her hither,
        That thou mightst join her hand with his
115   Whose heart within his bosom is.

---

87 **measured swords** (swords were measured before a duel) 88 **nomi-
nate** name 90 **by the book** according to the rules 99 **take up** settle
106 **stalking horse** (any object under cover of which a hunter pursues his
game) 107 **presentation** protection 107 s.d. **Hymen** god of marriage
107 s.d. **Still** soft 109 **made even** i.e., reconciled 110 **Atone together**
are set at one

Rosalind. [*To Duke*] To you I give myself, for I am yours.
    [*To Orlando*] To you I give myself, for I am yours.

Duke Senior. If there be truth in sight, you are my
    daughter.

Orlando. If there be truth in sight, you are my Rosalind.

Phebe. If sight and shape be true,   *120*
    Why then, my love adieu!

Rosalind. [*To Duke*] I'll have no father, if you be not he.
    [*To Orlando*] I'll have no husband, if you be not he.
    [*To Phebe*] Nor ne'er wed woman, if you be not she.

Hymen. Peace ho! I bar confusion: *125*
        'Tis I must make conclusion
          Of these most strange events.
        Here's eight that must take hands
        To join in Hymen's bands,
          If truth holds true contents.°   *130*
    [*To Orlando and Rosalind*]
        You and you no cross° shall part.
    [*To Oliver and Celia*]
        You and you are heart in heart.
    [*To Phebe*]
        You to his love must accord,°
        Or have a woman to your lord.
    [*To Touchstone and Audrey*]
        You and you are sure together°   *135*
        As the winter to foul weather.
    [*To all*]
        Whiles a wedlock hymn we sing,
        Feed yourselves with questioning,
        That reason wonder may diminish
        How thus we met, and these things finish.   *140*

Song.

    Wedding is great Juno's crown,
        O blessed bond of board and bed!

130 **If truth . . . contents** if the truth is true   131 **cross** quarrel   133 **accord** agree   135 **sure together** securely bound

> 'Tis Hymen peoples every town;
>> High° wedlock then be honorèd.
> Honor, high honor, and renown
>> To Hymen, god of every town!

145

Duke Senior. O my dear niece, welcome thou art to me,
Even daughter,° welcome, in no less degree!

Phebe. [*To Silvius*] I will not eat my word, now thou
art mine;
Thy faith my fancy to thee doth combine.°

150

    Enter Second Brother [*Jaques de Boys*].

Second Brother. Let me have audience for a word or two.
I am the second son of old Sir Rowland
That bring these tidings to this fair assembly.
Duke Frederick, hearing how that every day
Men of great worth resorted to this forest,
Addressed a mighty power,° which were on foot
In his own conduct,° purposely to take
His brother here and put him to the sword;
And to the skirts of this wild wood he came,
Where, meeting with an old religious man,°
After some question° with him, was converted
Both from his enterprise and from the world,
His crown bequeathing to his banished brother,
And all their lands restored to them again
That were with him exiled. This to be true
I do engage° my life.

155

160

165

Duke Senior.   Welcome, young man.
Thou offer'st fairly° to thy brothers' wedding:
To one, his lands withheld; and to the other,
A land itself at large, a potent° dukedom.
First, in this forest let us do those ends°
That here were well begun and well begot;
And after, every° of this happy number

170

---

144 **High** solemn   148 **Even daughter** i.e., even as a daughter   150 **combine** unite   156 **Addressed a mighty power** prepared a mighty army   157 **conduct** leadership   160 **old religious man** (a hermit?)   161 **question** talk   166 **engage** pledge   167 **offer'st fairly** bring a good gift   169 **potent** powerful   170 **do those ends** complete those purposes   172 **every** each one

That have endured shrewd° days and nights with us
Shall share the good of our returnèd fortune,
According to the measure° of their states.   *175*
Meantime forget this new-fall'n° dignity
And fall into our rustic revelry.
Play, music, and you brides and bridegrooms all,
With measure heaped in joy, to th' measures° fall.

Jaques. Sir, by your patience. If I heard you rightly,   *180*
The Duke hath put on a religious life
And thrown into neglect the pompous court.°

Second Brother. He hath.

Jaques. To him will I. Out of these convertites°
There is much matter to be heard and learned.   *185*
[*To Duke*] You to your former honor I bequeath;
Your patience and your virtue well deserves it.
[*To Orlando*] You to a love that your true faith doth
     merit;
[*To Oliver*] You to your land and love and great allies;
[*To Silvius*] You to a long and well-deservèd bed;   *190*
[*To Touchstone*] And you to wrangling, for thy loving
     voyage
Is but for two months victualled. So, to your pleas-
     ures:
I am for other than for dancing measures.

Duke Senior. Stay, Jaques, stay.

Jaques. To see no pastime I. What you would have   *195*
I'll stay to know at your abandoned cave.   *Exit.*

Duke Senior. Proceed, proceed. We will begin these
     rites,
As we do trust they'll end, in true delights.
                            Exit [*after the dance*].

[EPILOGUE]

Rosalind. It is not the fashion to see the lady the epilogue, but it is no more unhandsome° than to see the

173 **shrewd** hard   175 **measure** rank   176 **new-fall'n** newly acquired
179 **measures** dance steps   182 **thrown into . . . court** given up the cer-
emonious life of the court   184 **convertites** converts Epilogue.2
unhandsome unbecoming

lord the prologue. If it be true that good wine needs
no bush,° 'tis true that a good play needs no epilogue;
5 yet to good wine they do use good bushes, and good
plays prove the better by the help of good epilogues.
What a case am I in then, that am neither a good
epilogue, nor cannot insinuate with you° in the behalf
of a good play! I am not furnished° like a beggar;
10 therefore to beg will not become me. My way is to
conjure° you, and I'll begin with the women. I charge
you, O women, for the love you bear to men, to like
as much of this play as please you; and I charge you,
O men, for the love you bear to women—as I per-
15 ceive by your simpering none of you hates them—
that between you and the women the play may please.
If I were a woman,° I would kiss as many of you as
had beards that pleased me, complexions that liked°
me, and breaths that defied° not; and I am sure, as
20 many as have good beards, or good faces, or sweet
breaths, will, for my kind offer, when I make curtsy,
bid me farewell.°   *Exit.*

FINIS

---

4 **no bush** no advertisement (in Shakespeare's time vintners used an ivy
bush as a sign)   8 **insinuate with you** slyly get your approval   9 **furnished** dressed   11 **conjure** (1) solemnly entreat (2) charm (by
magic)   17 **If I were a woman** (Rosalind, of course, was played by a
boy)   18 **liked** pleased   19 **defied** disliked   22 **bid me farewell** i.e.,
applaud

Textual Note

As You Like It did not appear in print until the First Folio of 1623. The text is a good one and may represent a carefully prepared promptbook. Act and scene division is intelligent; exits and entrances are for the most part correctly indicated; and the stage directions are brief but generally adequate. The present edition follows the Folio text closely, admitting only those emendations that seem clearly necessary. A few directions not in the Folio but helpful in clarifying the action are placed in square brackets. Spelling and punctuation are modernized, speech prefixes are extended from abbreviations, obvious typographical errors and mislineation are corrected, and the Latin divisions into act and scene are translated. Other significant departures from the Folio (F) are listed below, the present reading in italics followed by F's reading in roman.

1.1.106 *she* hee   156 *Oliver* [F omits]

1.2.3 *yet I were* yet were   51 *goddesses and hath* goddesses, hath   80 *Celia* Ros   88 *Le Beau* the Beu   279 *Rosalind* Rosaline [from here on, F uses either form]

1.3.76 *her patience* per patience

2.1.49 *much* must   59 *of the country* of Countrie

2.3.10 *some* seeme   16 *Orlando* [F omits]   29 *Orlando* Ad[am]   71 *seventeen* seauentie

2.4.1 *weary* merry   42 *thy wound* they would   69 *you, friend* your friend

2.5.1 *Amiens* [F omits]   39–40 *no enemy . . . weather* &c   44 *Jaques* Amy [i.e., Amiens]

2.7.55 *Not to seem* Seeme   87 *comes* come   174 *Amiens* [F omits]
182 *Then* the

3.2.125 *this a desert* this Desert   145 *her* his   155 *pulpiter* Iupiter
255 *b' wi'* buy   356 *deifying* defying

3.4.28 *of a lover* of Louer

3.5.127–128 *yet I have* yet Haue

4.1.1 *me be better* me better   18 *my* by   29 *b'wi'* buy   201 *in, it* in, in

4.2.7 *Another Lord* Lord

4.3.5s.d. *Enter Silvius* [F places after "brain"]   8 *Phebe bid* Phebe, did
bid   143 *In* I   156 *his blood* this bloud

5.2.7 *nor her sudden* nor sodaine

5.3.18 *In spring time* In the spring time   15–32 [the fourth stanza here
appears as the second in F]   39 *b' wi'* buy

5.4.34s.d. *Enter ... Audrey* [F prints after line 33]   81 *so to the* so
ro   114 *her hand* his hand   164 *them* him   197 *we will* wee'l

The Source of
As You Like It

Shakespeare's source for *As You Like It* is Thomas Lodge's pastoral romance, *Rosalynde or Euphues' Golden Legacy*, printed in 1590. This romance in turn is based in part on a short narrative poem of the fourteenth century, "The Tale of Gamelyn," telling of the unjust treatment of Gamelyn by his older brother, the bloody fights between them, Gamelyn's flight to the greenwood, where he becomes the leader of a happy band of outlaws, and the eventual recovery of his land after his brother has been hanged. The only reference to love comes in the last lines, where we are told that Gamelyn took a "wyf bothe good and feyr."

To this rapid and brutally humorous narrative, Lodge added the story of a banished king, Gerismond, and three love stories: one of these concerns Rosader (Gamelyn of the early poem and Shakespeare's Orlando) and Rosalynde; the others, Alinda and Saladyne (Shakespeare's Celia and Oliver) and Phoebe and Montanus (Shakespeare's Phebe and Silvius). Interspersed throughout *Rosalynde* are elegant love poems. The whole, a medley of folk tale, pastoral love eclogue, and pastoral romance, is predominantly written in the highly mannered style known as Euphuism, a style made popular by John Lyly in the 1570s, but it is enlivened by homely phrases and proverbs.

Although there is no evidence that Shakespeare drew directly upon any work other than Lodge's, it is possible that three plays were in Shakespeare's mind when he came to write *As You Like It*. Two Robin Hood plays performed in 1598 by the Admiral's Company, *The Downfall of Robert Earl of Huntingdon* and *The Death of Robert Earl of*

Huntingdon, may have inspired Shakespeare's treatment of the singing outlaws, and *Sir Clyomon and Clamydes* (printed in 1599) may have suggested the rustics, Audrey and William. (In *Sir Clyomon* a princess disguised as a man meets a crude but amusing shepherd named Corin who describes in plain language the lovemaking of real shepherds and country girls.)

To return from conjecture to fact: *As You Like It* owes a great deal to *Rosalynde*. Shakespeare follows the outline of Lodge's plot closely and develops many of its situations, such as the enmity of two sets of characters, the wrestling match, the flight to the Forest, Orlando's desperate demand for food, the momentary hesitation of Orlando to save his brother from the lioness, the wooing of Rosalind disguised as Ganymede, the marriage of Celia and Oliver, the disdain of Phebe and her use of Silvius as messenger, and the return to the court. The title too may come from Lodge, who in a note to his "gentlemen readers," says, "If you like it, so."

It is not only in plot and situation that Shakespeare is indebted to Lodge. Lodge's two princesses possess in embryo almost all the characteristics of their counterparts, but compared to Shakespeare's heroine Lodge's Rosalynde is wooden. She does not master events as does Rosalind, and as a woman in love she is scarcely differentiated from Alinda (Shakespeare's Celia) or, at some points, from Phebe.

The differences are as striking as the resemblances. Some of the changes were required by the genre. For example, Shakespeare omits Rosader's internal debate on whether to save his brother, condensing the gist of this passage of over five hundred words into two and a half lines. Separate events are combined and compressed. Shakespeare omits the two reconciliations between Rosader and Saladyne and in place of the sequence where Rosader is chained as a lunatic by Saladyne and then set free by Adam with whose help he kills some of his brother's guests, Shakespeare has the brief third scene of the second act. Some material is rearranged so that major plot lines are not long lost to sight. Whereas in Lodge the Rosader–Saladyne plot is dropped for about fifteen pages when Alinda and Rosalynde appear in the forest, in Shakespeare Orlando flees to the forest at about the same time as the two girls. Lodge develops his three love affairs consecutively; one is virtually completed before the next is begun, and each is developed at almost equal length. Shakespeare quickly disposes of the Celia–Oliver romance and has Phebe fall in love with Ganymede much earlier than does Lodge. He is thus able to develop the love affairs concurrently, including the added one of Audrey and Touchstone, and to play them off one against the other. (Lodge has little of Shakespeare's ironic contrasts.)

Shakespeare retains little of the brutality of the novel. Orlando is far gentler than Rosader, the wrestler and his young opponents are injured rather than killed, and Saladyne's rescue of the ladies from a band of robbers is omitted. For the final battle in which Torismond, the usurper, dies, Shakespeare substitutes the miraculous conversion of Duke Frederick. The diminution of action and violence is in harmony with the spirit of the play and allows Shakespeare to develop contrasting emotions, values, and attitudes. Even when Shakespeare adheres to the general outline of a conversation in Lodge, he so alters the details that what is stilted in the novel becomes vivid, natural, engaging.

A few of Shakespeare's smaller changes can be mentioned here. In Lodge, the girls are not reluctant, as they are in Shakespeare, to watch the wrestling. Shakespeare gives far greater emphasis to Adam's age and long faithful service. He links the two groups of court characters by making the two Dukes brothers and the dead Sir Rowland de Boys an enemy of Duke Frederick. In Lodge, Rosalynde and Alinda see Rosader–Orlando in the forest at the same time; in Shakespeare, Celia sees him first, and her report to Rosalind allows us to see Rosalind's impulsive reaction and to hear some witty byplay.

Perhaps the most significant change is the addition of Jaques and Touchstone (Audrey, William, Martext, and Le Beau are far less important additions). Jaques and Touchstone have little effect on the development of the plot, but the Forest of Arden would be a duller and less realistic place without their presence. They help transform a piece of prose fiction, which is charming and often skillfully narrated but intellectually thin and sometimes tedious, into a play as rich in wisdom and knowledge as it is in laughter.

The following abridgment of Lodge's *Rosalynde* constitutes a little over a third of the whole. Summaries of the narrative portions omitted are given in brackets. The material reprinted is divided into fifteen sections, each preceded by a bracketed reference to the scene or passage from the play with which it can be compared.

THOMAS LODGE

Selections from Rosalynde

[Sir John of Bordeaux has gathered his three sons around his deathbed. After dividing his wealth among them, he bequeaths a moral legacy in which he cautions his sons to follow wisdom and to practice virtue.]

1. [1.1.1–166]

John of Bordeaux being thus dead was greatly lamented of his sons, and bewailed of his friends, especially of his fellow Knights of Malta, who attended on his funerals, which were performed with great solemnity. His obsequies done, Saladyne caused, next his epitaph, the contents of the scroll to be portrayed out, which were to this effect. . . .

Saladyne having thus set up the schedule [of moral axioms addressed by John of Bordeaux to his three sons], and hanged about his father's hearse many passionate poems, that France might suppose him to be passing sorrowful, he clad himself and his brothers all in black, and in such sable suits discoursed his grief; but as the hyena when she mourns is then most guileful, so Saladyne under this show of grief shadowed a heart full of contented thoughts. The tiger, though he hide his claws, will at last discover his rapine; the lion's looks are not the maps of his meaning, nor a man's physnomy is not the display of his secrets. Fire cannot be hid in the straw, nor the nature of man so concealed, but at last it will have his course. . . . So fared it with Saladyne, for after a month's mourning was passed, he fell to consideration of his father's testament; how he had bequeathed more to his younger brothers than himself, that Rosader was his father's darling, but now under his tuition, that as yet they were not come to years, and he being their guardian, might, if not defraud them of their due, yet make such havoc of their legacies and lands, as they should be a great deal the lighter; whereupon he began thus to meditate with himself:

"Saladyne, how art thou disquieted in thy thoughts, and perplexed with a world of restless passions, having thy mind troubled with the tenor of thy father's testament, and thy heart fired with the hope of present preferment! By the one thou art counseled to content thee with thy fortunes, by the other persuaded to aspire to higher wealth. Riches, Saladyne, is a great royalty, and there is no sweeter physic than store. . . . Thy brother is young, keep him now in awe; make him not checkmate with thyself, for

Nimia familiaritas contemptum parit.[1]

Let him know little, so shall he not be able to execute much; suppress his wits with a base estate, and though he be a gentleman by nature, yet form him anew, and make him a peasant by nurture; so shalt thou keep him as a slave, and reign thyself sole lord over all thy father's possessions. As for Fernandyne, thy middle brother, he is a scholar and hath no mind but on Aristotle; let him read on Galen while thou riflest with gold, and pore on his book till thou dost purchase lands. Wit is great wealth; if he have learning it is enough: and so let all rest."

In this humor was Saladyne, making his brother Rosader his footboy, for the space of two or three years, keeping him in such servile subjection, as if he had been the son of any country vassal. The young gentleman bore all with

[1]Too much familiarity breeds contempt.

patience, till on a day, walking in the garden by himself, he began to consider how he was the son of John of Bordeaux, a knight renowned for many victories, and a gentleman famoused for his virtues; how, contrary to the testament of his father, he was not only kept from his land and entreated as a servant, but smothered in such secret slavery, as he might not attain to any honorable actions.

"Ah," quoth he to himself, nature working these effectual passions, "why should I, that am a gentleman born, pass my time in such unnatural drudgery? Were it not better either in Paris to become a scholar, or in the court a courtier, or in the field a soldier, than to live a footboy to my own brother? Nature hath lent me wit to conceive, but my brother denied me art to contemplate; I have strength to perform any honorable exploit, but no liberty to accomplish my virtuous endeavors; those good parts that God hath bestowed upon me, the envy of my brother doth smother in obscurity; the harder is my fortune, and the more his forwardness."

With that, casting up his hand, he felt hair on his face, and perceiving his beard to bud, for choler he began to blush, and swore to himself he would be no more subject to such slavery. As thus he was ruminating of his melancholy passions in came Saladyne with his men, and seeing his brother in a brown study, and to forget his wonted reverence, thought to shake him out of his dumps thus:

"Sirrah," quoth he, "what is your heart on your half-penny, or are you saying a dirge for your father's soul? What, is my dinner ready?"

At this question Rosader, turning his head askance, and bending his brows as if anger there had ploughed the furrows of her wrath, with his eyes full of fire, he made this reply:

"Dost thou ask me, Saladyne, for thy cates? Ask some of thy churls who are fit for such an office. I am thine equal by nature, though not by birth, and though thou hast more cards in the bunch, I have as many trumps in my hands as thyself. Let me question with thee, why thou hast felled my woods, spoiled my manor houses, and made havoc of such utensils as my father bequeathed unto me? I tell thee, Saladyne, either answer me as a brother, or I will trouble thee as an enemy."

At this reply of Rosader's Saladyne smiled as laughing at his presumption, and frowned as checking his folly; he therefore took him up thus shortly:

"What, sirrah! Well, I see early pricks the tree that will prove a thorn; hath my familiar conversing with you made you coy, or my good looks drawn you to be thus contemptuous? I can quickly remedy such a fault, and I will bend the tree while it is a wand. In faith, sir boy, I have a snaffle for such a headstrong colt. You, sirs, lay hold on him and bind him, and then I will give him a cooling card for his choler."

This made Rosader half mad, that stepping to a great rake that stood in the garden, he laid such load upon his brother's men that he hurt some of them, and made the rest of them run away. Saladyne, seeing Rosader so resolute and with his resolution so valiant, thought his heels his best safety, and took him to a loft adjoining to the garden, whither Rosader pursued him hotly. Saladyne, afraid of his brother's fury, cried out to him thus:

"Rosader, be not so rash. I am thy brother and thine elder, and if I have done thee wrong I'll make thee amends. Revenge not anger in blood, for so shalt thou stain the virtue of old Sir John of Bordeaux. Say wherein thou art discontent and thou shalt be satisfied. Brothers' frowns ought not to be periods of wrath; what, man, look not so sourly; I know we shall be friends and better friends than we have been, for, *Amantium ira amoris redintegratio est*."[2]

These words appeased the choler of Rosader, for he was of a mild and courteous nature. . . . Upon these sugared reconciliations they went into the house arm in arm together, to the great content of all the old servants of Sir John of Bordeaux.

Thus continued the pad hidden in the straw, till it chanced that Torismond, king of France, had appointed for his pleasure a day of wrestling and of tournament to busy his commons' heads, lest, being idle, their thoughts should run

---

[2] The quarrels of friends lead to the renewing of love.

upon more serious matters, and call to remembrance their old banished king. A champion there was to stand against all comers, a Norman, a man of tall stature and of great strength—so valiant, that in many such conflicts he always bare away the victory, not only overthrowing them which he encountered, but often with the weight of his body killing them outright. Saladyne hearing of this, thinking now not to let the ball fall to the ground, but to take opportunity by the forehead, first by secret means convented with the Norman, and procured him with rich rewards to swear that if Rosader came within his claws he should never more return to quarrel with Saladyne for his possessions. The Norman desirous of pelf—as *Quis nisi mentis inops oblatum respuit aurum?*[3]—taking great gifts for little gods, took the crowns of Saladyne to perform the stratagem.

Having thus the champion tied to his villainous determination by oath, he prosecuted the intent of his purpose thus. He went to young Rosader, who in all his thoughts reached at honor, and gazed no lower than virtue commanded him, and began to tell him of this tournament and wrestling, how the king should be there, and all the chief peers of France, with all the beautiful damosels of the country.

"Now, brother," quoth he, "for the honor of Sir John of Bordeaux, our renowned father, to famous that house that never hath been found without men approved in chivalry, show thy resolution to be peremptory. For myself thou knowest, though I am eldest by birth, yet never having attempted any deeds of arms, I am youngest to perform any martial exploits, knowing better how to survey my lands than to charge my lance. My brother Fernandyne he is at Paris poring on a few papers, having more insight into sophistry and principles of philosophy, than any warlike endeavors. But thou, Rosader, the youngest in years but the eldest in valor, art a man of strength, and darest do what honor allows thee. Take thou my father's lance, his sword, and his horse, and hie thee to the tournament, and either there valiantly crack a spear, or try with the Norman for the palm of activity."

[3]Who in his right mind will refuse a gift of gold?

The words of Saladyne were but spurs to a free horse, for he had scarce uttered them, ere Rosader took him in his arms, taking his proffer so kindly, that he promised in what he might to requite his courtesy. . . .

[Torismond holds his tournament.]

2. [1.2.93–250]

At last, when the tournament ceased, the wrestling began, and the Norman presented himself as a challenger against all comers, but he looked like Hercules when he advanced himself against Achelous, so that the fury of his countenance amazed all that durst attempt to encounter with him in any deed of activity. Till at last a lusty franklin of the country came with two tall men that were his sons, of good lineaments and comely personage. The eldest of these doing his obeisance to the king entered the list, and presented himself to the Norman, who straight coped with him, and as a man that would triumph in the glory of his strength, roused himself with such fury, that not only he gave him the fall, but killed him with the weight of his corpulent personage; which the younger brother seeing, leaped presently into the place, and thirsty after the revenge, assailed the Norman with such valor, that at the first encounter he brought him to his knees; which repulsed so the Norman, that, recovering himself, fear of disgrace doubling his strength, he stepped so sternly to the young franklin, that taking him up in his arms he threw him against the ground so violently, that he broke his neck, and so ended his days with his brother. At this unlooked-for massacre the people murmured, and were all in a deep passion of pity; but the franklin, father unto these, never changed his countenance, but as a man of a courageous resolution took up the bodies of his sons without show of outward discontent.

All this while stood Rosader and saw this tragedy; who, noting the undoubted virtue of the franklin's mind, alighted off from his horse, and presently sat down on the grass, and commanded his boy to pull off his boots, making him ready to try the strength of this champion. Being furnished as he would, he clapped the franklin on the shoulder and said thus:

"Bold yeoman, whose sons have ended the term of their years with honor, for that I see thou scornest fortune with patience, and thwartest the injury of fate with content in brooking the death of thy sons, stand awhile, and either see me make a third in their tragedy, or else revenge their fall with an honorable triumph."

The franklin, seeing so goodly a gentleman to give him such courteous comfort, gave him hearty thanks, with promise to pray for his happy success. With that Rosader vailed bonnet to the king, and lightly leaped within the lists, where noting more the company than the combatant, he cast his eye upon the troop of ladies that glistered there like the stars of heaven; but at last, Love, willing to make him as amorous as he was valiant, presented him with the sight of Rosalynde, whose admirable beauty so inveigled the eye of Rosader, that forgetting himself, he stood and fed his looks on the favor of Rosalynde's face; which she perceiving blushed, which was such a doubling of her beauteous excellence, that the bashful red of Aurora at the sight of unacquainted Phaeton, was not half so glorious.

The Norman, seeing this young gentleman fettered in the looks of the ladies, drave him out of his *memento* with a shake by the shoulder. Rosader looking back with an angry frown, as if he had been wakened from some pleasant dream, discovered to all by the fury of his countenance that he was a man of some high thoughts: but when they all noted his youth and the sweetness of his visage, with a general applause of favors, they grieved that so goodly a young man should venture in so base an action: but seeing it were to his dishonor to hinder him from his enterprise, they wished him to be graced with the palm of victory.

After Rosader was thus called out of his *memento* by the Norman, he roughly clapped to him with so fierce an encounter, that they both fell to the ground, and with the violence of the fall were forced to breathe; in which space the Norman called to mind by all tokens, that this was he whom Saladyne had appointed him to kill; which conjecture made him stretch every limb, and try every sinew, that working his death he might recover the gold which so bountifully was promised him. On the contrary part, Rosader while he breathed was not idle, but still cast his eye upon Rosalynde, who to encourage him with a favor, lent him such an amorous look, as might have made the most coward desperate; which glance of Rosalynde so fired the passionate desires of Rosader, that turning to the Norman he ran upon him and braved him with a strong encounter. The Norman received him as valiantly, that there was a sore combat, hard to judge on whose side fortune would be prodigal. At last Rosader, calling to mind the beauty of his new mistress, the fame of his father's honors, and the disgrace that should fall to his house by his misfortune, roused himself and threw the Norman against the ground, falling upon his chest with so willing a weight, that the Norman yielded nature her due, and Rosader the victory.

The death of this champion, as it highly contented the franklin, as a man satisfied with revenge, so it drew the king and all the peers into a great admiration, that so young years and so beautiful a personage should contain such martial excellence; but when they knew him to be the youngest son of Sir John of Bordeaux, the king rose from his seat and embraced him and the peers entreated him with all favorable courtesy. . . .

As the king and lords graced him with embracing, so the ladies favored him with their looks, especially Rosalynde, whom the beauty and valor of Rosader had already touched; but she accounted love a toy, and fancy a momentary passion, that as it was taken in with a gaze, might be shaken off with a wink, and therefore feared not to dally in the flame; and to make Rosader know she affected him, took from her neck a jewel, and sent it by a page to the young gentleman. The prize that Venus gave to Paris was not half so pleasing to the Troyan as this gem was to Rosader; for if fortune had sworn to make him sole monarch of the world, he would rather have refused such dignity, than have lost the jewel sent him by Rosalynde. To return her with the like he was unfurnished, and yet that he might more than in his looks discover his affection, he stepped into a tent, and taking pen and paper wrote this fancy [love poem]. . . . This sonnet he sent to Rosalynde, which when she read she blushed, but with a sweet content in that she perceived love had allotted her so amorous a servant.

[Rosader and Saladyne again quarrel. Adam Spencer reconciles them. Rosalynde, debating her passion with herself, overcomes her doubts when she recalls the appearance and virtue of Rosader.]

3. [1.3.35 s.d.–136]

Scarce had Rosalynde ended her madrigal, before Torismond came in with his daughter Alinda and many of the peers of France, who were enamored of her beauty; which Torismond perceiving, fearing lest her perfection might be the beginning of his prejudice, and the hope of his fruit end in the beginning of her blossoms, he thought to banish her from the court: "for," quoth he to himself, "her face is so full of favor, that it pleads pity in the eye of every man; her beauty is so heavenly and divine, that she will prove to me as Helen did to Priam; some one of the peers will aim at her love, end the marriage, and then in his wife's right attempt the kingdom. To prevent therefore *had I wist* in all these actions, she tarries not about the court, but shall, as an exile, either wander to her father, or else seek other fortunes." In this humor, with a stern countenance full of wrath, he breathed out this censure unto her before the peers, that charged her that that night she were not seen about the court: "for," quoth he, "I have heard of thy aspiring speeches, and intended treasons." This doom was strange unto Rosalynde, and presently, covered with the shield of her innocence, she boldly brake out in reverent terms to have cleared herself; but Torismond would admit of no reason, nor durst his lords plead for Rosalynde, although her beauty had made some of them passionate, seeing the figure of wrath portrayed in his brow. Standing thus all mute, and Rosalynde amazed, Alinda, who loved her more than herself, with grief in her heart and tears in her eyes, falling down on her knees, began to entreat her father thus:

"If, mighty Torismond, I offend in pleading for my

friend, let the law of amity crave pardon for my boldness; for where there is depth of affection, there friendship alloweth a privilege. Rosalynde and I have been fostered up from our infancies, and nursed under the harbor of our conversing together with such private familiarities, that custom had wrought a union of our nature, and the sympathy of our affections such a secret love, that we have two bodies and one soul. Then marvel not, great Torismond, if, seeing my friend distressed, I find myself perplexed with a thousand sorrows; for her virtuous and honorable thoughts, which are the glories that maketh women excellent, they be such as may challenge love, and raze out suspicion. Her obedience to your majesty I refer to the censure of your own eye, that since her father's exile had smothered all griefs with patience, and in the absence of nature, hath honored you with all duty, as her own father by nurture, not in word uttering any discontent, nor in thought, as far as conjecture may reach, hammering on revenge; only in all her actions seeking to please you, and to win my favor. Her wisdom, silence, chastity, and other such rich qualities, I need not decipher: only it rests for me to conclude in one word, that she is innocent. If then, fortune, who triumphs in a variety of miseries, hath presented some envious person, as minister of her intended stratagem, to taint Rosalynde with any surmise of treason, let him be brought to her face, and confirm his accusation by witnesses; which proved, let her die, and Alinda will execute the massacre. If none can avouch any confirmed relation of her intent, use justice, my lord, it is the glory of a king, and let her live in your wonted favor; for if you banish her, myself, as copartner of her hard fortunes, will participate in exile some part of her extremities."

Torismond, at this speech of Alinda, covered his face with such a frown, as tyranny seemed to sit triumphant in his forehead, and checked her up with such taunts, as made the lords, that only were hearers, to tremble.

"Proud girl," quoth he, "hath my looks made thee so light of tongue, or my favors encouraged thee to be so forward, that thou darest presume to preach after thy father? Hath not my years more experience than thy youth, and the winter of mine age deeper insight into civil policy, than the prime of thy flourishing days? The old lion avoids the toils, where the young one leaps into the net; the care of age is provident and foresees much; suspicion is a virtue, where a man holds his enemy in his bosom. Thou, fond girl, measurest all by present affection, and as thy heart loves, thy thoughts censure; but if thou knowest that in liking Rosalynde thou hatchest up a bird to peck out thine own eyes, thou wouldst entreat as much for her absence as now thou delightest in her presence. But why do I allege policy to thee? Sit you down, housewife, and fall to your needle; if idleness make you so wanton, or liberty so mala-pert, I can quickly tie you to a sharper task. And you, maid, this night be packing, either into Arden to your father, or whither best it shall content your humor, but in the court you shall not abide."

This rigorous reply of Torismond nothing amazed Alinda, for still she prosecuted her plea in the defense of Rosalynde, wishing her father, if his censure might not be reversed, that he would appoint her partner of her exile; which if he refused to do, either she would by some secret means steal out and follow her, or else end her days with some desperate kind of death. When Torismond heard his daughter so reso-lute, his heart was so hardened against her, that he set down a definite and peremptory sentence, that they should both be banished, which presently was done, the tyrant rather choosing to hazard the loss of his only child than anyways to put in question the state of his kingdom; so suspicious and fearful is the conscience of an usurper. Well, although his lords persuaded him to retain his own daughter, yet his reso-lution might not be reversed, but both of them must away from the court without either more company or delay. In he went with great melancholy, and left these two ladies alone. Rosalynde waxed very sad, and sat down and wept. Alinda she smiled, and sitting by her friend began thus to comfort her:

"Why, how now, Rosalynde, dismayed with a frown of contrary fortune? Have I not oft heard thee say, that high minds were discovered in fortune's contempt, and heroical scene in the depth of extremities? Thou wert wont to tell others that complained of distress, that the sweetest salve for misery was patience, and the only medicine for want that precious implaister of content. Being such a good physician to others, wilt thou not minister receipts to thyself? . . . If then fortune aimeth at the fairest, be patient Rosalynde, for first by thine exile thou goest to thy father; nature is higher prized than wealth, and the love of one's parents ought to be more precious than all dignities. Why then doth my Rosalynde grieve at the frown of Torismond, who by offering her a prejudice proffers her a greater pleasure? And more, mad lass, to be melancholy, when thou hast with thee Alinda, a friend who will be a faithful copartner of all thy misfortunes, who hath left her father to follow thee, and chooseth rather to brook all extremities than to forsake thy presence. . . . Cheerly, woman; as we have been bedfellows in royalty, we will be fellow mates in poverty. I will ever be thy Alinda, and thou shalt ever rest to me Rosalynde; so shall the world canonize our friendship, and speak of Rosalynde and Alinda, as they did of Pylades and Orestes. . . ."

At this Rosalynde began to comfort her, and after she had wept a few kind tears in the bosom of her Alinda, she gave her hearty thanks, and then they sat them down to consult how they should travel. Alinda grieved at nothing but that they might have no man in their company, saying it would be their greatest prejudice in that two women went wandering without either guide or attendant.

"Tush," quoth Rosalynde, "art thou a woman, and hast not a sudden shift to prevent a misfortune? I, thou seest, am of a tall stature, and would very well become the person and apparel of a page; thou shalt be my mistress, and I will play the man so properly, that, trust me, in what company soever I come I will not be discovered. I will buy me a suit, and have my rapier very handsomely at my side, and if any knave offer wrong, your page will show him the point of his weapon."

At this Alinda smiled, and upon this they agreed, and presently gathered up all their jewels, which they trussed up in a casket, and Rosalynde in all haste provided her of robes, and Alinda, from her royal weeds, put herself in more homelike attire. Thus fitted to the purpose, away go these two friends, having now changed their names, Alinda being called Aliena, and Rosalynde Ganymede. They traveled along the vineyards, and by many byways at last got to the forest side. . . .

[In the forest Aliena and Ganymede find the verses of Montanus engraved on a tree.]

4. [4.1.141–68, 192–95]

"No doubt," quoth Aliena, "this poesy is the passion of some perplexed shepherd, that being enamored of some fair and beautiful shepherdess, suffered some sharp repulse, and therefore complained of the cruelty of his mistress."

"You may see," quoth Ganymede, "what mad cattle you women be, whose hearts sometimes are made of adamant that will touch with no impression, and sometime of wax that is fit for every form. They delight to be courted, and then they glory to seem coy, and when they are most desired then they freeze with disdain; and this fault is so common to the sex, that you see it painted out in the shepherd's passions, who found his mistress as froward as he was enamored."

"And I pray you," quoth Aliena, "if your robes were off, what mettle are you made of that you are so satirical against women? Is it not a foul bird defiles the own nest? Beware, Ganymede, that Rosader hear you not; if he do, perchance you will make him leap so far from love, that he will anger every vein in your heart."

"Thus," quoth Ganymede, "I keep decorum. I speak now as I am Aliena's page, not as I am Gerismond's daughter; for put me into a petticoat, and I will stand in defiance to the uttermost, that women are courteous, constant, virtuous, and what not."

"Stay there," quoth Aliena, "and no more words. . . ."

[Aliena and Ganymede overhear the eclogue in which Montanus, the young shepherd, describes his love for Phoebe and Corydon, the older shepherd, warns against the pains and follies of love.]

5. [2.4.18–100; 3.2.23–31, 73–77]

The shepherds having thus ended their eclogue, Aliena
stepped with Ganymede from behind the thicket; at whose
sudden sight the shepherds arose, and Aliena saluted them
thus:

"Shepherds, all hail, for such we deem you by your flocks,
and lovers, good luck, for such you seem by your passions, our
eyes being witness of the one, and our ears of the other.
Although not by love, yet by fortune, I am a distressed gentlewoman, as sorrowful as you are passionate, and as full of woes
as you of perplexed thoughts. Wandering this way in a forest
unknown, only I and my page, wearied with travel, would
fain have some place of rest. May you appoint us any place of
quiet harbor, be it never so mean, I shall be thankful to you,
contented in myself, and grateful to whosoever shall be mine
host."

Corydon, hearing the gentlewoman speak so courteously,
returned her mildly and reverently this answer:

"Fair mistress, we return you as hearty a welcome as you
gave us a courteous salute. A shepherd I am, and this a lover,
as watchful to please his wench as to feed his sheep; full of
fancies, and therefore, say I, full of follies. Exhort him I
may, but persuade him I cannot; for love admits neither of
counsel nor reason. But leaving him to his passions, if you
be distressed, I am sorrowful such a fair creature is crossed
with calamity; pray for you I may, but relieve you I cannot.
Marry, if you want lodging, if you vouch to shroud your-
selves in a shepherd's cottage, my house for this night shall
be your harbor."

Aliena thanked Corydon greatly, and presently sat her
down and Ganymede by her. Corydon looking earnestly
upon her, and with a curious survey viewing all her perfections applauded in his thought her excellence, and pitying
her distress was desirous to hear the cause of her misfortunes, began to question her thus:

"If I should not, fair damosel, occasion offense, or renew
your griefs by rubbing the scar, I would fain crave so much
favor as to know the cause of your misfortunes, and why,

and whither you wander with your page in so dangerous a forest?"

Aliena, that was as courteous as she was fair, made this reply:

"Shepherd, a friendly demand ought never to be offensive, and questions of courtesy carry privileged pardons in their foreheads. Know, therefore, to discover my fortunes were to renew my sorrows, and I should, by discoursing my mishaps, but rake fire out of the cinders. Therefore let this suffice, gentle shepherd. My distress is as great as my travel is dangerous, and I wander in this forest to light on some cottage where I and my page may dwell: for I mean to buy some farm, and a flock of sheep, and so become a shepherdess, meaning to live low, and content me with a country life; for I have heard the swains say, that they drunk without suspicion, and slept without care."

"Marry, mistress," quoth Corydon, "if you mean so you came in good time, for my landlord intends to sell both the farm I till, and the flock I keep, and cheap you may have them for ready money; and for a shepherd's life, O mistress, did you but live awhile in their content, you would say the court were rather a place of sorrow than of solace. Here, mistress, shall not fortune thwart you, but in mean misfortunes, as the loss of a few sheep, which, as it breeds no beggary, so it can be no extreme prejudice; the next year may mend all with a fresh increase. Envy stirs not us, we covet not to climb, our desires mount not above our degrees, nor our thoughts above our fortunes. Care cannot harbor in our cottages, nor do our homely couches know broken slumbers. As we exceed not in diet, so we have enough to satisfy; and, mistress, I have so much Latin, *Satis est quod sufficit.*"[4]

"By my troth, shepherd," quoth Aliena, "thou makest me in love with your country life, and therefore send for thy landlord, and I will buy thy farm and thy flocks, and thou shalt still under me be overseer of them both. Only for pleasure sake I and my page will serve you, lead the flocks to the field, and fold them. Thus will I live quiet, unknown, and contented."

[4]Sufficient is enough.

This news so gladdened the heart of Corydon, that he should not be put out of his farm, that putting off his shepherd's bonnet, he did her all the reverence that he might. But all this while sat Montanus in a muse, thinking of the cruelty of his Phoebe, whom he wooed long, but was in no hope to win. Ganymede, who still had the remembrance of Rosader in his thoughts, took delight to see the poor shepherd passionate, laughing at Love, that in all his actions was so imperious.

[Aliena and Ganymede question Montanus about his love. They happily tend their flocks every day. Back at court Rosader has been chained by Saladyne. Freed by Adam, Rosader fights with Saladyne and the sheriff, after which he takes flight with Adam. They wander in the forest, where they almost perish for hunger.]

6. [2.6.; 2.7.87s.d.–200]

As he [Adam] was ready to go forward in his passion, he looked earnestly on Rosader, and seeing him change color, he rose up and went to him, and holding his temples, said:

"What cheer, master? Though all fail, let not the heart faint; the courage of a man is showed in the resolution of his death."

At these words Rosader lifted up his eye, and looking on Adam Spencer, began to weep.

"Ah, Adam," quoth he, "I sorrow not to die, but I grieve at the manner of my death. Might I with my lance encounter the enemy, and so die in the field, it were honor and content; might I, Adam, combat with some wild beast and perish as his prey, I were satisfied; but to die with hunger, Oh Adam, it is the extremest of all extremes!"

"Master," quoth he, "you see we are both in one predicament, and long I cannot live without meat; seeing therefore we can find no food, let the death of the one preserve the life of the other. I am old, and overworn with age, you are young, and are the hope of many honors. Let me then die; I will presently cut my veins, and, master, with the warm blood relieve your fainting spirits; suck on that till I end, and you be comforted."

With that Adam Spencer was ready to pull out his knife, when Rosader full of courage, though very faint, rose up, and wished Adam Spencer to sit there till his return; "for my mind gives me," quoth he, "I shall bring thee meat." With that, like a madman, he rose up, and ranged up and down the woods, seeking to encounter some wild beast with his rapier, that either he might carry his friend Adam food, or else pledge his life in pawn for his loyalty.

It chanced that day, that Gerismond, the lawful king of France banished by Torismond, who with a lusty crew of outlaws lived in that forest, that day in honor of his birth made a feast to all his bold yeomen, and frolicked it with store of wine and venison, sitting all at a long table under the shadow of lemon trees. To that place by chance fortune conducted Rosader, who seeing such a crew of brave men, having store of that for want of which he and Adam perished, he stepped boldly to the board's end, and saluted the company thus:

"Whatsoever thou be that art master of these lusty squires, I salute thee as graciously as a man in extreme distress may; know that I and a fellow friend of mine are here famished in the forest for want of food; perish we must, unless relieved by thy favors. Therefore, if thou be a gentleman, give meat to men, and to such men as are every way worthy of life. Let the proudest squire that sits at thy table rise and encounter with me in any honorable point of activity whatsoever, and if he and thou prove me not a man, send me away comfortless. If thou refuse this, as a niggard of thy cates, I will have amongst you with my sword; for rather will I die valiantly, than perish with so cowardly an extreme."

Gerismond, looking him earnestly in the face, and seeing so proper a gentleman in so bitter a passion, was moved with so great pity, that rising from the table, he took him by the hand and bad him welcome, willing him to sit down in his place, and in his room not only to eat his fill, but be lord of the feast.

"Grammercy, sir," quoth Rosader, "but I have a feeble friend that lies hereby famished almost for food, aged and therefore less able to abide the extremity of hunger than myself, and dishonor it were for me to taste one crumb, before I made him partner of my fortunes; therefore I will run and fetch him, and then I will gratefully accept of your proffer."

Away hies Rosader to Adam Spencer, and tells him the news, who was glad of so happy fortune, but so feeble he was that he could not go; whereupon Rosader got him up on his back, and brought him to the place. Which when Gerismond and his men saw, they greatly applauded their league of friendship; and Rosader, having Gerismond's place assigned him, would not sit there himself, but set down Adam Spencer. Well, to be short, those hungry squires fell to their victuals, and feasted themselves with good delicates, and great store of wine. As soon as they had taken their repast, Gerismond, desirous to hear what hard fortune drave them into those bitter extremes, requested Rosader to discourse, if it were not any way prejudicial unto him, the cause of his travel. Rosader, desirous any way to satisfy the courtesy of his favorable host, first beginning his exordium with a volley of sighs, and a few lukewarm tears, prosecuted his discourse, and told him from point to point all his fortunes: how he was the youngest son of Sir John of Bordeaux, his name Rosader, how his brother sundry times had wronged him, and lastly how, for beating the sheriff and hurting his men, he fled.

"And this old man," quoth he, "whom I so much love and honor, is surnamed Adam Spencer, an old servant of my father's, and one, that for his love, never failed me in all my misfortunes."

When Gerismond heard this, he fell on the neck of Rosader, and next discoursing unto him how he was Gerismond their lawful king exiled by Torismond, what familiarity had ever been betwixt his father, Sir John of Bordeaux, and him, how faithful a subject he lived, and how honorable he died, promising, for his sake, to give both him and his friend such courteous entertainment as his present estate could minister, and upon this made him one of his foresters. Rosader seeing it was the king, craved pardon for his boldness, in that he did not do him due reverence, and humbly gave him thanks for his favorable courtesy. Gerismond, not satisfied yet with news, began to inquire if he had been

lately in the court of Torismond, and whether he had seen
his daughter Rosalynde or no? At this Rosader fetched a
deep sigh, and shedding many tears, could not answer. Yet
at last, gathering his spirits together, he revealed unto the
king, how Rosalynde was banished. . . . This news drave the
king into a great melancholy, that presently he arose from all
the company, and went into his privy chamber, so secret as
the harbor of the woods would allow him. The company was
all dashed at these tidings and Rosader and Adam Spencer,
having such opportunity, went to take their rest. Where we
leave them, and return again to Torismond.

[To get Saladyne's land, Torismond uses the pretext of Saladyne's
cruelty to Rosader. Thrown into prison, Saladyne repents of his
wickedness. In the forest Rosader carves verses on trees celebrating
Rosalynde.]

7. [3.2.1–10, 86–249]

One day among the rest, finding a fit opportunity and
place convenient, desirous to discover his woes to the
woods, he engraved with his knife on the bark of a myrtle
tree, this pretty estimate of his mistress' perfection . . . In
these and such like passions Rosader did every day eternize
the name of his Rosalynde; and this day especially when
Aliena and Ganymede, enforced by the heat of the sun to
seek for shelter, by good fortune arrived in that place, where
this amorous forester registered his melancholy passions.
They saw the sudden change of his looks, his folded arms,
his passionate sighs; they heard him often abruptly call on
Rosalynde, who, poor soul, was as hotly burned as himself,
but that she shrouded her pains in the cinders of honorable
modesty. Whereupon, guessing him to be in love, and
according to the nature of their sex being pitiful in that
behalf, they suddenly brake off his melancholy by their
approach, and Ganymede shook him out of his dumps thus:

"What news, forester? Hast thou wounded some deer, and
lost him in the fall? Care not man for so small a loss; thy
fees was but the skin, the shoulder, and the horns; 'tis
hunter's luck to aim fair and miss; and a woodman's fortune
to strike and yet go without the game."

"Thou art beyond the mark, Ganymede," quoth Aliena: "his passions are greater, and his sighs discovers more loss; perhaps in traversing these thickets, he hath seen some beautiful nymph, and is grown amorous."

"It may be so," quoth Ganymede, "for here he hath newly engraven some sonnet; come, and see the discourse of the forester's poems."

Reading the sonnet over, and hearing him name Rosa-lynde, Aliena looked on Ganymede and laughed, and Ganymede looking back on the forester, and seeing it was Rosader, blushed; yet thinking to shroud all under her page's apparel, she boldly returned to Rosader, and began thus:

"I pray thee tell me, forester, what is this Rosalynde for whom thou pinest away in such passions? Is she some nymph that waits upon Diana's train, whose chastity thou hast deciphered in such epithets? Or is she some shepherdess that haunts these plains whose beauty hath so bewitched thy fancy, whose name thou shadowest in covert under the figure of Rosalynde, as Ovid did Julia under the name of Corinna? Or say me forsooth, is it that Rosalynde, of whom we shepherds have heard talk, she, forester, that is the daughter of Gerismond, that once was king, and now an outlaw in the forest of Arden?"

At this Rosader fetched a deep sigh, and said:

"It is she, O gentle swain, it is she; that saint it is whom I serve, that goddess at whose shrine I do bend all my devotions; the most fairest of all fairs, the phoenix of all that sex, and the purity of all earthly perfection."

"And why, gentle forester, if she be so beautiful, and thou so amorous, is there such a disagreement in thy thoughts? Happily she resembleth the rose, that is sweet but full of prickles? Or the serpent Regius that hath scales as glorious as the sun and a breath as infectious as the Aconitum is deadly? So thy Rosalynde may be most amiable and yet unkind; full of favor and yet froward, coy without wit, and disdainful without reason."

[Rosader denies this and reads a poem describing Rosalynde's beauty.]

"Believe me," quoth Ganymede, "either the forester is an

exquisite painter, or Rosalynde far above wonder; so it makes me blush to hear how women should be so excellent, and pages so unperfect."

Rosader beholding her earnestly, answered thus:

"Truly, gentle page, thou hast cause to complain thee wert thou the substance, but resembling the shadow content thyself; for it is excellence enough to be like the excellence of nature."

"He hath answered you, Ganymede," quoth Aliena. "It is enough for pages to wait on beautiful ladies, and not to be beautiful themselves."

"O mistress," quoth Ganymede, "hold you your peace, for you are partial. Who knows not, but that all women have desire to tie sovereignty to their petticoats, and ascribe beauty to themselves, where, if boys might put on their garments, perhaps they would prove as comely; if not as comely, it may be more courteous. . . ."

[Rosader agrees to meet Ganymede and Aliena the next day to read them some more sonnets addressed to Rosalynde.]

"So Ganymede," said Aliena, the forester being gone, "you are mightily beloved; men make ditties in your praise, spend sighs for your sake, make an idol of your beauty. Believe me, it grieves me not a little to see the poor man so pensive, and you so pitiless."

"Ah, Aliena," quoth she, "be not peremptory in your judgments. I hear Rosalynde praised as I am Ganymede, but were I Rosalynde, I could answer the forester. If he mourn for love, there are medicines for love; Rosalynde cannot be fair and unkind. And so, madam, you see it is time to fold our flocks, or else Corydon will frown and say you will never prove good housewife."

[Rosalynde meditates on whether to serve Diana or Venus. She decides not to arouse the ire of Venus.]

The sun was no sooner stepped from the bed of Aurora, but Aliena was wakened by Ganymede, who, restless all night, had tossed in her passions, saying it was then time to go to the field to unfold their sheep. Aliena, that spied where the hare was by the hounds, and could see day at a little hole, thought to be pleasant with her Ganymede, and therefore replied thus:

"What, wanton! The sun is but new up, and as yet Iris' riches lie folded in the bosom of Flora; Phoebus hath not dried up the pearled dew, and so long Corydon hath taught me, it is not fit to lead the sheep abroad, lest, the dew being unwholesome, they get the rot. But now see I the old proverb true: he is in haste whom the devil drives, and where love pricks forward, there is no worse death than delay. Ah, my good page, is there fancy in thine eye, and passions in thy heart? What, hast thou wrapt love in thy looks, and set all thy thoughts on fire by affection: I tell thee, it is a flame as hard to be quenched as that of Aetna. . . .

"Come on," quoth Ganymede, "this sermon of yours is but a subtlety to lie still a-bed, because either you think the morning cold, or else I being gone, you would steal a nap. This shift carries no palm, and therefore up and away. And for Love, let me alone; I'll whip him away with nettles, and set disdain as a charm to withstand his forces: and therefore look you to yourself; be not too bold, for Venus can make you bend, nor too coy, for Cupid hath a piercing dart, that will make you cry *Peccavi*."

"And that is it," quoth Aliena, "that hath raised you so early this morning." And with that she slipped on her petticoat, and start up; and as soon as she had made her ready, and taken her breakfast, away go these two with their bag and bottles to the field, in more pleasant content of mind than ever they were in the court of Torismond.

They came no sooner nigh the folds, but they might see where their discontented forester was walking in his melancholy. As soon as Aliena saw him, she smiled and said to Ganymede:

"Wipe your eyes, sweeting, for yonder is your sweetheart this morning in deep prayers, no doubt, to Venus, that she may make you as pitiful as he is passionate. Come on, Ganymede, I pray thee, let's have a little sport with him."

[Rosader again speaks of his love and reads some of his love poems to Aliena and Ganymede.]

8. [3.2.338–90]

"Now, surely, forester," quoth Aliena, "when thou madest this sonnet, thou wert in some amorous quandary, neither too fearful as despairing of thy mistress' favors, nor too gleesome as hoping in thy fortunes."

"I can smile," quoth Ganymede, "at the sonettos, canzones, madrigals, rounds, and roundelays, that these pensive patients pour out when their eyes are more full of wantonness, than their hearts of passions. Then, as the fishers put the sweetest bait to the fairest fish, so these Ovidians, holding *amo* in their tongues, when their thoughts come at haphazard, write that they be rapt in an endless labyrinth of sorrow, when walking in the large lease of liberty, they only have their humors in their inkpot. If they find women so fond, that they will with such painted lures come to their lust, then they triumph till they be full-gorged with pleasures; and then fly they away, like ramage kites, to their own content, leaving the tame fool, their mistress, full of fancy, yet without even a feather. If they miss, as dealing with some wary wanton, that wants not such a one as themselves, but spies their subtlety, they end their amours with a few feigned sighs: and so their excuse is, their mistress is cruel, and they smother passions with patience. Such, gentle forester, we may deem you to be, that rather pass away the time here in these woods with writing amorets, than to be deeply enamored, as you say, of your Rosalynde. If you be such a one, then I pray God, when you think your fortunes at the highest, and your desires to be most excellent, then that you may with Ixion embrace Juno in a cloud, and have nothing but a marble mistress to release your martyrdom; but if you be true and trusty, eye-pained and heartsick, then accursed be Rosalynde if she prove cruel; for, forester, I flatter not, thou art worthy of as fair as she." Aliena, spying the storm by the wind, smiled to see how Ganymede flew to the first without any call; but Rosader, who took him flat for a shepherd's swain, made him this answer:

"Trust me, swain," quoth Rosader, "but my canzon was written in no such humor; for mine eye and my heart are relatives, the one drawing fancy by sight, the other entertaining her by sorrow. If thou sawest my Rosalynde, with what beauties nature hath favored her, with what perfection the heavens hath graced her, with what qualities the gods have endued her, then wouldst thou say, there is none so fickle that could be fleeting unto her. If she had been Aeneas' Dido, had Venus and Juno both scolded him from Carthage, yet her excellence, despite of them, would have detained him at Tyre. . . .

[After further conversation Rosader reads the last of his poems.]

9. [3.2.391–425; 4.1.64–151]

Ganymede, pitying her Rosader, thinking to drive him out of this amorous melancholy, said that now the sun was in his meridional heat and that it was high noon, "therefore we shepherds say, 'tis time to go to dinner; for the sun and our stomachs are shepherds' dials. Therefore, forester, if thou wilt take such fare as comes out of our homely scrips, welcome shall answer whatsoever thou wantest in delicates."

Aliena took the entertainment by the end, and told Rosader he should be her guest. He thanked them heartily, and sat with them down to dinner, where they had such cates as country state did allow them, sauced with such content, and such sweet prattle, as it seemed far more sweet than all their courtly junkets.

As soon as they had taken their repast, Rosader, giving them thanks for his good cheer, would have been gone; but Ganymede, that was loath to let him pass out of her presence, began thus:

"Nay, forester," quoth he, "if thy business be not the greater, seeing thou sayest thou art so deeply in love, let me see how thou canst woo; I will represent Rosalynde, and thou shalt be as thou art, Rosader. See in some amorous eclogue, how if Rosalynde were present, how thou couldst court her; and while we sing of love, Aliena shall tune her pipe and play us melody."

"Content," quoth Rosader, and Aliena, she, to show her

willingness, drew forth a recorder, and began to wind it.
Then the loving forester began thus:

Rosader

I pray thee, nymph, by all the working words,
By all the tears and sighs that lovers know,
Or what or thoughts or faltering tongue affords,
I crave for mine in ripping up my woe.
Sweet Rosalynde, my love—would God, my love—
My life—would God, my life—aye, pity me!
Thy lips are kind, and humble like the dove,
And but with beauty pity will not be.
Look on mine eyes, made red with rueful tears,
From whence the rain of true remorse descendeth,
All pale in looks am I though young in years,
And nought but love or death my days befriendeth.
Oh let no stormy rigor knit thy brows,
Which love appointed for his mercy seat:
The tallest tree by Boreas' breath it bows;
The iron yields with hammer, and to heat.
   O Rosalynde, then be thou pitiful,
   For Rosalynde is only beautiful.

Rosalynde

Love's wantons arm their trait'rous suits with tears,
With vows, with oaths, with looks, with showers of gold;
But when the fruit of their affects appears,
The simple heart by subtle sleights is sold. . . .

When thus they had finished their courting eclogue in
such a familiar clause, Ganymede, as augur of some good
fortunes to light upon their affections, began to be thus
pleasant:

"How now, forester, have I not fitted your turn? Have I
not played the woman handsomely, and showed myself as
coy in grants as courteous in desires, and been as full of suspicion as men of flattery? And yet to salve all, jumped I not
all up with the sweet union of love? Did not Rosalynde content her Rosader?"

The forester at this smiling, shook his head, and folding his arms made this merry reply:

"Truth, gentle swain, Rosader hath his Rosalynde; but as Ixion had Juno, who, thinking to possess a goddess, only embraced a cloud. In these imaginary fruitions of fancy I resemble the birds that fed themselves with Zeuxis' painted grapes; but they grew so lean with pecking at shadows, that they were glad, with Aesop's cock, to scrape for a barley kernel. So fareth it with me, who to feed myself with the hope of my mistress's favors, sooth myself in thy suits, and only in conceit reap a wished-for content; but if my food be no better than such amorous dreams, Venus at the year's end shall find me but a lean lover. Yet do I take these follies for high fortunes, and hope these feigned affections do divine some unfeigned end of ensuing fancies."

"And thereupon," quoth Aliena, "I'll play the priest. From this day forth Ganymede shall call thee husband, and thou shalt call Ganymede wife, and so we'll have a marriage."

"Content," quoth Rosader, and laughed.

"Content," quoth Ganymede, and changed as red as a rose; and so with a smile and a blush, they made up this jesting match, that after proved to a marriage in earnest, Rosader full little thinking he had wooed and won his Rosalynde.

[Rosader rescues Saladyne from a lion and the two brothers are reconciled. They spend three days together, in which time Rosader is sorely missed by Ganymede. Shortly after he appears and accounts for his absence, a band of robbers sets upon them, hoping to steal Aliena. Rosader is wounded, but Saladyne, who is passing by, hears their cries and saves them. He and Aliena fall in love. Meditating on the pains and perils of love, Aliena consents in her mind to accept Saladyne. Ganymede praises Saladyne. While the two are tending their flocks and thinking of their loves, Corydon approaches and tells them where they can observe Montanus pleading with Phoebe.]

10. [5.2.82–98; 3.5.1–83]

Montanus, hearing the cruel resolution of Phoebe, was so overgrown with passions, that from amorous ditties he fell flat into these terms:

"Ah, Phoebe," quoth he, "whereof art thou made, that thou regardest not my malady? Am I so hateful an object that thine eyes condemn me for an abject? Or so base, that thy desires cannot stoop so low as to lend me a gracious look? My passions are many, my loves more, my thoughts loyalty, and my fancy faith: all devoted in humble devoir to the service of Phoebe; and shall I reap no reward for such fealties. ... If, Phoebe, time may plead the proof of my truth, twice seven winters have I loved fair Phoebe; if constancy be a cause to farther my suit, Montanus' thoughts have been sealed in the sweet of Phoebe's excellence, as far from change as she from love. If outward passions may discover inward affections, the furrows in my face may decipher the sorrows of my heart, and the map of my looks the griefs of my mind. ... If Phoebe cannot love, let a storm of frowns end the discontent of my thoughts, and so let me perish in my desires, because they are above my deserts; only at my death this favor cannot be denied me, that all shall say Montanus died for love of hardhearted Phoebe."

At these words she filled her face full of frowns, and made him this short and sharp reply:

"Importunate shepherd, whose loves are lawless, because restless, are thy passions so extreme that thou canst not conceal them with patience? Or art thou so folly-sick, that thou must needs be fancy-sick, and in thy affection tied to such an exigent, as none serves but Phoebe? Well, sir, if your market may be made nowhere else, home again, for your mart is at the fairest. Phoebe is no lettuce for your lips, and her grapes hangs so high, that gaze at them you may, but touch them you cannot. Yet, Montanus, I speak not this in pride, but in disdain; not that I scorn thee, but that I hate love; for I count it as great honor to triumph over fancy as over fortune. Rest thee content therefore, Montanus. Cease from thy loves, and bridle thy looks, quench the sparkles before they grow to a further flame; for in loving me thou shalt live by loss, and what thou utterest in words are all written in the wind. Wert thou, Montanus, as fair as Paris, as hardy as Hector, as constant as Troilus, as loving as

Leander, Phoebe could not love, because she cannot love at all. . . .

Ganymede, overhearing all these passions of Montanus, could not brook the cruelty of Phoebe, but starting from behind the bush said:

"And if, damsel, you fled from me, I would transform you as Daphne to a bay, and then in contempt trample your branches under my feet."

Phoebe at this sudden reply was amazed, especially when she saw so fair a swain as Ganymede; blushing therefore, she would have been gone, but that he held her by the hand, and prosecuted his reply thus:

"What, shepherdess, so fair and so cruel? Disdain beseems not cottages, nor coyness maids; for either they be condemned to be too proud, or too froward. Take heed, fair nymph, that in despising love, you be not overreached with love, and in shaking off all, shape yourself to your own shadow, and so with Narcissus prove passionate and yet unpitied. Oft have I heard, and sometimes have I seen, high disdain turned to hot desires. Because thou art beautiful be not so coy; as there is nothing more fair, so there is nothing more fading—as momentary as the shadows which grows from a cloudy sun. Such, my fair shepherdess, as disdain in youth desire in age, and then are they hated in winter, that might have been loved in the prime. A wrinkled maid is like to a parched rose, that is cast up in coffers to please the smell, not worn in the hand to content the eye. There is no folly in love to *had I wist,* and therefore be ruled by me. Love while thou art young, lest thou be disdained when thou art old. Beauty nor time cannot be recalled, and if thou love, like of Montanus; for if his desires are many, so his deserts are great."

Phoebe all this while gazed on the perfection of Ganymede, as deeply enamored on his perfection as Montanus inveigled with hers; for her eye made survey of his excellent feature, which she found so rare, that she thought the ghost of Adonis had been leaped from Elysium in the shape of a swain. When she blushed at her own folly to look so long on a stranger, she mildly made answer to Ganymede thus:

"I cannot deny, sir, but I have heard of Love, though I never felt love; and have read of such a goddess as Venus, though I never saw any but her picture; and perhaps"—and with that she waxed red and bashful, and withal silent; which Ganymede perceiving, commended in herself the bashfulness of the maid, and desired her to go forward.

"And perhaps, sir," quoth she, "mine eye hath been more prodigal today than ever before"—and with that she stayed again, as one greatly passionate and perplexed.

Aliena seeing the hare through the maze, bade her forward with her prattle, but in vain; for at this abrupt period she broke off, and with her eyes full of tears, and her face covered with a vermilion dye, she sat down and sighed. Whereupon Aliena and Ganymede, seeing the shepherdess in such a strange plight, left Phoebe with her Montanus, wishing her friendly that she would be more pliant to Love, lest in penance Venus joined her to some sharp repentance. Phoebe made no reply, but fetched such a sigh, that Echo made relation of her plaint, giving Ganymede such an adieu with a piercing glance, that the amorous girl-boy perceived Phoebe was pinched by the heel.

[Saladyne woos and wins Aliena. Phoebe becomes ill for love of Ganymede.]

II. [3.5.84–139; 4.3.7–75]

The news of her sickness was bruited abroad through all the forest, which no sooner came to Montanus' ear, but he, like a madman, came to visit Phoebe. Where sitting by her bedside he began his exordium with so many tears and sighs, that she, perceiving the extremity of his sorrows, began now as a lover to pity them, although Ganymede held her from redressing them. Montanus craved to know the cause of her sickness, tempered with secret plaints, but she answered him, as the rest, with silence, having still the form of Ganymede in her mind, and conjecturing how she might reveal her loves. To utter it in words she found herself too bashful; to discourse by any friend she would not trust any in her amours; to remain thus perplexed still and conceal all, it was a double death. Whereupon, for her last refuge, she resolved to write unto Ganymede, and therefore desired Montanus to absent himself a while, but not to depart, for she would see if she could steal a nap. He was no sooner gone out of the chamber, but reaching to her standish, she took pen and paper, and wrote a letter to this effect. . . .

This letter and the sonnet being ended, she could find no fit messenger to send it by, and therefore she called in Montanus, and entreated him to carry it to Ganymede. Although poor Montanus saw day at a little hole, and did perceive what passion pinched her, yet, that he might seem dutiful to his mistress in all service, he dissembled the matter, and became a willing messenger of his own martyrdom. And so, taking the letter, went the next morn very early to the plains where Aliena fed her flocks, and there he found Ganymede, sitting under a pomegranate tree, sorrowing for the hard fortunes of her Rosader. Montanus saluted him, and according to his charge delivered Ganymede the letters, which, he said, came from Phoebe. At this the wanton blushed, as being abashed to think what news should come from an unknown shepherdess; but taking the letters, unripped the seals and read over the discourse of Phoebe's fancies. When she had read and overread them Ganymede began to smile, and looking on Montanus, fell into a great laughter, and with that called Aliena, to whom she showed the writings. Who, having perused them, conceited them very pleasantly, and smiled to see how love had yoked her, who before would not stoop to the lure; Aliena whispering Ganymede in the ear, and saying, "Knew Phoebe what want there were in thee to perform her will, and how unfit thy kind is to be kind to her, she would be more wise, and less enamored. But leaving that, I pray thee let us sport with this swain." At that word Ganymede, turning to Montanus, began to glance at him thus:

"I pray thee, tell me, shepherd, by those sweet thoughts and pleasing sighs that grow from my mistress' favors, art thou in love with Phoebe?"

"Oh, my youth," quoth Montanus, "were Phoebe so far in love with me, my flocks would be more fat and their master more quiet; for through the sorrows of my discontent grows the leanness of my sheep."

"Alas, poor swain," quoth Ganymede, "are thy passions so extreme or thy fancy so resolute that no reason will blemish the pride of thy affection, and raze out that which thou strivest for without hope?"

"Nothing can make me forget Phoebe, while Montanus forget himself; for those characters which true love hath stamped, neither the envy of time nor fortune can wipe away."

"Why but, Montanus," quoth Ganymede, "enter with a deep insight into the despair of thy fancies, and thou shalt see the depth of thine own follies. . . . I tell thee, Montanus, in courting Phoebe, thou barkest with the wolves of Syria against the moon, and rovest⁵ at such a mark, with thy thoughts, as is beyond the pitch of thy bow, praying to Love, when Love is pitiless, and thy malady remediless. For proof, Montanus, read these letters, wherein thou shalt see thy great follies and little hope."

With that Montanus took them and perused them, but with such sorrow in his looks, as they betrayed a source of confused passions in his heart; at every line his color changed, and every sentence was ended with a period of sighs.

At last, noting Phoebe's extreme desire toward Ganymede and her disdain toward him, giving Ganymede the letter, the shepherd stood as though he had neither won nor lost. Which Ganymede perceiving wakened him out of his dream thus:

"Now, Montanus, dost thou see thou vowest great service and obtainest but little reward. . . . Then drink not willingly of that potion wherein thou knowest is poison; creep not to her that cares not for thee. . . ."

"I tell thee, Ganymede," quoth Montanus. . . . "Persuasions are bootless, reason lends no remedy, counsel no comfort, to such whom fancy hath made resolute; and therefore though Phoebe loves Ganymede, yet Montanus must honor none but Phoebe."

"Then," quoth Ganymede, "may I rightly term thee a

⁵ shoot wildly

despairing lover, that livest without joy, and lovest without hope. But what shall I do, Montanus, to pleasure thee? Shall I despise Phoebe, as she disdains thee?"

"Oh," quoth Montanus, "that were to renew my griefs, and double my sorrows; for the sight of her discontent were the censure of my death. Alas, Ganymede, though I perish in my thoughts, let not her die in her desires. . . .

[Ganymede decides to visit Phoebe to cure her of her sickness and win her love for Montanus. Phoebe confesses her love to Ganymede.]

12. [5.2.76–122]

At this she held down her head and wept, and Ganymede rose as one that would suffer no fish to hang on his fingers, made this reply.

"Water not thy plants, Phoebe, for I do pity thy plaints, nor seek not to discover thy loves in tears, for I conjecture thy truth by thy passions; sorrow is no salve for loves, nor sighs no remedy for affection. Therefore frolic, Phoebe; for if Ganymede can cure thee, doubt not of recovery. . . . Therefore, Phoebe, seek not to suppress affection, and with the love of Montanus quench the remembrance of Ganymede; strive thou to hate me as I seek to like of thee, and ever have the duties of Montanus in thy mind, for I promise thee thou mayest have one more wealthy, but not more loyal." These words were corrosives to the perplexed Phoebe, that sobbing out sighs, and straining out tears, she blubbered out these words:

"And shall I then have no salve of Ganymede but suspense, no hope but a doubtful hazard, nor comfort, but be posted off to the will of time? Justly have the gods balanced my fortunes, who, being cruel to Montanus, found Ganymede as unkind to myself; so in forcing him perish for love, I shall die myself with overmuch love."

"I am glad," quoth Ganymede, "you look into your own faults, and see where your shoe wrings you, measuring now the pains of Montanus by your own passions."

"Truth," quoth Phoebe, "and so deeply I repent me of

my frowardness toward the shepherd, that could I cease to love Ganymede, I would resolve to like Montanus."

"What, if I can with reason persuade Phoebe to mislike of Ganymede, will she then favor Montanus?"

"When reason," quoth she, "doth quench that love I owe to thee, then will I fancy him; conditionally, that if my love can be suppressed with no reason, as being without reason Ganymede will only wed himself to Phoebe."

"I grant it, fair shepherdess," quoth he; "and to feed thee with the sweetness of hope, this resolve on: I will never marry myself to woman but unto thyself."

And with that Ganymede gave Phoebe a fruitless kiss, and such words of comfort, that before Ganymede departed she arose out of her bed, and made him and Montanus such cheer, as could be found in such a country cottage; Ganymede in the midst of their banquet rehearsing the promises of either in Montanus' favor, which highly pleased the shepherd.

[Ganymede goes to join Aliena, who is with Rosader and Saladyne.]

13. [5.2.13–74]

At last Corydon, who was with them, spied Ganymede, and with that the clown rose, and, running to meet him, cried:

"Oh sirrah, a match, a match! Our mistress shall be married on Sunday."

Thus the poor peasant frolicked it before Ganymede, who coming to the crew saluted them all, and especially Rosader, saying that he was glad to see him so well recovered of his wounds.

"I had not gone abroad so soon," quoth Rosader, "but that I am bidden to a marriage, which, on Sunday next, must be solemnized between my brother and Aliena. I see well where love leads delay is loathsome, and that small wooing serves where both the parties are willing."

"Truth," quoth Ganymede; "but a happy day should it be, if Rosader that day might be married to Rosalynde."

"Ah, good Ganymede," quoth he, "by naming Rosalynde, renew not my sorrows; for the thought of her perfections is the thrall of my miseries."

"Tush, be of good cheer, man," quoth Ganymede; "I have a friend that is deeply experienced in necromancy and magic; what art can do, shall be acted for thine advantage. I will cause him to bring in Rosalynde, if either France or any bordering nation harbor her; and upon that take the faith of a young shepherd."

Aliena smiled to see how Rosader frowned, thinking that Ganymede had jested with him. But, breaking off from those matters, the page, somewhat pleasant, began to discourse unto them what had passed between him and Phoebe; which, as they laughed, so they wondered at, all confessing that there is none so chaste but love will change. Thus they passed away the day in chat, and when the sun began to set they took their leaves and departed; Aliena providing for their marriage day such solemn cheer and handsome robes as fitted their country estate, and yet somewhat the better, in that Rosader had promised to bring Gerismond thither as a guest. Ganymede, who then meant to discover herself before her father, had made her a gown of green, and a kirtle of the finest sendal, in such sort that she seemed some heavenly nymph harbored in country attire.

[The characters assemble for the wedding of Aliena and Saladyne. Phoebe and Montanus speak of their unrequited loves to Gerismond.]

14. [5.4.1–34; 107s.d.–148]

Gerismond, desirous to prosecute the end of these passions, called in Ganymede, who, knowing the case, came in graced with such a blush, as beautified the crystal of his face with a ruddy brightness. The king noting well the physnomy of Ganymede, began by his favors to call to mind the face of his Rosalynde, and with that fetched a deep sigh. Rosader, that was passing familiar with Gerismond, demanded of him why he sighed so sore.

"Because, Rosader," quoth he, "the favor of Ganymede puts me in mind of Rosalynde."

At this word Rosader sighed so deeply, as though his heart would have burst.

"And what's the matter," quoth Gerismond, "that you quite me with such a sigh?"

"Pardon me, sir," quoth Rosader, "because I love none but Rosalynde."

"And upon that condition," quoth Gerismond, "that Rosalynde were here, I would this day make up a marriage betwixt her and thee."

At this Aliena turned her head and smiled upon Ganymede, and she could scarce keep countenance. Yet she salved all with secrecy; and Gerismond, to drive away his dumps, questioned with Ganymede, what the reason was he regarded not Phoebe's love, seeing she was as fair as the wanton that brought Troy to ruin. Ganymede mildly answered:

"If I should affect the fair Phoebe, I should offer poor Montanus great wrong to win that from him in a moment, that he hath labored for so many months. Yet have I promised to the beautiful shepherdess to wed myself never to woman except unto her; but with this promise, that if I can by reason suppress Phoebe's love toward me, she shall like of none but of Montanus."

"To that," quoth Phoebe, "I stand; for my love is so far beyond reason, as will admit no persuasion of reason."

"For justice," quoth he, "I appeal to Gerismond."

"And to his censure will I stand," quoth Phoebe.

"And in your victory," quoth Montanus, "stands the hazard of my fortunes; for if Ganymede go away with conquest, Montanus is in conceit love's monarch; if Phoebe win, then am I in effect most miserable."

"We will see this controversy," quoth Gerismond, "and then we will to church. Therefore, Ganymede, let us hear your argument."

"Nay, pardon my absence a while," quoth she, "and you shall see one in store."

In went Ganymede and dressed herself in woman's attire . . . upon her head she wore a chaplet of roses, which gave her such a grace that she looked like Flora perked in the pride of all her flowers. Thus attired came Rosalynde in, and presented herself at her father's feet, with her eyes full of tears, craving his blessing, and discoursing unto him all her fortunes, how she was banished by Torismond, and how ever since she lived in that country disguised.

[Gerismond gives Rosalynde to Rosader and Phoebe accepts Montanus. After the three couples are married in church, Corydon sings a song, the first two lines of which are "A blithe and bonny country lass, / Heigh ho, the bonny lass!"]

15. [5.4.150s.d.–198]

As they were in the midst of their jollity, word was brought in to Saladyne and Rosader that a brother of theirs, one Fernandyne, was arrived, and desired to speak with them. Gerismond overhearing this news, demanded who it was.

"It is, sir," quoth Rosader, "our middle brother, that lives a scholar in Paris; but what fortune hath driven him to seek us out I know not."

. . . Fernandyne, as one that knew as many manners as he could points of sophistry, and was as well brought up as well lettered, saluted them all. But when he espied Gerismond, kneeling on his knee he did him what reverence belonged to his estate, and with that burst forth into these speeches:

"Although, right mighty prince, this day of my brother's marriage be a day of mirth, yet time craves another course; and therefore from dainty cates rise to sharp weapons. And you, the sons of Sir John of Bordeaux, leave off your amours and fall to arms. . . . For know, Gerismond, that hard by at the edge of this forest the twelve peers of France are up in arms to recover thy right; and Torismond, trooped with a crew of desperate runagates, is ready to bid them battle. The armies are ready to join; therefore show thyself in the field to encourage thy subjects. . . .

When the peers perceived that their lawful king was there, they grew more eager; and Saladyne and Rosader so behaved themselves, that none durst stand in their way, nor abide the fury of their weapons. To be short, the peers were conquerors, Torismond's army put to flight, and himself slain in battle. The peers then gathered themselves together, and saluted their king, conducted him royally into Paris, where he was received with great joy of all the citizens. As soon as all was quiet and he had received again the crown, he sent for Alinda and Rosalynde to the court, Alinda being very passionate for the death of her father, yet brooking it with the more patience, in that she was contented with the welfare of her Saladyne.

Well, as soon as they were come to Paris, Gerismond made a royal feast for the peers and lords of his land, which continued thirty days, in which time summoning a parliament, by the consent of his nobles he created Rosader heir apparent to the kingdom; he restored Saladyne to all his father's land and gave him the Dukedom of Nemours; he made Fernandyne principal secretary to himself; and that fortune might every way seem frolic, he made Montanus lord over all the forest of Arden, Adam Spencer captain of the King's Guard, and Corydon master of Alinda's flocks.

Commentaries

ARTHUR COLBY SPRAGUE

From Shakespeare and the Actors

Early in 1723, Charles Johnson's *Love in a Forest*, a version of *As You Like It* with interpolated passages from other Shakespearean plays, especially *A Midsummer Night's Dream*, was put on at Drury Lane. Only some eighteen years later was *As You Like It* itself revived. The play prospered in the years to come, and of course accumulated traditions. But the oldest of these traditions go back only to a time long after any recollection of Elizabethan ways had vanished.

Almost at once we have a physical encounter. "Wilt thou lay hands on me?" Oliver cries (1.1.54). "Wert thou not my brother," says Orlando, "I would not take this hand from thy throat" (57–59). Oliver, one is sure, is the first to pass from words to deeds; but what precisely he does, there is no way of telling. "Going to strike" is written, evidently by some early actor, in a copy of the 1794 acting edition. Most frequently, Oliver has "advanced and laid hold of him." In like manner, I have seen an attempt by Adam to help Oliver to his feet made the pretext for the latter's "Get you with him, you old dog" (79).

In 1890, exception was taken to Ada Rehan's "rushing rapidly on the stage with a face all smiles, followed, after an interval sufficient to give the audience time to applaud, by Celia coming on in much the same manner, as if the two ladies were playing at a lively game of hide-and-seek." But leading ladies, like low comedians, have their privileges. Another note concerns Le Beau, who, at the St. James's five years before, carried "a live falcon on his wrist." This bit of antiquarianism worked out badly, for the bird flapped its wings "persistently through all his speeches."[1]

The Duke's guard form a ring. This was sometimes done with ropes and spears, sometimes by the guards kneeling and crossing their spears.[2] Then the wrestling begins. Godfrey Turner, writing in 1883, could remember only two occasions upon which it was done successfully: once at Drury Lane, in Macready's time; once at Sadler's Wells. There "Marston, a Lancashire lad, wrestled superbly, and was as agile as a cat." He

> allowed himself to be caught up by Charles, so as to lean over the wrestler's shoulder, while his own feet, being lifted clear above the ground, were coiled round the giant's firmly planted leg. For a few moments this statuesque position was retained; and then, just as Orlando appeared in utmost peril of being thrown, he suddenly regained his footing, reversed the situation, cross-buttocked Charles, and flung him heavily to earth.

Winter describes in detail Daly's arrangement of the bout. Hobart Bosworth, "who played *Charles,* was a large man of commanding presence, an athlete and a trained wrestler." He brought out "the savage animosity" Charles feels toward his adversary. After hurling Orlando from him twice, he rushed upon him "like a maddened bull." Whereupon, Orlando,

> stepping suddenly forward . . . whirled upon his heel, reaching over his own shoulder, grasped *Charles* about the neck, and, using as an aid the momentum of that swiftly rushing attack, heaved his body aloft and seemed to dash it upon

the ground with killing force. The feat was, in reality, performed by Bosworth, using *Orlando's* shoulder to pivot upon.

Benson "in his earlier days . . . would lift Oscar Asche, even then no light weight, and throw him clear over his head."[3]

After the defeat of the wrestler come these speeches:

> *Duke Frederick.* How dost thou, Charles?
> *Le Beau.* He cannot speak, my lord.
> *Duke Frederick.* Bear him away.   (1.2.208–10)

But as early as 1774 (when Bell's edition appeared), Touchstone had appropriated Le Beau's line, and he continued in possession of it for more than a century. He even gagged it, in course of time, so that it became "*He says* he cannot speak, my lord."[4] Likewise, he took charge of the removal of Charles's body—and in one instance seems actually to have dragged it off himself.[5] Usually, however, following Kemble's direction (1810), the guards have carried away Charles, with Touchstone going, or rather, strutting before. In James Lewis's copy, the comedian wrote at "He cannot speak, my lord:"—"Puts End of Staff on Chas breast &c."

Rosalind rewards Orlando by hanging a chain about his neck. Helen Faucit stealthily kissed the chain in doing so. Mary Anderson, at Stratford in 1885, approached Orlando carrying a victor's wreath as well as her own chain, and, as she pressed the chain endearingly into his hand, Orlando let the wreath "drop unheeded to the ground."[6] One further variation comes from the so-called "William Warren Edition," based on Julia Marlowe's promptbook, where Orlando goes out at the end of the scene, *"kissing cross on chain."*

A single note must suffice for the next three scenes. When Celia pleads with her father (1.3.67ff.), Julia Marlowe's Rosalind *"goes to bench and sits, weeping."* Rosalind must do something here—or do nothing very well. But the actress was criticized for abandoning "herself to such a prone state of sobbing as she did, lying prostrate . . . after the

tyrannical Duke's stumping exit up the terrace-steps." She
might have "taken her banishment with no less apprehension
but with less collapse."[7]

Act 2, Scene 3, begins with Adam [*sic*] saying "Who's
there?" and presently he warns Orlando not to come "within
these doors." Francis Gentleman, in 1770, speaks of the
scene's changing "to Oliver's house, Orlando appears
knocking at the door, and is answered by Adam." Orlando
not implausibly continued to knock on doors for over a century.[8] In two early promptbooks, Adam goes into the house
for the gold. Later, he usually carried it about with him in a
bag, going in, however, to fetch a staff and other small
objects in preparation for his journey.[9]

Rosalind, Celia, and Touchstone find themselves in the
Forest of Arden, at the beginning of Scene 4. Rosalind has
a boar spear, of course, and should have a cutlass, instead
of the little ax she was accustomed to wear at her belt in
nineteenth-century performances. Celia often carried a shepherd's crook—and leaned heavily on Touchstone.[10] Touchstone has sometimes, indeed, quite forgotten his place. Thus,
Lionel Brough, in 1880, laid Celia's "head on his shoulder,
put his arm around her waist," and patted her cheek, as they
went out together, at the end of the scene.[11] "Business and
then Change Scene" is Buckstone's promptnote at this point.
The word "Business" standing alone can be most tanta-
lizing—but not here! "Rosalind follows Corin off," reads the
Howard Athenaeum (Boston) Promptbook, "Touchstone is
following slowly when Celia calls, 'Touchstone,' he turns,
recollects, goes back for her and they Exit together." The
same pleasant bit of byplay turns up in at least three later
acting versions.[12]

Daly's treatment of the songs in Scene 5 was justly
praised:

> Sung as they were by Amiens half lying on the ground,
> with his brother exiles stretched on the sward around him . . .
> they fitted naturally into the action. . . . As usually given by a
> gentleman who advances to the footlights and sings not to his
> companions but across the orchestra to the audience, all the
> dramatic value of these lyrics is lost.[13]

Next we have Orlando and Adam; and Orlando should carry Adam off. Not infrequently, however, he has shirked his assignment and merely led the old man away.[14] In the last scene in the act, it may be worth noting that in Lester Wallack's promptbook: "Duke—blesses—repast," just before Orlando rushes in (2.7.87); and "Jaq. Eats" after Orlando has forbidden it—which occasions his "but forbear, I say" (97). At the end, it was usual for Amiens and Jaques to help Adam away, Orlando being now deeply engaged in talk with the Duke.[15]

As for the Seven Ages Speech, the old way was to accompany the "reading" of it with a full display of the actor's powers of mimicry. Darbyshire, in his *Art of the Victorian Stage*, describes a talk he had with Irving after a performance of *As You Like It* at the Prince's Theatre, Manchester, in 1902. " 'If these people are right,' " Irving is quoted as saying,

"how terribly wrong we must have been; who ever heard of or saw Jaques on a rustic stool at a table, from which he gave the seven age speech, and never rose from it, not even on the delivery of the final line." . . . I reminded Sir Henry . . . that he gave the "To be or not to be" speech from an arm chair.

Oscar Asche was to carry informality a step further, and munch an apple during the delivery of the lines—a feat which took, he observes, much rehearsing.[16]

Upon his entrance in the second scene in Act 3, Orlando certainly hangs his verses on a tree—or, in Elizabethan performances, on one of "the pillars of the heavens"—and the natural sequence is for Rosalind, when she appears, to find these verses rather than bring others with her. So, at any rate, she does in *Love in a Forest* and in most of the later acting editions.[17] Winter, in a characteristic effusion, describes Ada Rehan's entrance:

When she dashed through the trees of Arden, snatching the verses of Orlando from their boughs, and cast herself at the foot of a great elm, to read those fond messages . . . her whole person, in its graceful abandonment of posture, seemed to express an ecstasy of happy vitality and of victorious delight; her hands that held the written scrolls trembled with eager, tumultuous, and grateful joy.[18]

Mary Anderson had entered singing and sauntering, continued to sing negligently after she read Orlando's poem, then stopped singing as she read it. It may be added that Ben Greet's Touchstone, in 1896, was pounced upon by Mr. Bernard Shaw for picking up and reading—as if they were still another of Orlando's compositions—"the impromptu burlesque" beginning "If a hart do lack a hind."[19]

Soon afterwards, Celia dismisses Corin and Touchstone. In Daly's version, Touchstone has been impertinently "*looking over her shoulder and reading in dumb show, winking* at Corin." At Celia's "Shepherd, go off a little" (3.2.158–59), Touchstone "*orders Corin off with a gesture, when he turns—and is ordered off himself. He goes with comic abruptness, first picking up the paper, which he carries off, reading dumb show.*" In the "William Warren Edition" when Celia says "Go with him, sirrah," Touchstone "*points to himself inquiringly*; Celia *points* L.; Corin *laughs.*"

Celia names Orlando as the writer of the verses, and Rosalind exclaims, "Alas the day! what shall I do with my doublet and hose?" (217–18) At this point, the Victorian actress was likely to make a great to-do about her own legs. Mrs. Kendal put "her hands over her face" at "Alas the day," then after a pause crossed to where Celia was sitting and spoke, "half whispering in Celia's ear, 'What shall I do with my doublet and hose?' "[20] To a writer in *Blackwood's* for September 1890, Rosalind's words are merely an expression

of natural embarrassment, suddenly to find that here is the man to whom she has lost her heart, by whom "she would be woo'd, and not unsought be won," and that her man's attire stands in the way of her being so. . . . What can Miss Rehan mean by pulling down her doublet as she speaks the words, as though she would accomplish the impossible feat of hiding her legs under it,—an indelicacy of suggestion at which one can only shudder?

A. B. Walkley, playing "Devil's Advocate," complains that the American actress "made as much fuss as though she had been Susannah surprised by the Elders."[21] On the other hand, W. Graham Robertson writes of Mrs. Langtry that, as Rosalind, she gave "no new readings," spoke her lines

> simply, not chopping them up with "business" or strangling them with "suppressed emotion." ... In short, she gave Shakespeare a chance. ... One bit of original business I remember which I have never noticed in another Rosalind. She carefully avoided all vulgar clowning in passages referring to her male attire, but when she spoke the line—"Here, on the skirts of the forest, like fringe on a petticoat," she put out her hand with a perfectly natural gesture to pick up her own petticoat, and finding none, paused awkwardly for half a second.[22]

Meanwhile, Jaques and Orlando have entered, and Rosalind has overheard their talk (Ada Rehan could not forbear clapping her hands "vivaciously, though softly, on hearing Orlando's sentiments"). On the departure of "Monsieur Melancholy," the lover may well begin to "mar trees" once more[23]—and Rosalind will attract his attention with difficulty. Helen Faucit was praised for the manner in which she hugged Orlando's verses to her heart, as she talked with Orlando himself about them; and Mary Anderson used very similar business.[24]

On January 6, 1825, *The Edinburgh Dramatic Review*, in commenting upon a performance at the Theatre Royal the night before, praises the Audrey of Mrs. Nicol as

> most rich and felicitous. There was perhaps an anachronism in her munching a turnip; but, to be sure, since Shakespeare treated the forest of *Ardennes* with a lion, a little thing like this may be overlooked; *argale,* we were very much pleased with the effect of the turnip.

From the terms used, it is conceivable that the eating of turnips was new to Audrey, in Edinburgh, at any rate, but once she had begun it was long indeed before she tired of them. In the Boston, Howard Athenaeum Promptbook, of 1852, she is furnished at her entrance—arm in arm with Touchstone—with a "clasp knife, turnip and large sunflower." At "Well, the gods give us joy" (3.3.45), Cumberland's old direction, *"Capers clumsily up the Stage,"* is kept, with the added note: "during this Sc Audrey produces a knife & turnip and after peeling it cuts and eats it occasionally offering Touchstone a piece." And at the end: "He takes her arm and they go up and off R3E she dancing and singing 'The gods give us joy &c.' "[25]

The natural affinity existing between Audrey and her turnip is made the subject of some highly curious reflections by Arthur Matthison in his essay, "Theatrical Properties," in *The Era Almanack* for 1882. "Woe to the day for *As You Like It*," he exclaims, "should Audrey venture on alone, or the turnip in a rash moment rush on its fate discoupled from its Audrey." That day was fast approaching. In 1885, when Mary Anderson played Rosalind at Stratford, Audrey, indeed, not only "gnawed" a turnip, but one which "had been plucked near Anne Hathaway's cottage." But Marion Lea, Mrs. Langtry's Audrey in 1890, spoke "Is it honest in deed and word? Is it a true thing?" simply and well, instead of drawling it "with a leer between two bites at a property turnip." And in Isabel Irving's performance with the Daly Company, "for the first time *Audrey* became a possible mate for *Touchstone*, and no mere turnip-munching, cherry-cheeked clod."[26] Daly's acting edition has her in the course of devouring *"a huge turnip,"* early in the scene. "Touchstone, *annoyed, snatches it and throws it off.*" Then she produces a succession of apples! In the "William Warren Edition" these apples again figure—but there is no turnip.

The scene of the mock marriage, early in Act 4, needs taste and tact if it is to be right. I fancy we should have liked the Orlando of Forbes-Robertson, which puzzled and somewhat offended *The Athenaeum* (27 October 1888):

What can we make of an Orlando who accepts his mistress's challenge to woo her in her disguise as a Girton graduate might accept a proposal to analyze a case of modern witchcraft; who declines, until compelled, to kiss the small gloved hand?

But we read, too, of Adelaide Neilson that "her utterance of the simple words 'Woo me! woo me!' to Orlando, as her cheek was laid upon his shoulder, and her arm stole coyly about his neck, was sweet as a blackbird's call to his mate." And when all allowance has been made for the sentimentality of the description, the action described still seems wrong. In Fanny Davenport's promptbook, when Rosalind, hearing that Orlando must be away from her until two o'clock, says, " 'Tis but one cast away, and so, come death!" (4.1.176–77) she "cries—Orlando taps her on shoulder—she turns laughing—he retreats"; and on his exit, "Ros. coughs—Orlando reenters—kisses her hand and then runs off." Both bits of business found their way into later acting texts.[27]

As for the episode of Rosalind's fainting near the end of the act, it is enough to note that Oliver had better not catch her, or do more than Celia asks him to do, take her by the arm; that he has sometimes slapped "Ganymede" cheerfully on the back, at "take a good heart and counterfeit to be a man" (4.3.173–74); and that Rosalind has occasionally indulged in a second (pretended) swoon, at "I pray you tell your brother how well I counterfeited. Heigh-ho!" (67–68) Fanny Davenport, indeed, to get a strong curtain, closed with: "Ros. faints on back C. Oliver on R & Celia on L. of bank. . . . Picture."[28]

In the first scene in Act 5, Touchstone has been accustomed to follow William about, threateningly, during the speech beginning "He, sir, that must marry this woman" (45), the clown shrinking before him.[29]

In the concluding scene, Robson's Touchstone, at Cincinnati in 1885, is described with relish by Frederick Warde: "He strutted, he crowed, and to continue the simile, he flapped his wings with the triumphant satisfaction of a barnyard rooster."[30] "Salutation and greeting to you all," says Touchstone (5.4.39)—and James Lewis wrote against the words, in his copy of *As You Like It*, "bows. Makes Audrey curtsy &c." What she does to occasion his reproving, "Bear your body more seeming, Audrey" (69–70) is for the actress to decide. I have seen her hanging upon Touchstone here.[31] Or perhaps she merely stands in some ungainly posture gaping at the courtiers? The stage direction in Cumberland's edition, "Audrey, L. assumes a stiff and formal air," presupposes some such display of loutishness. On the other hand, the observant, if censorious author of "*As You Like It*, à l'Américaine," in *Blackwood's* for September 1890, after remarking that the words are a hint to Audrey "not to slouch in country fashion before the great folks," is shocked to find that in Daly's production Touchstone here "turned round to Audrey, who is flirting with two courtiers (*proh pudor!*) and with these words swings her round to him with the roughness of an angry boor."[32]

Rosalind's final entrance, in early nineteenth-century editions, is slightly postponed. Hymen delivers his first stanza, then "*goes to the Top of the Stage, brings forward* Rosalind, *and presents her to the Duke.*" Anna Seward, in a letter dated 20 July 1786, describes Mrs. Siddons at this moment in the play:

> One of those rays of exquisite and original discrimination, which her genius so perpetually elicits, shone out on her first rushing upon the stage in her own resumed person and dress: when she bent her knee to her father, the Duke, and said—
> "To you I give myself—for I am yours";
> and when, falling into Orlando's arms, she repeated the same words,—
> "To *you* I give myself—for I am *yours!*" . . .
> The tender joy of filial love was in the first [line]; the whole soul of enamoured transport in the second.

A century and more later, Julia Arthur was inspired to bring upon the stage "a lot of monks in an attempt to make the all-round marriage at the end realistic and spectacular." Norman Hapgood, who liked her production, calls this the "only impertinence" in it.[33]

Bibliographical Notes

PROMPTBOOKS

(a)   ? Eighteenth Century Promptbook (N. Y. P.).
[Bell ed. annotated in old hand. What looks like "Carvers Gar:" (*sc.* "Garden" at beginning of I, 1—cf. Robert Carver, the scene painter, died 1791. Very few properties—e.g., a single "gilt chair" in 1, 2.]

(b)   Marked Copy of 1794 acting edition (Harvard).
[Old hand and faded ink. An actor's name (?) against "Oliver," p. 63, but this is in pencil and perhaps later, as is "write this myself," p. 51.]

(c)   Aberdeen 1806 Promptbook (N. Y. P.).
[1774 ed. inscribed "Aberdeen Jany 1806."]

(d)   "Prompt Book Theatres Sheffield & Doncaster. Novr 1834" (N. Y. P.).

(e)   "Prompt Copy Marked & Corrected by Robert Jones Stage Manager Howard Athenaeum Boston 1852" (N. Y. P.).
[Jones became stage manager at the opening of the season of 1852–53 when *As You Like It* was played with Miss Kimberly as Rosalind, Oct. 4 and 15—Van Lennep.]

(f)   Buckstone's Haymarket 1867 Inscribed Promptbook (A. G. S.).
[Stage directions in Lacy's Acting Edition almost invariably retained. Some penciled additions refer to Manchester performances.]

(g)   Lester Wallack's Promptbook (N. Y. P.).
[Penciled cast that of the important revival Sept. 30, 1880—see Odell, xi, 220. Twice described as "Wallack's Copy."]

(h)   James L. Carhart's Marked Copy (Harvard).
[Ed. "As Played by Mrs. Langtry," New York and London, c. 1883, with printed cast including Carhart as Duke. This part and that of Adam are marked.]

(i)   Fanny Davenport's 1886 Promptbook (Harvard).

[Handwriting, cuts, business, etc. identify it with "j" and the Fanny Davenport–J. H. Barnes tour of 1886–87. See *Much Ado* "f."]

(j)   Wilton Lackaye's Marked Copy (Harvard).
["Property of Miss Davenport," and "Oliver" (in pencil, "Lackaye") on cover. Lackaye appeared with Miss Davenport on 1886–87 tour. Two other marked copies are for "Phoebe" and "Banished Duke."]

(k)   James Lewis's Marked Copy (Harvard).
["French's Standard Drama" ed. "James Lewis" on wrapper, and the part of Touchstone marked throughout. He played it, under Daly, in 1889.]

The "William Warren Edition," Boston [1907], is "based upon the Prompt Book of Miss Julia Marlowe."

Notes

[[Professor Sprague has the following introduction to his notes. "In order to cut down the number of notes as much as possible, references to authorities have frequently been grouped in sequences corresponding to those of the text, with semicolons used to distinguish one set of references from another. Thus, on page 66 of the text, I have written:

Mamillius, early in the nineteenth century, was contented with such playthings as a horse and drum. But Ellen Terry, playing the part in Charles Kean's production, drew about a toy cart 'from an actual one, in terra-cotta, preserved in the British Museum.'232

Note 232 reads: 'Oxberry's edition; Kean's edition, William Archer, "The Winter's Tale," *The Nineteenth Century*, October 1887, Ellen Terry, *The Story of My Life*, photograph opposite page 12, etc.' Here 'Oxberry's edition' is my authority for the early toys; whereas 'Kean's edition' and the other two citations refer to Ellen Terry's go-cart."

Material in double brackets has been added by editor.]]

1. *"As You Like It* à l'Américaine," *Blackwood's,* September 1890; *Dramatic Review,* 1 February 1885.

2. Daly's acting edition (1890); Lester Wallack's promptbook, "William Warren Edition."

3. "Pittite Memories," *The Theatre,* 1 November 1883; [[William Winter]], *Shakespeare on the Stage,* Second Series [[New York, 1915]], pp. 278 ff.; [[Gordon]] Crosse, *Fifty Years of Shakespearean Playgoing* [[London, 1941]], 31. For an ingenious modern expedient for avoiding the danger of ridicule here, see Harcourt Williams, *Four Years at the Old Vic*, London [1935], pp. 189, 190.

4. He spoke the line as recently as 1886 (Lackaye's Marked Copy). For the gag, see [[Frederick]] Warde, *The Fools of Shakespeare* [[New York, 1913]], 48.

5. 1794 Marked Copy.

6. [Margaret Stokes,] "Helen Faucit," *Blackwood's,* December 1885, cf. Helen Faucit, *On Some of Shakespeare's Female Characters,* Edinburgh and London, 1891, p. 244; Winter, *Shakespeare on the Stage,* Second Series, p. 296.

7. "William Warren Edition"; C[harlotte] P[orter], in *Poet-Lore,* I (1889), p. 142.

8. *The Dramatic Censor,* I, 465. James Carhart's marked copy of Mrs. Langtry's acting edition (c. 1883) still has the knocking. It is absent in the Daly and "William Warren" editions.

9. Eighteenth Century (?) Promptbook in New York Public Library, Sheffield and Doncaster Promptbook; Howard Athenaeum and Wallack Promptbooks, Carhart's Marked Copy.

10. Cf. I, 3, 119, and R. G. White, *Studies in Shakespeare,* Boston and New York, 1886, p. 245; and, for the crook, Howard Athenaeum and other promptbooks, Daly's edition.

11. *The Theatre,* April 1, 1880, *Athenaeum,* 6 March 1880.

12. Wallack and Fanny Davenport Promptbooks, Daly's edition.

13. "*As You Like It* à l'Américaine," *Blackwood's,* September 1890.

14. As, e.g., in *Love in a Forest,* where, though Orlando still says, "Come I will bear thee to some Shelter," he goes out, and later returns, merely "*leading* Adam."

15. "Eighteenth Century," Howard Athenaeum, and Wallack Promptbooks.

16. E.g., *The Monthly Mirror,* N.S., viii (1810), p. 466, *Shakespeariana,* V (1888), p. 223, J. R. Towse, *Sixty Years of the Theater,* New York and London, 1916, p. 113; [[A.]] Darbyshire [[*The Art of the Victorian Stage,* London and Manchester, 1907]], 77, 78; Max Beerbohm, *Around Theatres,* New York 1930, II, 616, Oscar Asche *His Life,* London [1929], p. 119. At "Even in the cannon's mouth . . ." Daly's edition has the listeners "nod to each other."

17. Exceptions are Bell's and the "William Warren" editions. Dover Wilson has Rosalind find the verses. Kittredge has her bring them.

18. *Shadows of the Stage,* Second Series, New York, 1893 (1898), p. 251, repeated in his *Wallet of Time,* II, 155. Ada Rehan carried one paper with her and took another from the tree (Daly's edition).

19. *Dramatic Review,* 5 September 1885, Winter, *Shakespeare on the Stage,* Second Series, p. 299; *Our Theatres in the Nineties,* II, 122.

20. *The Dramatic Review,* 1 February 1885.

21. *Playhouse Impressions,* London, 1892, p. 32, Clement Scott, *Thirty Years at the Play and Dramatic Table Talk,* London [1891], p. 216. See also, *The Athenaeum,* 4 March 1871 (on Mrs. Rousby), and the Daly and "William Warren" editions.

22. *Life Was Worth Living,* New York and London [1931], p. 71.

23. *Saturday Review,* 26 July 1890, "*As You Like It* à l'Américaine"; Wallack's promptbook, cf. Daly and "William Warren" editions.

24. [[Joseph]] Knight, *Theatrical Notes* [[London, 1893]], 17; Winter, *Shakespeare on the Stage,* Second Series, pp. 299, 300.

25. Cumberland's *British Theatre* (1826). Wallack's promptbook also gives her the sunflower, knife, and turnip. The sunflower is wanting in Fanny Davenport's promptbook.

26. Mary Anderson, *A Few Memories,* New York, 1896, p. 197; W. G. Robertson, *Life Was Worth Living,* 72; *The Theatre,* 1 February 1894. See also Dutton Cook, *Nights at the Play,* 2 vols., London, 1883, I, 247, and *The Theatre,* 1 May 1894. Much later, Elizabeth Fagan always ate "a big raw turnip," as Audrey with Benson's Company (*From the Wings,* London, etc. [1922,] p. 73.

27. L. Clarke Davis, "Gossip about Actors," *The Galaxy,* May 1873; "William Warren Edition," cf. *Poet-Lore,* I (1889), p. 144; Daly's edition. For the deer carried across the stage at many Stratford performances, in IV, 2, see C. E. Flower in [[*As You Like It*]], "Memorial Theatre Edition" [[London, 1885]], p. vi.

28 Mary Anderson's acting edition, New York, c. 1885, "William Warren Edition," cf. *"As You Like It* à l'Américaine"; Davenport Promptbook, Daly and "William Warren" editions; *Monthly Mirror,* XV (1803), p. 276, Daly's edition.

29. Lacy's Acting Edition (c. 1842), Howard Athenaeum Promptbook, etc.

30. *The Fools of Shakespeare,* 67, 68.

31. As reproduced in Daly's edition, the accompanying photograph [[in Sprague]] of Lewis and Isabel Irving has for text the words under discussion.

32. Cf. C. D., "Audrey—A Country Wench," in *The Theatre,* 1 May 1894. Later in the scene, Daly's edition has "Touchstone *seeing* Jaques de Bois, *seizes* Audrey, *puts her arm in his, and drags her up the stage.*"

33. Mrs. Inchbald's *British Theatre* (1808), Cumberland, etc.; Hesketh Pearson (ed.), *The Swan of Lichfield,* New York, 1937, pp. 91, 92; Hapgood, *The Stage in America* [[New York, 1901]], 169.

HELEN GARDNER

"As You Like It"

As its title declares, this is a play to please all tastes. It is the last play in the world to be solemn over, and there is more than a touch of absurdity in delivering a lecture, particularly on a lovely summer morning, on this radiant blend of fantasy, romance, wit and humor. The play itself provides its own ironic comment on anyone who attempts to speak about it: "You have said; but whether wisely or no, let the forest judge" (3.2.121–22).

For the simple, it provides the stock ingredients of romance: a handsome, well-mannered young hero, the youngest of three brothers, two disguised princesses to be wooed and wed, and a banished, virtuous Duke to be restored to his rightful throne. For the more sophisticated, it propounds, in the manner of the old courtly literary form of the *débat*, a question which is left to us to answer: Is it better to live in the court or the country? "How like you this shepherd's life, Master Touchstone?" asks Corin, and receives a fool's answer: "Truly, shepherd, in respect of itself, it is a good life; but in respect that it is a shepherd's life, it is naught. In respect that it is solitary, I like it very well; but in respect that it is private, it is a very vile life" (3.2.11–17). Whose society would you prefer, Le Beau's or

From *More Talking of Shakespeare,* ed. John Garrett. (New York: Theatre Arts Books; London: Longmans, Green & Company, Ltd., 1959). © Longmans, Green and Co. Ltd. and Contributors, 1959. Reprinted by permission of the publishers.

Audrey's? Would you rather be gossiped at in the court or gawped at in the country? The play has also the age-old appeal of the pastoral, and in different forms. The pastoral romance of princesses playing at being a shepherd boy and his sister is combined with the pastoral love-eclogue in the wooing of Phebe, with the burlesque of this in the wooing of Audrey, and with the tradition of the moral eclogue, in which the shepherd is the wise man, in Corin. For the learned and literary this is one of Shakespeare's most allusive plays, uniting old traditions and playing with them lightly. Then there are the songs—the forest is full of music—and there is spectacle: a wrestling match to delight lovers of sport, the procession with the deer, which goes back to old country rituals and folk plays, and finally the masque of Hymen, to end the whole with courtly grace and dignity. This is an image of civility and true society, for Hymen is a god of cities, as Milton knew:

> There let *Hymen* oft appear
> In Saffron robe, with Taper clear,
> And pomp, and feast, and revelry,
> With mask, and antique Pageantry.   (*L'Allegro*, 125–28)

The only thing the play may be said to lack, when compared with Shakespeare's other comedies, is broad humor, the humor of gross clowns. William makes only a brief appearance. The absence of clowning may be due to an historic reason, the loss of Kempe, the company's funnyman. But if this was the original reason for the absence of pure clowning, Shakespeare has turned necessity to glorious gain and made a play in which cruder humors would be out of place. *As You Like It* is the most refined and exquisite of the comedies, the one which is most consistently played over by a delighted intelligence. It is Shakespeare's most Mozartian comedy.

The basic story is a folk tale. The ultimate sources for the plots of Shakespeare's greatest tragedy and his most unflawed comedy are stories of the same kind. The tale of the old king who had three daughters, of whom the elder two were wicked and the youngest was good, belongs to the

same primitive world of the imagination as the tale of the
knight who had three sons, the eldest of whom was wicked
and robbed the youngest, who was gallant and good, of his
inheritance. The youngest son triumphed, like Jack the
Giant Killer, over a strongman, a wrestler, joined a band
of outlaws in the forest, became their king, and with the
aid of an old servant of his father, the wily Adam Spencer, in
the end had his revenge on his brother and got his rights.
Lodge retained some traces of the boisterous elements of
this old story; but Shakespeare omitted them. His Orlando
is no bully, threatening and blustering and breaking down
the doors to feast with his boon companions in his brother's
house. He is brave enough and quick-tempered; but he is
above all gentle. On this simple story Lodge grafted a
pastoral romance in his *Rosalynde*. He made the leader of
the outlaws a banished duke, and gave both exiled duke
and tyrant usurper only daughters, as fast friends as their
fathers are sworn enemies. The wrestling match takes place
at the tyrant's court and is followed by the banishment of
Rosalynde and the flight of the two girls to the forest,
disguised as shepherd and shepherdess. There the shepherd
boy is wooed by the gallant hero, and arouses a passion of
lovesickness in a shepherdess who scorns her faithful lover.
The repentance of the wicked brother and his flight to the
forest provide the necessary partner for the tyrant's good
daughter, and all ends happily with marriages and the
restoration of the good duke. Shakespeare added virtually
nothing to the plot of Lodge's novel. There is no comedy in
which, in one sense, he invents so little. He made the two
dukes into brothers. Just as in *King Lear* he put together
two stories of good and unkind children, so here he gives
us two examples of a brother's unkindness. This adds to the
fairy-tale flavor of the plot, because it turns the usurping
duke into a wicked uncle. But if he invents no incidents,
he leaves out a good deal. Besides omitting the blusterings
of Rosader (Orlando), he leaves out a final battle and the
death in battle of the usurping duke, preferring to have him
converted offstage by a chance meeting with a convenient
and persuasive hermit. In the same way he handles very
cursorily the repentance of the wicked brother and his good

fortune in love. In Lodge's story, the villain is cast into prison by the tyrant who covets his estates. In prison he repents, and it is as a penitent that he arrives in the forest. Shakespeare also omits the incident of the attack on Ganymede and Aliena by robbers, in which Rosader is overpowered and wounded and Saladyne (Oliver) comes to the rescue and drives off the assailants. As has often been pointed out, this is both a proof of the genuineness of his repentance and a reason, which many critics of the play have felt the want of, for Celia's falling in love. Maidens naturally fall in love with brave young men who rescue them. But Shakespeare needs to find no "reasons for loving" in this play in which a dead shepherd's saw is quoted as a word of truth: "Who ever loved that loved not at first sight?" (3.5.82). He has far too much other business in hand at the center and heart of his play to find time for mere exciting incidents. He stripped Lodge's plot down to the bare bones, using it as a kind of frame, and created no subplot of his own. But he added four characters. Jaques, the philosopher, bears the same name as the middle son of Sir Rowland de Boys—the one whom Oliver kept at his books—who does not appear in the play until he turns up casually at the end as a messenger. It seems possible that the melancholy Jaques began as this middle son and that his melancholy was in origin a scholar's melancholy. If so, the character changed as it developed, and by the time that Shakespeare had fully conceived his cynical spectator he must have realized that he could not be kin to Oliver and Orlando. The born solitary must have no family: Jaques seems the quintessential only child. To balance Jaques, as another kind of commentator, we are given Touchstone, critic and parodist of love and lovers and of court and courtiers. And, to make up the full consort of pairs to be mated, Shakespeare invented two rustic lovers, William and Audrey, dumb yokel and sluttish goat-girl. These additional characters add nothing at all to the story. If you were to tell it you would leave them out. They show us that story was not Shakespeare's concern in this play; its soul is not to be looked for there. If you were to go to *As You Like It* for the story you would, in Johnson's phrase, "hang yourself."

In an essay called "The Basis of Shakespearian Comedy"[1] Professor Nevill Coghill attempted to "establish certain things concerning the nature of comic form, as it was understood at Shakespeare's time." He pointed out that there were two conceptions of comedy current in the sixteenth century, both going back to grammarians of the fourth century, but radically opposed to each other. By the one definition a comedy was a story beginning in sadness and ending in happiness. By the other it was, in Sidney's words, "an imitation of the common errors of our life" represented "in the most ridiculous and scornefull sort that may be; so that it is impossible that any beholder can be content to be such a one." Shakespeare, he declared, accepted the first; Jonson, the second. But although *As You Like It*, like *A Midsummer Night's Dream*, certainly begins in sadness and ends with happiness, I do not feel, when we have said this, that we have gone very far toward defining the play's nature, and I do not think that the plot in either of these two lovely plays, or in the enchanting early comedy *Love's Labor's Lost*, which indeed was hardly any plot at all, can be regarded as the "soul" or animating force of Shakespeare's most original and characteristic comedies. Professor Coghill's formula fits plays which we feel rather uneasy about, *The Merchant of Venice* and *Measure for Measure*. It is precisely the stress on the plot which makes us think of these as being more properly described as tragicomedies than comedies. Neither of them is a play which we would choose as a norm of Shakespeare's genius in comedy. In *As You Like It* the plot is handled in the most perfunctory way. Shakespeare crams his first act with incident in order to get everyone to the forest as soon as he possibly can and, when he is ready, he ends it all as quickly as possible. A few lines dispose of Duke Frederick, and leave the road back to his throne empty for Duke Senior. As for the other victim of a wicked brother, it is far more important that Orlando should marry Rosalind than that he should be restored to his rights.

Mrs. Suzanne Langer, in her brilliant and suggestive

[1] *Essays and Studies* (English Association: John Murray, 1950).

book *Feeling and Form,*[2] has called comedy an image of life triumphing over chance. She declares that the essence of comedy is that it embodies in symbolic form our sense of happiness in feeling that we can meet and master the changes and chances of life as it confronts us. This seems to me to provide a good description of what we mean by "pure comedy," as distinct from the corrective or satirical comedy of Jonson. The great symbol of pure comedy is marriage by which the world is renewed, and its endings are always instinct with a sense of fresh beginnings. Its rhythm is the rhythm of the life of mankind, which goes on and renews itself as the life of nature does. The rhythm of tragedy, on the other hand, is the rhythm of the individual life which comes to a close, and its great symbol is death. The one inescapable fact about every human being is that he must die. No skill in living, no sense of life, no inborn grace or acquired wisdom can avert this individual doom. A tragedy, which is played out under the shadow of an inevitable end, is an image of the life pattern of every one of us. A comedy, which contrives an end which is not implicit in its beginning, and which is, in itself, a fresh beginning, is an image of the flow of human life. The young wed, so that they may become in turn the older generation, whose children will wed, and so on, as long as the world lasts. Comedy pictures what Rosalind calls "the full stream of the world." At the close of a tragedy we look back over a course which has been run: "the rest is silence." The end of a comedy declares that life goes on: "Here we are all over again." Tragic plots must have a logic which leads to an inescapable conclusion. Comic plots are made up of changes, chances and surprises. Coincidences can destroy tragic feeling: they heighten comic feeling. It is absurd to complain in poetic comedy of improbable encounters and characters arriving pat on their cue, of sudden changes of mind and mood by which an enemy becomes a friend. Puck, who creates and presides over the central comedy of *A Midsummer Night's Dream*, speaks for all comic writers and lovers of true comedy when he says:

[2]Routledge, 1953.

And those things do best please me
That befall prepost'rously.   (3.2.120–21)

   This aspect of life, as continually changing and presenting
fresh opportunities for happiness and laughter, poetic
comedy idealizes and presents to us by means of fantasy.
Fantasy is the natural instrument of comedy, in which
plot, which is the "soul" of tragedy, is of secondary impor-
tance, an excuse for something else. After viewing a tragedy
we have an "acquist of true experience" from a "great
event." There are no "events" in comedy; there are only
"happenings." Events are irreversible and comedy is not
concerned with the irreversible, which is why it must always
shun the presentation of death. In adapting Lodge's story
Shakespeare did not allow Charles the wrestler to kill the
Franklin's sons. Although they are expected to die, we may
hope they will recover from their broken ribs. And he
rejected also Lodge's ending in which the wicked duke was
killed in battle, preferring his improbable conversion by a
hermit. But why should we complain of its improbability? It
is only in tragedy that second chances are not given.
Comedy is full of purposes mistook, not "falling on the
inventor's head" but luckily misfiring altogether. In comedy,
as often happens in life, people are mercifully saved from
being as wicked as they meant to be.
   Generalization about the essential distinctions between
tragedy and comedy is called in question, when we turn to
Shakespeare, by the inclusiveness of his vision of life. In the
great majority of his plays the elements are mixed. But just
as he wrote one masterpiece which is purely tragic, dominated by the conception of Fate, in *Macbeth*, so he wrote
some plays which embody a purely comic vision. Within the
general formula that "a comedy is a play with a happy
ending," which can, of course, include tragicomedies, he
wrote some plays in which the story is a mere frame and the
essence of the play lies in the presentation of an image of
human life, not as an arena for heroic endeavor but as a
place of encounters.
   Tragedy is presided over by time, which urges the hero
onward to fulfill his destiny. In Shakespeare's comedies

time goes by fits and starts. It is not so much a movement onward as a space in which to work things out: a midsummer night, a space too short for us to feel time's movement, or the unmeasured time of *As You Like It* or *Twelfth Night*. The comedies are dominated by a sense of place rather than of time. In Shakespeare's earliest comedy it is not a very romantic place: the city of Ephesus. Still, it is a place where two pairs of twins are accidentally reunited, and their old father, in danger of death at the beginning, is united to his long-lost wife at the close. The substance of the play is the comic plot of mistakings, played out in a single place on a single day. The tragicomic story of original loss and final restoration provides a frame. In what is probably his second comedy, *The Two Gentlemen of Verona*, Shakespeare tried a quite different method. The play is a dramatization of a *novella*, and it contains no comic place of encounters where time seems to stand still. The story begins in Verona, passes to Milan, and ends in a forest between the two cities. None of these places exerts any hold upon our imaginations. The story simply moves forward through them. In *Love's Labor's Lost*, by contrast, Shakespeare went as far as possible in the other direction. The whole play is a kind of ballet of lovers and fantastics, danced out in the King of Navarre's park. Nearby is a village where Holofernes is the schoolmaster, Nathaniel the curate, and Dull the constable. In this play we are given, as a foil to the lords and ladies, not comic servants, parasitic on their masters, but a little comic world, society in miniature, going about its daily business while the lovers are engaged in the discovery of theirs. Shakespeare dispensed with the tragicomic frame altogether here. There is no sorrow at the beginning, only youthful male fatuity; and the "putting right" at the close lies in the chastening of the lords by the ladies. The picture of the course of life as it appears to the comic vision, with young men falling in love and young women testing their suitors, and other men "laboring in their vocations" to keep the world turning and to impress their fellows, is the whole matter of the play. Much more magical than the sunlit park of the King of Navarre is the wood near Athens where Puck plays the part of chance. Shakespeare reverted here to the structural pattern of his earliest comedy, beginning with the cruel fury of Egeus against his daughter, the rivalry of Lysander and Demetrius and the unhappiness of the scorned Helena, and ending with Theseus's overriding of the father's will and the proper pairing of the four lovers. But here he not only set his comic plot of mistakings within a frame of sorrow turning to joy, he also set his comic place of encounters apart from the real world, the palace where the play begins and ends. All the center of the play takes place in the moonlit wood where lovers immortal and mortal quarrel, change partners, are blinded, and have their eyes purged.

Having created a masterpiece, Shakespeare, who never repeated a success, went back in his next play to the tragicomedy, allowing the threat of terrible disaster to grow through the play up to a great dramatic fourth act. *The Merchant of Venice* has what *The Two Gentlemen of Verona* lacks, an enchanted place. Belmont, where Bassanio goes to find his bride, and where Lorenzo flees with Jessica, and from which Portia descends like a goddess to solve the troubles of Venice, is a place apart, "above the smoke and stir." But it is not, like the wood near Athens, a place where the changes and chances of our mortal life are seen mirrored. It stands too sharply over against Venice, a place of refuge rather than a place of discovery. *Much Ado About Nothing* reverts to the single place of *The Comedy of Errors* and *Love's Labor's Lost*; and its tragicomic plot, which also comes to a climax in a dramatic scene in the fourth act, is lightened not by a shift of scene but by its interweaving with a brilliant comic plot, and by all kinds of indications that all will soon be well again. The trouble comes in the middle of this play: at the beginning, as at the end, all is revelry and happiness. A sense of holiday, of time off from the world's business, reigns in Messina. The wars are over, peace has broken out, and Don Pedro and the gentlemen have returned to where the ladies are waiting for them to take up again the game of love and wit. In the atmosphere created by the first act Don John's malice is a cloud no bigger than a man's hand. And although it grows as the play proceeds, the crisis of the fourth act is like a heavy summer thunderstorm which darkens the sky for a time but will, we know, soon pass. The brilliant lively city of Messina is a true place of mistakings and discoveries, like the park of the King of Navarre; but, also like the park of the King of Navarre, it lacks enchantment. It is too near the ordinary world to seem more than a partial image of human life. In *As You Like It* Shakespeare returned to the pattern of *A Midsummer Night's Dream*, beginning his play in sorrow and ending it with joy, and making his place of comic encounters a place set apart from the ordinary world.

The Forest of Arden ranks with the wood near Athens and Prospero's island as a place set apart, even though, unlike them, it is not ruled by magic. It is set over against the envious court ruled by a tyrant, and a home which is no home because it harbors hatred, not love. Seen from the court it appears untouched by the discontents of life, a place where they "fleet the time carelessly as they did in the golden world" (1.1.114–15), the gay greenwood of Robin Hood. But, of course, it is no such Elysium. It contains some unamiable characters. Corin's master is churlish and Sir Oliver Martext is hardly sweet-natured; William is a dolt and Audrey graceless. Its weather, too, is by no means always sunny. It has a bitter winter. To Orlando, famished with hunger and supporting the fainting Adam, it is "an uncouth forest" (2.6.6) and a desert where the air is bleak. He is astonished to find civility among men who

> in this desert inaccessible,
> Under the shade of melancholy boughs,
> Lose and neglect the creeping hours of time. (2.7.110–12)

In fact Arden does not seem very attractive at first sight to the weary escapers from the tyranny of the world. Rosalind's "Well, this is the forest of Arden" (2.4.14) does not suggest any very great enthusiasm; and to Touchstone's "Ay, now I am in Arden; the more fool I: when I was at home, I was in a better place: but travelers must be content," she can only reply "Ay, be so, good Touchstone" (15–18). It is as if they all have to wake up after a good night's rest to find what a pleasant place they have come to. Arden is not a place for the young only. Silvius, forever young and forever

loving, is balanced by Corin, the old shepherd, who reminds
us of that other "penalty of Adam" besides "the seasons' difference": that man must labor to get himself food and
clothing. Still, the labor is pleasant and a source of pride: "I
am a true laborer: I earn that I eat, get that I wear, owe no
man hate, envy no man's happiness, glad of other men's
good, content with my harm; and the greatest of my pride is
to see my ewes graze and my lambs suck" (3.2.73–77).
Arden is not a place where the laws of nature are abrogated
and roses are without their thorns. If, in the world, Duke
Frederick has usurped on Duke Senior, Duke Senior is
aware that he has in his turn usurped upon the deer, the
native burghers of the forest. If man does not slay and kill
man, he kills the poor beasts. Life preys on life. Jaques, who
can suck melancholy out of anything, points to the callous-
ness that runs through nature itself as a mirror of the cal-
lousness of men. The herd abandons the wounded deer, as
·prosperous citizens pass with disdain the poor bankrupt, the
failure. The race is to the swift. But this is Jaques' view.
Orlando, demanding help for Adam, finds another image
from nature:

> Then but forbear your food a little while,
> Whiles, like a doe, I go to find my fawn
> And give it food. There is an poor old man
> Who after me hath many a weary step
> Limped in pure love. Till he be first sufficed,
> Oppressed with two weak evils, age and hunger,
> I will not touch a bit.   (2.7.127–33)

The fact that they are both derived ultimately from folk
tale is not the only thing that relates *As You Like It* to *King
Lear*. Adam's somber line, "And unregarded age in corners
thrown" (2.3.42), which Quiller-Couch said might have
come out of one of the greater sonnets, sums up the fate
of Lear:

> Dear daughter, I confess that I am old;
> Age is unnecessary: on my knees I beg
> That you'll vouchsafe me raiment, bed, and food.

At times Arden seems a place where the same bitter lessons can be learned as Lear has to learn in his place of exile, the blasted heath. Corin's natural philosophy, which includes the knowledge that "the property of rain is to wet" (3.2.26), is something which Lear has painfully to acquire:

> When the rain came to wet me once and the wind to make me chatter; when the thunder would not peace at my bidding; there I found 'em, there I smelt 'em out. Go to, they are not men o' their words: they told me I was everything; 'tis a lie, I am not ague-proof.   (*King Lear*, 4.6.101–7)

He is echoing Duke Senior, who smiles at the "icy fang / And churlish chiding of the winter's wind," saying:

> This is no flattery: these are counselors
> That feelingly persuade me what I am.   (2.1.6–7, 10–11)

Amiens's lovely melancholy song:

> Blow, blow, thou winter wind,
> Thou art not so unkind
>   As man's ingratitude. . . .
>
> Freeze, freeze, thou bitter sky,
> That dost not bite so nigh
>   As benefits forgot   (2.7.174–76, 184–86)

is terribly echoed in Lear's outburst:

> Blow, winds, and crack your cheeks! rage! blow!
> .   .   .   .
> Rumble thy bellyful! Spit, fire! spout, rain!
> Nor rain, wind, thunder, fire, are my daughters:
> I tax not you, you elements, with unkindness;
> I never gave you kingdom, call'd you children. . . .
>   (*Lear*, 3.2.1, 14–17)

And Jaques's reflection that "All the world's a stage" (2.7.139ff.) becomes in Lear's mouth a cry of anguish:

When we are born, we cry that we are come
To this great stage of fools.   (*Lear*, 4.6.184–85)

It is in Arden that Jaques presents his joyless picture of
human life, passing from futility to futility and culminating
in the nothingness of senility—"sans everything"; and in
Arden also a bitter judgment on human relations is lightly
passed in the twice repeated "Most friendship is feigning,
most loving mere folly" (2.7.181). But then one must add
that hard on the heels of Jaques' melancholy conclusion
Orlando enters with Adam in his arms, who, although he
may be "sans teeth" and at the end of his usefulness as a servant, has, besides his store of virtue and his peace of conscience, the love of his master. And the play is full of signal
instances of persons who do not forget benefits: Adam,
Celia, Touchstone—not to mention the lords who chose to
leave the court and follow their banished master to the
forest. In a recent number of the *Shakespeare Survey* Professor Harold Jenkins has pointed out how points of view
put forward by one character find contradiction or correction
by another, so that the whole play is a balance of sweet
against sour, of the cynical against the idealistic, and life is
shown as a mingling of hard fortune and good hap. The lords
who have "turned ass, leaving their wealth and ease a stub-
born will to please" (2.6.46–48), are happy in their gross
folly, as Orlando is in a lovesickness which he does not wish
to be cured of. What Jaques has left out of his picture of
man's strange eventful pilgrimage is love and companion-
ship, sweet society, the banquet under the boughs to which
Duke Senior welcomes Orlando and Adam. Although life in
Arden is not wholly idyllic, and this place set apart from the
world is yet touched by the world's sorrows and can be
mocked by the worldly wise, the image of life which the
forest presents is irradiated by the conviction that the gay
and the gentle can endure the rubs of fortune and that this
earth is a place where men can find happiness in themselves
and in others.

The Forest of Arden is, as has often been pointed out, a
place which all the exiles from the court, except one, are
only too ready to leave at the close. As, when the short mid-

summer night is over, the lovers emerge from the wood, in their right minds and correctly paired, and return to the palace of Theseus; and, when Prospero's magic has worked the cure, the enchanted island is left to Caliban and Ariel, and its human visitors return to Naples and Milan; so the time of holiday comes to an end in Arden. The stately masque of Hymen marks the end of this interlude in the greenwood, and announces the return to a court purged of envy and baseness. Like other comic places, Arden is a place of discovery where the truth becomes clear and where each man finds himself and his true way. This discovery of truth in comedy is made through errors and mistakings. The trial and error of which we come to knowledge of ourselves and of our world is symbolized by the disguisings which are a recurrent element in all comedy, but are particularly common in Shakespeare's. Things have, as it were, to become worse before they become better, more confused and farther from the proper pattern. By misunderstandings men come to understand, and by lies and feignings they discover truth. If Rosalind, the princess, had attempted to "cure" her lover Orlando, she might have succeeded. As Ganymede, playing Rosalind, she can try him to the limit in perfect safety, and discover that she cannot mock or flout him out of his "mad humor of love to a living humor of madness," and drive him "to forswear the full stream of the world, and to live in a nook merely monastic" (3.2.409–11). By playing with him in the disguise of a boy, she discovers when she can play no more. By love of a shadow, the mere image of a charming youth, Phebe discovers that it is better to love than to be loved and scorn one's lover. This discovery of truth by feigning, and of what is wisdom and what folly by debate, is the center of *As You Like It*. It is a play of meetings and encounters, of conversations and sets of wit: Orlando versus Jaques, Touchstone versus Corin, Rosalind versus Jaques, Rosalind versus Phebe, and above all Rosalind versus Orlando. The truth discovered is, at one level, a very "earthy truth": Benedick's discovery that "the world must be peopled." The honest toil of Corin, the wise man of the forest, is mocked at by Touchstone as "simple sin." He brings "the

ewes and the rams together" and gets his living "by the copulation of cattle" (3.2.78–80). The goddess Fortune seems
similarly occupied in this play: "As the ox hath his bow, the
horse his curb, and the falcon her bells, so man hath his
desires; and as pigeons bill, so wedlock would be nibbling"
(3.3.76–79). Fortune acts the role of a kindly bawd. Touchstone's marriage to Audrey is a mere coupling. Rosalind's
advice to Phebe is brutally frank: "Sell when you can, you
are not for all markets" (3.5.60). The words she uses to
describe Oliver and Celia "in the very wrath of love"
(5.2.39) are hardly delicate, and after her first meeting with
Orlando she confesses to her cousin that her sighs are for her
"child's father" (1.3.11). Against the natural background of
the life of the forest there can be no pretense that the love of
men and women can "forget the He and She." But Rosalind's behavior is at variance with her bold words. Orlando
has to prove that he truly is, as he seems at first sight, the
right husband for her, and show himself gentle, courteous,
generous and brave, and a match for her in wit, though a
poor poet. In this, the great coupling of the play, there is a
marriage of true minds. The other couplings run the gamut
downward from it, until we reach Touchstone's image of "a
she-lamb of a twelve-month" and "a crooked-pated, old,
cuckoldy ram" (3.2.81–82), right at the bottom of the scale.
As for the debate as to where happiness is to be found, the
conclusion come to is again, like all wisdom, not very star-
tling or original: that "minds innocent and quiet" can find
happiness in court or country:

> happy is your Grace,
> That can translate the stubbornness of fortune
> Into so quiet and so sweet a style.   (2.1.18)

And, on the contrary, those who wish to can "suck melancholy" out of anything, "as a weasel sucks eggs" (2.5.10–11).
    In the pairing one figure is left out. "I am for other
than for dancing measures," says Jaques (5.4.193). Leaving
the hateful sight of reveling and pastime, he betakes himself
to the Duke's abandoned cave, on his way to the house of

penitents where Duke Frederick has gone. The two commentators of the play are nicely contrasted. Touchstone is the parodist, Jaques the cynic. The parodist must love what he parodies. We know this from literary parody. All the best parodies are written by those who understand, because they love, the thing they mock. Only poets who love and revere the epic can write mock-heroic and the finest parody of classical tragedy comes from Housman, a great scholar. In everything that Touchstone says and does gusto, high spirits and a zest for life ring out. Essentially comic, he can adapt himself to any situation in which he may find himself. Never at a loss, he is life's master. The essence of clowning is adaptability and improvisation. The clown is never baffled and is marked by his ability to place himself at once *en rapport* with his audience, to be all things to all men, to perform the part which is required at the moment. Touchstone sustains many different roles. After hearing Silvius's lament and Rosalind's echo of it, he becomes the maudlin lover of Jane Smile; with the simple shepherd Corin he becomes the cynical and worldly-wise man of the court; with Jaques he is a melancholy moralist, musing on the power of time and the decay of all things; with the pages he acts the lordly amateur of the arts, patronizing his musicians. It is right that he should parody the rest of the cast, and join the procession into Noah's ark with his Audrey. Jaques is his opposite. He is the cynic, the person who prefers the pleasures of superiority, cold-eyed and cold-hearted. The tyrannical Duke Frederick and the cruel Oliver can be converted; but not Jaques. He likes himself as he is. He does not wish to plunge into the stream, but prefers to stand on the bank and "fish for fancies as they pass." Sir Thomas Elyot said that dancing was an image of matrimony: "In every daunse, of a most auncient custome, there daunseth together a man and a woman, holding eche other by the hande or the arme, which betokeneth concorde." There are some who will not dance, however much they are piped to, any more than they will weep when there is mourning. "In this theater of man's life," wrote Bacon, "it is reserved only for God and angels to be lookers on." Jaques arrogates to himself the divine role. He has opted out from the human condition.

It is characteristic of Shakespeare's comedies to include an element that is irreconcilable, which strikes a lightly discordant note, casts a slight shadow, and by its presence questions the completeness of the comic vision of life. In *Love's Labor's Lost* he dared to allow the news of a death to cloud the scene of revels at the close, and, through Rosalind's rebuke to Berowne, called up the image of a whole world of pain and weary suffering where "Mirth cannot move a soul in agony" (5.2.858). The two comedies whose main action is motivated by hatred end with malice thwarted but not removed. In *The Merchant of Venice* and *Much Ado About Nothing*, Shakespeare asks us to accept the fact that the human race includes not only a good many fools and rogues but also some persons who are positively wicked, a fact which comedy usually ignores. They are prevented from doing the harm they wish to do. They are not cured of wishing to do harm. Shylock's baffled exit and Don John's flight to Messina leave the stage clear for lovers and well-wishers. The villains have to be left out of the party at the close. At the end of *Twelfth Night* the person who is left out is present. The impotent misery and fury of the humiliated Malvolio's last words, "I'll be reveng'd on the whole pack of you" (5.1.380), call in question the whole comic scheme by which, through misunderstandings and mistakes, people come to terms with themselves and their fellows. There are some who cannot be "taught a lesson." In Malvolio pride is not purged; it is fatally wounded and embittered. It is characteristic of the delicacy of temper of *As You Like It* that its solitary figure, its outsider, Jaques, does nothing whatever to harm anyone, and is perfectly satisfied with himself and happy in his melancholy. Even more, his melancholy is a source of pleasure and amusement to others. The Duke treats him as virtually a court entertainer, and he is a natural butt for Orlando and Rosalind. Anyone in the play can put him down and feel the better for doing so. All the same his presence casts a faint shadow. His criticism of the world has its sting drawn very early by the Duke's rebuke to him as a former libertine, discharging his filth upon the world, and he is to some extent discredited before he opens his mouth by the unpleasant implication of his name. But he cannot be wholly dismissed. A certain sour distaste for life is voided through him, something most of us feel at some time or other. If he were not there to give expression to it, we might be tempted to find the picture of life in the forest too sweet. His only action is to interfere in the marriage of Touchstone and Audrey; and this he merely postpones. His effect, whenever he appears, is to deflate: the effect does not last and cheerfulness soon breaks in again. Yet as there is a scale of love, so there is a scale of sadness in the play. It runs down from the Duke's compassionate words:

Thou seest we are not all alone unhappy:
This wide and universal theater
Presents more woeful pageants than the scene
Wherein we play in,   (2.7.136–39)

through Rosalind's complaint "O, how full of briers is this working-day world" (1.3.12), to Jaques' studied refusal to find anything worthy of admiration or love.

One further element in the play I would not wish to stress, because though it is pervasive it is unobtrusive: the constant natural and easy reference to the Christian ideal of loving-kindness, gentleness, pity and humility and to the sanctions which that ideal finds in the commands and promises of religion. In this fantasy world, in which the world of our experience is imaged, this element in experience finds a place with others, and the world is shown not only as a place where we may find happiness, but as a place where both happiness and sorrow may be hallowed. The number of religious references in *As You Like It* has often been commented on, and it is striking when we consider the play's main theme. Many are of little significance and it would be humorless to enlarge upon the significance of the "old religious man" who converted Duke Frederick, or of Ganymede's "old religious uncle." But some are explicit and have a serious, unforced beauty: Orlando's appeal to outlawed men,

If ever you have looked on better days,
If ever been where bells have knolled to church . . . ;
                                                      (2.7.113–14)

Adam's prayer,

> he that doth the ravens feed,
> Yea, providently caters for the sparrow,
> Be comfort to my age;   (2.3.43–45)

and Corin's recognition, from St. Paul, that we have to find the way to heaven by doing deeds of hospitality. These are all in character. But the God of Marriage, Hymen, speaks more solemnly than we expect and his opening words with their New Testament echo are more than conventional:

> Then is there mirth in heaven
> When earthly things made even
> Atone together.   (5.4.108–10)

The appearance of the god to present daughter to father and to bless the brides and grooms turns the close into a solemnity, an image of the concord which reigns in Heaven and which Heaven blesses on earth. But this, like much else in the play, may be taken as you like it. There is no need to see any more in the god's appearance with the brides than a piece of pageantry which concludes the action with a graceful spectacle and sends the audience home contented with a very pretty play.

PETER B. ERICKSON

From Sexual Politics and Social Structure in *As You Like It*

Before entering the forest of Arden, Rosalind's companion Celia/Aliena redefines this pastoral space to mean opportunity rather than punishment: "Now go we in content / To liberty, and not to banishment" (1.3.135–36). This "liberty" implies overcoming the restrictions of the female role. The idea of the male disguise originates as a strategy for avoiding the normal vulnerability to male force: "Alas, what danger will it be to us, / Maids as we are, to travel forth so far! / Beauty provoketh thieves sooner than gold" (106–8). Rosalind's male costume, as it evolves, expands her identity so that she can play both male and female roles. Yet the costume is problematic. Though it gives her freedom of action and empowers her to take the initiative with Orlando, it simultaneously serves as a protective device, which temptingly offers excessive security, even invulnerability. In order to love, Rosalind must reveal herself directly to Orlando, thereby making herself vulnerable. She must give up the disguise and appear—as she ultimately promises Orlando—"human as she is" (5.2.67). But in giving up the disguise, she also gives up the strength it symbolizes. As the disguise begins to break down before its official removal, Rosalind's transparent femininity

From *Patriarchal Structures in Shakespeare's Drama* by Peter B. Erickson. (Berkeley, Calif.: University of California Press, 1985), pp. 22–37.

takes the form of fainting—a sign of weakness that gives her away: "You a man? / You lack a man's heart" (4.3.164–65). This loss of control signals that Rosalind can no longer deny her inner feminine self. The capacity for love that we find so admirable in Rosalind is compromised by the necessity that she resume a traditional female role in order to engage in love.

This traditional image has been present all along. Rosalind willingly confides to Celia that she remains a woman despite the male costume: ". . . in my heart / Lie there what hidden woman's fear there will, / We'll have a swashing and a martial outside" (1.3.116–18); "Good my complexion! Dost thou think, though I am caparisoned like a man, I have a doublet and hose in my disposition?" (3.2.193–95); and "Do you not know I am a woman?" (247). By virtue of the costume, Rosalind does have access to both male and female attributes, but the impression she conveys of androgynous wholeness is misleading. Neither Rosalind nor the play questions the conventional categories of masculine and feminine. She does not reconcile gender definitions in the sense of integrating or synthesizing them. Her own insistence on the metaphor of exterior (male) and interior (female) keeps the categories distinct and separable. The liberation that Rosalind experiences in the forest has built into it the conservative countermovement by which, as the play returns to the normal world, she will be reduced to the traditional woman who is subservient to men.

Rosalind is shown working out in advance the terms of her return. Still protected by her disguise yet allowing herself to come closer to the decisive moment, she instructs Orlando to "woo me" (4.1.64) and subsequently tells him what to say in a wedding rehearsal while she practices yielding. Though she teases Orlando with the wife's power to make him a cuckold and then to conceal her duplicity with her "wayward wit" (154–77), this is good fun, and it is only that. It is clear to the audience, if not yet to Orlando, that Rosalind's flaunting of her role as disloyal wife is a put-on rather than a genuine threat. She may playfully delay the final moment when she becomes a wife, but we are reassured that, once married, she will in fact be faithful. Her humor has the effect of exorcising and renouncing her potential weapon. The uncertainty concerns not her loyalty but Orlando's, as her sudden change of tone when he announces his departure indicates: "Alas, dear love, I cannot lack thee two hours!" (170). Her exuberance and control collapse in fears of his betrayal: "Ay, go your ways, go your ways; I knew what you would prove" (173–74). Her previous wit notwithstanding, for Rosalind the scene is less a demonstration of power than an exercise in vulnerability. She is once again consigned to anxious waiting for her tardy man: "But why did he swear he would come this morning, and comes not?" (3.4.18–19).

Rosalind's own behavior neutralizes her jokes about cuckoldry, but this point is sharply reinforced by the brief account of the male hunt that immediately follows Act 4, Scene 1. The expected negative meaning of horns as the sign of a cuckold is transformed into a positive image of phallic potency that unites men. Changing the style of his literary response to deer killing, Jaques replaces his earlier lament (2.1.26–66) with a celebration of male hunt and conquest: "Let's present him to the Duke like a Roman conqueror; and it would do well to set the deer's horns upon his head, for a branch of victory" (4.2.3–5).[1] The rousing song occasioned by this moment suggests the power of an all-male activity to provide a self-sufficient male heritage, thus to defend against male insecurity about humiliation by women.

The final scene, orchestrated by Rosalind, demonstrates her power in a paradoxical way. She is the architect of a resolution that phases out the control she has wielded and prepares the way for the patriarchal status quo. She accedes to the process by which, in the transition from courtship to marriage, power passes from the female to the male: the man is no longer the suitor who serves, obeys, and begs but is now the husband who commands. Rosalind's submission is explicit but not ironic, though her tone may be high-spirited. To each of the two men in her life she declares: "To you I give myself, for I am yours" (5.4.116–17). Her casting herself in the role of male possession is all the more charming because she does not have to be forced to adopt it:

her self-taming is voluntary. We may wish to give Rosalind credit for her cleverness in forestalling male rivalry between her father and her fiancé. Unlike Cordelia, she is smart enough to see that in order to be gratified, each man needs to feel that he is the recipient of all her love, not half of it. Yet Rosalind is not really in charge here because the potential hostility between the younger and older man has already been negotiated in the forest in Act 2, Scene 7, a negotiation that results in the formation of an idealized male alliance. Rosalind submits not only to two individual men but also to the patriarchal society that they embody. Patriarchy is not a slogan smuggled in from the twentieth century and imposed on the play but an exact term for the social structure that close reading reveals within the play.

II

We are apt to assume that the green world is more free than it actually is. In the case of *As You Like It*, the green world cannot be interpreted as a space apart where a youthful rebellion finds a refuge from the older generation. The forest of Arden includes a strong parental presence: Duke Senior's is the first voice we hear there. Moreover, the green world has a clear political structure. Freed from the constraints of courtly decorum, Duke Senior can afford to address his companions as "brothers" (2.1.1), but he nonetheless retains a fatherly command. Fraternal spirit is not equivalent to democracy, as is clarified when the duke dispenses favor on a hierarchical basis: "Shall share the good of our returnèd fortune, / According to the measure of their states" (5.4.174–75).

Although interpretations of *As You Like It* often stress youthful love, we should not neglect the paternal context in which the love occurs. Both Rosalind and Orlando acknowledge Duke Senior. Rosalind is aware, as she finds herself attracted to Orlando, that "My father loved Sir Rowland [Orlando's father] as his soul" (1.2.225) and hence that her affection is not incompatible with family approval. Orlando, for his part, does not go forward in pursuit of love until after he has become friends with Duke Senior.

Rosalind and Orlando approach the forest in strikingly different ways. Rosalind's mission is love. Upon entering the forest, she discovers there the love "passion" she has brought with her: "Alas, poor shepherd, searching of thy wound, / I have by hard adventure found mine own" (2.4.42–43). Orlando, by contrast, has two projects (though he does not consciously formulate them) to complete in the forest: the first is his quest to reestablish the broken connection with his father's legacy; the second is the quest for Rosalind. The sequence of these projects is an indication of priority. Orlando's outburst—"But heavenly Rosalind!" (1.2.279)—is not picked up again until he opens Act 3, Scene 2, with his love poem. The interim is reserved for his other, patriarchal business.

In the first scene of the play, Orlando makes it clear, in a melodramatic but nonetheless poignant way, that he derives his sense of identity from his dead father, an identity that is not yet fulfilled. In protesting against his older brother's mistreatment, Orlando asserts the paternal bond: "The spirit of my father grows strong in me, and I will no longer endure it" (1.1.67–69). His first step toward recovery of the connection with his lost father is the demolition of Charles the wrestler: "How dost thou, Charles?" / "He cannot speak, my lord" (1.2.208–9). This victory earns Orlando the right to proclaim his father's name as his own:

Duke Frederick.   What is thy name, young man?
   Orlando. Orlando, my liege, the youngest son of Sir Rowland
               de Boys. . . .
          I am more proud to be Sir Rowland's son.

                                        (210–13, 222)

Frederick's negative reaction to Orlando's statement of identity confirms the concept of heritage being evoked here: "Thou shouldst have better pleased me with this deed / Hadst thou descended from another house" (217–18). The significance of the wrestling match is that Orlando has undergone a traditional male rite of passage, providing an established channel for the violence he has previously expressed by collaring Oliver in the opening scene. Yet aggression is the epitome of a rigid masculinity that Shake-speare characteristically condemns as too narrow a basis for identity. Orlando's aggressiveness is instantly rendered inappropriate by his falling in love. Moreover, his recourse to violence simply mirrors the technique of the tyrannical Duke Frederick. As it turns out, Orlando must give up violence in order to meet the "good father."

While Rosalind's confidante Celia provides the opportunity to talk about love, Orlando is accompanied by Adam, who serves a very different function since he is a living link to Orlando's father. The paternal inheritance blocked by Oliver is received indirectly from Adam when he offers the money "I saved under your father, / Which I did store to be my foster nurse" (2.3.39–40). The motif of nurturance implied by the "foster nurse" image is continued as Orlando, through Adam's sudden collapse from lack of food, is led to Duke Senior's pastoral banquet. Treating this new situation as another trial of "the strength of my youth," Orlando imag-ines an all-or-nothing "adventure" (1.2.161–2, 166) similar to the wrestling match: "If this uncouth forest yield any thing savage, I will either be food for it, or bring it for food to thee" (2.6.6–7). In Act 2, Scene 7, he enters with drawn sword. Unexpectedly finding a benevolent father figure, Orlando effects as gracefully as possible a transition from toughness to tenderness: "Let gentleness my strong enforce-ment be; / In the which hope I blush, and hide my sword" (118–19). This display of nonviolence is the precondition for Orlando's recovery of patriarchal lineage. Duke Senior aids this recovery by his recognition of the father's reflection in the son and by his declaration of his own loving connec-tion with Orlando's father. This transaction concludes the scene:

> If that you were the good Sir Rowland's son,
> As you have whispered faithfully you were,
> And as mine eye doth his effigies witness
> Most truly limned and living in your face,
> Be truly welcome hither. I am the Duke
> That loved your father.

>   (191–96)

The confirmation of Orlando's identity has the effect of a ritual blessing that makes this particular father-son relation the basis for social cohesion in general. There is much virtue in Orlando's "If":

> *Orlando.* If ever you have looked on better days,
>   If ever been where bells have knolled to church,
>   If ever sat at any good man's feast,
>   If ever from your eyelids wiped a tear
>   And know what 'tis to pity and be pitied. . . .
> *Duke Senior.* True is it that we have seen better days,
>   And have with holy bell been knolled to church,
>   And sat at good men's feasts, and wiped our eyes
>   Of drops that sacred pity hath engend'red.
>
> (2.7.113–17, 120–23)

The liturgy of male utopia, ruthlessly undercut in *Love's Labor's Lost*, is here allowed to stand. Virgilian piety, founded on ideal father-son relations and evoked visually when, like Aeneas with Anchises, Orlando carries Adam on his back, can achieve what Navarre's academe with its spurious abstinence could not. Orlando's heroic language as he goes off to rescue Adam is as clumsy as any he uses in the poems to Rosalind, but whereas the play pokes fun at the love poetry, the expression of duty to Adam is not subject to irony: "Then but forbear your food a little while, / Whiles, like a doe, I go to find my fawn / And give it food" (127–29). We are invited simply to accept the doe-fawn metaphor that Orlando invokes for his obligation to reciprocate Adam's "pure love" (131).

Just as there is an unlimited supply of food in this scene, so there seems to be more than enough "pure love" to go around, Jaques excepted. Love is expressed in terms of food, and men gladly take on nurturant roles. Duke Senior's abundant provision of food and of "gentleness" creates an image of a self-sustaining patriarchal system. The men take over the traditional female prerogative of maternal nurturance, negatively defined by Jaques: "At first the infant, / Mewling and puking in the nurse's arms" (2.7.143–44). Such discomfort has been purged from the men's nurturance as it is dramatized in this scene, which thus offers a new perspective on Duke Senior's very first speech in the play. We now see that it is the male feast, not the biting winter wind, that "feelingly persuades me what I am" (2.1.11). "Sweet are the uses of adversity" because, as Orlando discovers, adversity disappears when men's "gentleness" prevails, "translating the stubbornness of fortune / Into so quiet and sweet a style" (12, 19–20). This sweetness explains why "loving lords have put themselves into voluntary exile" with the duke and why "many young gentlemen flock to him every day" (1.1.99, 113–14).

The idealized male enclave founded on "sacred pity" in Act 2, Scene 7, is not an isolated incident. The power of male pity extends beyond this scene to include the evil Oliver, who is threatened by a symbol of maternal nurturance made hostile by depletion: "A lioness, with udders all drawn dry" (4.3.115) and "the sucked and hungry lioness" (127). The motif of eating here creates a negative image that might disturb the comfortable pastoral banquet, but the lioness's intrusion is quickly ended. Responding with a kindness that can be traced back to his meeting with Duke Senior, Orlando rescues his brother: "But kindness, nobler ever than revenge, / And nature, stronger than his just occasion, / Made him give battle to the lioness" (129–31). Oliver's oral fulfillment follows: "my conversion / So sweetly tastes" (137–38). The tears "that sacred pith hath engendered" (2.7.123) are reiterated by the brothers' reconciliation—"Tears our recountments had most kindly bathed" (4.3.141)—and their reunion confirmed by a recapitulation of the banquet scene: "he led me to the gentle Duke, / Who gave me fresh array and entertainment, / Committing me unto my brother's love" (143–45). Again the pattern of male reconciliation preceding love for women is seen in Oliver's confession of his desire to marry Celia (5.2.1–12) coming after his admission to the brotherhood.

The male community of Act 2, Scene 7, is also vindicated by the restoration of patriarchal normalcy in the play's final scene. In the end, as Rosalind's powers are fading, the relationship between Duke Senior and Orlando is reasserted and completed as the duke announces the inheritance to

which marriage entitles Orlando: "A land itself at large, a
potent dukedom" (5.4.169). Like the "huswife Fortune"
who "doth most mistake in her gifts to women" (1.2.30, 36),
Rosalind plays her part by rehearsing the men in their political roles:

> *Rosalind.* You say, if I bring in your Rosalind,
>   You will bestow her on Orlando here?
> *Duke Senior.* That would I, had I kingdoms to give with her.
> *Rosalind.* And you say you will have her, when I bring her.
> *Orlando.* That would I, were I of all kingdoms king.
>
> (5.4.6–10)

The reference the two men make to kingdoms is shortly
to be fulfilled, but this bounty is beyond Rosalind's power
to give. For it is not her magic that produces the surprise
entrance of Jaques de Boys with the news of Duke Senior's
restoration. In completing the de Boys family reunion, the
middle brother's appearance reverses the emblematic fate
of the three sons destroyed by Charles the wrestler: "Yonder they lie, the poor old man, their father, making such
pitiful dole over them that all the beholders take his part
with weeping" (1.2.121–23). The image of three de Boys
sons reestablishes the proper generational sequence, ensur-
ing continuity.

III

C. L. Barber has shown that the "Saturnalian Pattern" that
gives structure to festive comedy is intrinsically conservative since it involves only "a temporary license, a 'misrule'
which implied rule."[2] But in *As You Like It* the conservatism
of comic form does not affect all characters equally. In
the liberal opening out into the forest of Arden, both men
and women are permitted an expansion of sexual identity that transcends restrictive gender roles. Just as Rosalind
gains access to the traditional masculine attributes of
strength and control through her costume, so Orlando gains
access to the traditional female attributes of compassion and
nurturance. However, the conservative countermovement

built into comic strategy applies exclusively to Rosalind. Her possession of the male costume and of the power it symbolizes is only temporary. But Orlando does not have to give up the emotional enlargement he has experienced in the forest. Discussions of androgyny in *As You Like It* usually focus on Rosalind whereas in fact it is the men rather than the women who are the lasting beneficiaries of androgyny. It is Orlando, not Rosalind, who achieves a synthesis of attributes traditionally labeled masculine and feminine when he combines compassion and aggression in rescuing his brother from the lioness.

This selective androgyny demands an ambivalent response: it is a humanizing force for the men, yet it is based on the assumption that men have power over women.[3] Because androgyny is available only to men, we are left with a paradoxical compatibility of androgyny with patriarchy, that is, benevolent patriarchy. In talking about male power in *As You Like It*, we must distinguish between two forms of patriarchy. The first and most obvious is the harsh, mean-spirited version represented by Oliver, who abuses primogeniture, and by Duke Frederick, who after usurping power holds on to it by arbitrary acts of suppression. Driven by greed, envy, suspicion, and power for power's sake, neither man can explain his actions. In an ironic demonstration of the consuming nature of evil, Duke Frederick expends his final rage against Oliver, who honestly protests: "I never loved my brother in my life" (3.1.14). In contrast to good men, bad men are incapable of forming alliances. Since Frederick's acts of banishment have now depopulated the court, he himself must enter the forest in order to seek the enemies so necessary to his existence (5.4.154–58). But of course this patriarchal tyranny is a caricature and therefore harmless. Oliver and Frederick are exaggerated fairy-tale villains whose hardened characters are unable to withstand the wholesome atmosphere of the forest and instantly dissolve (4.3.136–38; 5.4.159–65). The second, more serious version of patriarchy is the political structure headed by Duke Senior. To describe it, we seek adjectives like "benevolent," "humane," and "civilized." Yet we cannot leave it at that. A benevolent patriarchy still requires women to be subordinate, and Rosalind's final performance is her enactment of this subordination.

We can now summarize the difference between the conclusions of *Love's Labor's Lost* and *As You Like It*. In order to assess the sense of an ending, we must take into account the perspective of sexual politics and correlate formal harmony or disharmony with patriarchal stability or instability. Unlike Rosalind, the women in *Love's Labor's Lost* do not give up their independence.[4] The sudden announcement of the death of the princess's father partially restrains her wit. But this news is a *pater ex machina* attempt to even the score and to equalize the situation between the men and the women because nothing has emerged organically within the play to challenge the women's predominance. The revelation that the "decrepit, sick, and bed-rid" father (1.1.138) has died is not an effective assertion of his presence but, on the contrary, advertises his weakness. The princess submits to the "new-sad soul" (5.2.732) that mourning requires, but this provides the excuse for going on to reject the suitors as she has all along. Her essential power remains intact, whereas patriarchal authority is presented as weak or nonexistent. The death of the invalid father has a sobering impact because it mirrors the vacuum created by the four lords' powerlessness within the play. There is no relief from the fear that dominant women inspire in a patriarchal sensibility, and this continuing tension contributes to the uneasiness at the play's end.

Like the princess, Rosalind confronts her father in the final scene. But in her case paternal power is vigorously represented by Duke Senior and by the line of patriarchal authority established when Senior makes Orlando his heir. Festive celebration is now possible because a dependable, that is, patriarchal, social order is securely in place. It is Duke Senior's voice that legitimates the festive closure: "Play, music, and you brides and bridegrooms all, / With measure heaped in joy, to th' measures fall" (5.4.178–79). Orlando benefits from this social structure because, in contrast to the lords of *Love's Labor's Lost*, he has a solid political resource to offset the liability of a poetic convention that dictates male subservience. *As You Like It* achieves marital closure not by eliminating male ties but rather by strengthening them.[5]

A further phasing out of Rosalind occurs in the Epilogue when it is revealed that she is male: "If I were a woman I would kiss as many of you as had beards that pleased me" (18–19). This explicit breaking of theatrical illusion forces us to reckon with the fact of an all-male cast. The boy-actor convention makes it possible for males to explore the female other (I use the term *other* here in the sense given by Simone de Beauvoir in *The Second Sex* of woman as the other). Vicariously taking on the female role enables male spectators to make an experimental contact with what otherwise might remain unknown, forbidden territory. Fear of women can be encountered in the relatively safe environment of the theater, acted out, controlled (when it can be controlled as in *As You Like It*), and overcome. A further twist of logic defuses and reduces the threat of female power: Rosalind is no one to be frightened of since, as the Epilogue insists, she is male after all; she is only a boy and clearly subordinate to men in the hierarchy of things.

The convention of males playing female roles gives men the opportunity to imagine sex-role fluidity and flexibility. Built into the conditions of performance is the potential for male acknowledgment of a "feminine self" and thus for male transcendence of a narrow masculinity. In the particular case of *As You Like It*, the all-male cast provides a theatrical counterpart for the male community at Duke Senior's banquet in Act 2, Scene 7. This theatrical dimension reinforces the conservative effect of male androgyny within the play. Acknowledgment of the feminine within the male is one thing, the acknowledgment of individual women another: the latter does not automatically follow from the former. In the boy-actor motif, woman is a metaphor for the male discovery of the feminine within himself, of those qualities suppressed by a masculinity strictly defined as aggressiveness. Once the tenor of the metaphor has been attained, the vehicle can be discarded—just as Rosalind is discarded. The sense of the patriarchal ending in *As You Like It* is that male androgyny is affirmed whereas female "liberty" in the person of Rosalind is curtailed.

There is, finally, a studied ambiguity about heterosexual versus homoerotic feeling in the play, Shakespeare allowing himself to have it both ways. The Epilogue is heterosexual in its bringing together of men and women: "and I charge you, O men, for the love you bear to women (as I perceive by your simp'ring, none of you hates them), that between you and the women the play may please" (13–16). The "simp'ring" attributed to men in their response to women is evoked in a good-natured jocular spirit; yet the tone conveys discomfort as well. In revealing the self-sufficient male acting company, the Epilogue also offers the counterimage of male bonds based on the exclusion of women.

Though he is shown hanging love poems on trees only after achieving atonement with Rosalind's father, Orlando never tries, like the lords of *Love's Labor's Lost*, to avoid women. The social structure of *As You Like It*, in which political power is vested in male bonds, can include heterosexual love because marriage becomes a way of incorporating women since Rosalind is complicit in her assimilation by patriarchal institutions. However, in spite of the disarming of Rosalind, resistance to women remains. It is as though asserting the priority of relations between men over relations between men and women is not enough, as though a fall-back position is needed. The Epilogue is, in effect, a second ending that provides further security against women by preserving on stage the image of male ties in their pure form with women absent. Not only are women to be subordinate; they can, if necessary, be imagined as nonexistent. Rosalind's art does not, as is sometimes suggested, coincide with Shakespeare's: Shakespeare uses his art to take away Rosalind's female identity and thereby upstages her claim to magic power.

We can see the privileged status accorded to male bonds by comparing Shakespeare's treatment of same-sex relations for men and for women. Men originally divided are reunited as in the instance of Oliver and Orlando, but women undergo the reverse process. Rosalind and Celia are initially inseparable: "never two ladies loved as they do" (1.1.108–9); "whose loves / Are dearer than the natural bond of sisters" (1.2.265–66); "And whereso'er we went, like

Juno's swans, / Still we went coupled and inseparable" (1.3.73–74); and "thou and I am one. / Shall we be sund'red? shall we part, sweet girl? / No, let my father seek another heir" (95–97). Yet the effect of the play is to separate them by transferring their allegiance to husbands. Celia ceases to be a speaking character at the end of Act 4, her silence coinciding with her new role as fiancée. The danger of female bonding is illustrated when Shakespeare diminishes Rosalind's absolute control by mischievously confronting her with the unanticipated embarrassment of Phebe's love for her. Rosalind is of course allowed to devise an escape from the pressure of this undesirable entanglement, but it is made clear in the process that such ardor is taboo and that the authorized defense against it is marriage. "And I for no woman," Rosalind insists (5.2.87). A comparable prohibition is not announced against male friendship.[6]

In conclusion, we must ask: what is Shakespeare's relation to the sexual politics of *As You Like It*? Is he taking an ironic and critical stance toward the patriarchal solution of his characters, or is he heavily invested in this solution himself? I think there are limits to Shakespeare's critical awareness in this play. The sudden conversions of Oliver and Duke Frederick have a fairy-tale quality that Shakespeare clearly intends as an aspect of the wish fulfillment to which he calls attention in the play's title. Similarly, Jaques' commentary in the final scene is a deliberate foil to the neatness of the ending that allows Shakespeare as well as Jaques a modicum of distance. However, in fundamental respects Shakespeare appears to be implicated in the fantasy he has created for his characters.

As You Like It enacts two rites of which Shakespeare did not avail himself in *Love's Labor's Lost*. We have too easily accepted the formulation that says that Shakespeare in the mature history plays concentrates on masculine development whereas in the mature festive comedies he gives women their due by allowing them to play the central role.[7] *As You Like It* is primarily a defensive action against female power rather than a celebration of it. Second, Shakespeare portrays an ideal male community based on "sacred pity." This idealized vision of relationships between men can be seen as sentimental and unrealistic, but in contrast to his undercutting of academe in *Love's Labor's Lost*, Shakespeare is here thoroughly engaged and endorses the idealization. These two elements—female vitality kept manageable and male power kept loving—provided a resolution that at this particular moment was "As Shakespeare Liked It."

Notes

1. Norman O. Brown employs this passage in his own celebration of the horn: "Metamorphoses II: Actaeon," *American Poetry Review* 1 (1972): 38–40.

2. C. L. Barber, *Shakespeare's Festive Comedy* (Princeton, N.J.: Princeton University Press, 1959).

3. Adrienne Rich provides a critique of the conservative use of the concept *androgyny* and a summary of recent writing on the subject in *Of Woman Born: Motherhood as Experience and Institution* (New York: W. W. Norton, 1976), pp. 62–63. Rich's poem "The Stranger," in *Diving into the Wreck* (New York: W. W. Norton, 1973), declares proudly: "I am the androgyne" (p. 19). But the revaluation of androgyny in her prose work leads Rich to disavow the term in "Natural Resources," in *The Dream of a Common Language* (New York: W. W. Norton, 1978): "There are words I cannot choose again: / humanism androgyny (p. 66).

4. I do not mean to suggest that this is a positive ending in the sense of being the best possible outcome, but the women's continued assertion of independence is a valid response to the less-than-ideal circumstances with which they must deal. It allows them to retain their integrity—an alternative preferable to capitulation.

5. In Anne Barton's judgment, *As You Like It* "stands as the fullest and most stable realization of Shakespearean comic form" (" 'As You Like It' and 'Twelfth Night': Shakespeare's Sense of an Ending," in *Shakespearean Comedy: Stratford-Upon-Avon Studies 14,* ed. Malcolm Bradbury and David Palmer [New York: Crane, Russak & Co., 1972] p. 161). Barton speaks of Shakespeare's loss of "faith" in comic endings after the perfection of *As You Like It* and of the "renewed faith" made possible by his "readjustment of form" in the late romances (pp. 179–80). Both the loss and the recovery of faith involve Shakespeare's changing attitudes toward the viability of benign patriarchy. In particular, *The Winter's Tale* restores this faith (after its shattering in the tragedies) by reestablishing patriarchal harmony in a believable form.

6. In this regard *The Merchant of Venice* offers a useful contrast. The conclusion of *Love's Labor's Lost* presents a three-way stalemate. Marital bonds, male bonds, and female bonds are all sources of vague discomfort: none can be affirmed. *As You Like It* affirms marriage by strengthening male bonds and eliminating female bonds. *The Merchant of Venice* breaks the stalemate in a different way. Marriage is achieved by disrupting the bond between Antonio and Bassanio, but the alliance between Portia and Nerissa remains in effect, as their comparatively sharp deployment of

the cuckold motif attests. The source of uneasiness in *The Merchant of Venice,* however, is Portia's defeat of a Jewish father in the earlier court scene and, in particular, her problematic speech about Christian bounty (4.1.184–202), problematic partly because her own behavior toward Shylock fails to exhibit the mercy she recommends to him.

7. For an example of this contrast between comedies and histories, see R. J. Dorius, "Shakespeare's Dramatic Modes and *Antony and Cleopatra*" in *Literatur als Kritik des Lebens: Festschrift zum 65. Geburtstag von Ludwig Borinski* (Heidelberg: Quelle & Meyer, 1975), pp. 83–96. Dorius's overview is useful but overdrawn in the way I have suggested.

JEAN E. HOWARD

Cross-dressing in *As You Like It*

More complex still [than *The Merchant of Venice*] is *As You Like It*, which explicitly invites, through its epilogue, a consideration of how secure even the most recuperative representations of cross-dressing could be in a theater in which male actors regularly played women's roles. Rosalind's cross-dressing, of course, occurs in the holiday context of the pastoral forest, and, as Natalie Davis has argued, holiday inversions of order can spur social change or, in other instances, can merely reconfirm the existing order.[1] The representation of Rosalind's holiday humor has the primary effect, I think, of confirming the gender system and perfecting rather than dismantling it by making a space for mutuality within relations of dominance.[2] Temporarily lording it over Orlando, teaching him how to woo and appointing the times of his coming and going, she *could* be a threatening figure if she did not constantly, contrapuntally,

From "Crossdressing, The Theatre, and Gender Struggle in Early Modern England," *Shakespeare Quarterly* 43 (1988), reprinted by permission of the author and *Shakespeare Quarterly*. The title of this extract is the editor's.

[1] Natalie Zemon Davis, "Women on Top: Symbolic Sexual Inversion and Political Disorder in Early Modern Europe," in *The Reversible World: Symbolic Inversion in Art and Society*, ed. Barbara Babcock (Ithaca, N.Y.: Cornell University Press, 1978), pp. 147–90.

[2] For the view that the romantic comedies champion mutuality between the sexes, see Marianne Novy's *Love's Argument: Gender Relations in Shakespeare* (Chapel Hill: University of North Carolina Press, 1984), especially Chapter 2, " 'An You Smile Not, He's Gagged': Mutuality in Shakespearean Comedy," pp. 21–44.

reveal herself to the audience as the not-man, as in actuality a lovesick maid whose love "hath an unknown bottom, like the bay of Portugal" (4.1.198–99) and who faints at the sight of blood. Crucially, like Viola, Rosalind retains a properly feminine subjectivity: "Dost thou think, though I am caparisoned like a man, I have a doublet and hose in my disposition?" (3.2.193–95) As Annette Kuhn has argued, in certain circumstances cross-dressing intensifies, rather than blurs, sexual difference, sometimes by calling attention to the woman's failure to perform the masculine role signified by her dress.[3] Rosalind's fainting constitutes such a reminder, endearing her to earlier generations of readers and audiences for her true "womanliness." And, as in *Twelfth Night*, the thrust of the narrative is toward that long-delayed moment of disclosure, orchestrated so elaborately in Act 5, when the heroine will doff her masculine attire along with the saucy games of youth and accept the position of wife, when her biological identity, her gender identity, and the semiotics of dress will coincide.

Where this account of the consequences of Rosalind's cross-dressing becomes too simple, however, is in a close consideration of the particular *way* in which Rosalind plays with her disguise. Somewhat like Portia, Rosalind uses her disguise to redefine (albeit in a limited way) the position of woman in a patriarchal society. The most unusual aspect of her behavior is that while dressed as a man, Rosalind impersonates a woman, and that woman is herself—or, rather, a self that is the logical conclusion of Orlando's romantic, Petrarchan construction of her. Saucy, imperious, and fickle by turns, Rosalind plays out masculine constructions of femininity, in the process showing Orlando their limitations. Marianne Doane has argued that "masquerade," the self-conscious staging, parody, exaggeration of cultural constructions of self, offers women a choice between simple identification with male selves—which is how she reads the meaning of cross-dressing—or simple inscription within

[3] "Sexual Disguise and Cinema," *The Power of the Image: Essays on Representation and Sexuality* (London: Routledge and Kegan Paul, 1985), pp. 48–73, especially pp. 55–57.

patriarchal constructions of the feminine.[4] In my view, the figure of Rosalind dressed as a boy engages in playful masquerade as, in playing Rosalind for Orlando, she acts out the parts scripted for women by her culture. Doing so does not release Rosalind from patriarchy but reveals the constructed nature of patriarchy's representations of the feminine and shows a woman manipulating those representations in her own interest, theatricalizing for her own purposes what is assumed to be innate, teaching her future mate how to get beyond certain ideologies of gender to more enabling ones.

Moreover, this play, more than other Shakespearean comedies, deliberately calls attention to the destabilizing fact that it is boy actors playing the roles of all the women in the play, including Rosalind. There is a permanent gap on the stage between the incipiently masculine identity of the boy actors and their appropriation of the "grace, / Voice, gait, and action of a gentlewoman"—to borrow a definition of the actor's task from the job assigned the Page in the Induction to *The Taming of the Shrew* (Ind.1.131–32). I agree with Kathleen McLuskie that at some level boy actors playing women must simply have been accepted in performance as a convention.[5] Otherwise, audience involvement with dramatic narratives premised on heterosexual love and masculine/feminine difference would have been minimal. It is also true, as McLuskie and others suggest, that the convention of the boy actor playing a girl can, at any moment, be unmasked *as* a convention and the reality (that the fictional woman is played by a boy) can be revealed. One of those moments occurs at the end of *As You Like It*. The play has achieved closure in part by re-inscribing everyone into his or her "proper" social position. The duke is now again a duke and not a forest outlaw, Rosalind is now Rosalind and not Ganymede, and so forth. But when in the Epilogue the character playing Rosalind reminds us that she is played by a boy, the neat convergence of biological sex and culturally

---

[4] "Film and the Masquerade: Theorizing the Female Spectator," *Screen* 23 (1982), 74–89.

[5] "The Act, the Role, and the Actor: Boy Actresses on the Elizabethan Stage," *New Theatre Quarterly* 3 (1987), 120–30, especially 121.

constructed gender is once more severed. If a boy can so successfully personate the voice, gait, and manner of a woman, how stable are those boundaries separating one sexual kind from another, and thus how secure are those powers and privileges assigned to the hierarchically superior sex, which depends upon notions of difference to justify its dominance?[6] The Epilogue playfully invites this question. That it does so suggests something about the contradictory nature of the theater as a site of ideological production, an institution that can circulate recuperative fables of cross-dressing, re-inscribing sexual difference and gender hierarchy, and at the same time can make visible on the level of theatrical practice the contamination of sexual kinds.

[6] For good discussions of the disruptive effects of the Epilogue, see Catherine Belsey's "Disrupting Sexual Difference," *Alternative Shakespeares*, ed. John Drakakis (1985), pp. 166–90, and Phyllis Rackin's "Androgyny, Mimesis, and the Marriage of the Boy Heroine on the English Renaissance Stage," *PMLA* 102 (1987), 29–41.

SYLVAN BARNET

As You Like It on Stage and Screen

> Rosalind is to the actress what Hamlet is to the actor—a part
> in which, reasonable presentability being granted, failure is
> hardly possible.
>
> —GEORGE BERNARD SHAW,
> reviewing a performance in 1896

True; and it is almost true that, given an adequate
Rosalind, one will get an adequate production of *As You
Like It*. Orlando, delightfully deprecated in the play as "a
dropped acorn," is not a part that demands a great performer, though in fact the role has been played in their
salad days by Gielgud, Olivier (in a weak film of 1935),
and Michael Redgrave. It is Rosalind (whose part is twice
as long as that of any other character's in the play, and is
considerably longer than Macbeth's or Prospero's) who
carries the play, and in our century the role has been
marvelously performed by Edith Evans, Peggy Ashcroft,
and Vanessa Redgrave. Still, a good Rosalind is not
always enough to save a production. Sometimes, in this age
of "director's theater," the director sets forth a bright idea
that sinks this all-but-unsinkable play. Modern dress, of
course, is occasionally used, as in the production at Stratford, Connecticut, in 1961, where Orlando, in overalls,
courted a Rosalind in jeans. Unnecessary, but harmless
enough. But think, for instance, of a production at the
Tyrone Guthrie Theater in Minneapolis in 1966, set in the
years just after the Civil War. The exiled duke was a sort of
Robert E. Lee, living in retirement attended by former Con-
federate soldiers; the Forest of Arden was a great brown

tree, hung with Spanish moss. According to the director, the setting was a "visual metaphor that expresses the essence of the play." Hearing this, with Touchstone we might drily say, "Thus men may grow wiser every day." Or consider another example, this one a San Diego production in 1976, set in colonial French Canada. The banished duke's attendants now were North American Indians, as were Adam, Audrey, William, and Amiens. When Amiens sang "Under the green-wood tree," the chorus, arranged in a circle, passed a peace pipe. Some changes were made in the text—for instance "court" became "fort"—so that the lines did not seem utterly incongruous with the director's idea, but the whole seemed a travesty.

In general, however, most productions of *As You Like It* are more or less straight, and more or less (if they have a passable Rosalind) successful. For a fairly brief but packed survey, see the admirable discussion by Richard Knowles, in his *New Variorum Edition of Shakespeare: As You Like It*, pages 629–62.

We know nothing of the earliest productions of the play, though a couple of early seventeenth-century references to productions for the court may refer to *As You Like It*. Also conjectural, but probably true, is the idea that Robert Armin played Touchstone. Armin, a noted player of witty fools, in 1599 replaced Will Kemp, the member of Shakespeare's theatrical company who had specialized in playing clownish types such as Bottom in *A Midsummer Night's Dream*. It is an article of modern scholarly faith that Armin's gift was for a sensitive rather than coarse kind of fool, and that Shakespeare therefore wrote such parts as Touchstone, Feste (in *Twelfth Night*), and the Fool (in *King Lear*) for Armin. What is the evidence that Shakespeare tailored the parts for Armin? The parts themselves. The reasoning is circular, but since Armin was indeed a member of the company when the play was first performed, and since he did play fools, we can conjecture that he played Touchstone. Nothing else is known, or can even be conjectured, about the early history of the play—unless one wants to conjecture that for unknown reasons the play was not performed in Shakespeare's day.

In 1723 *As You Like It* underwent a curious transformation at the hands of Charles Johnson, who omitted Touchstone, Silvius, Phebe, Audrey, William, and Sir Oliver Martext, and renamed some other characters. He added to the text some passages from *Much Ado About Nothing*, *Twelfth Night*, and even *Richard II* (the wrestling match between Charles and Orlando, converted into a duel, is tricked out with some lines from the combat between Mowbray and Bolingbroke in *Richard II*); Oliver commits suicide when Charles confesses plotting with Oliver against Orlando; and Jaques marries Celia—though not before a play of Pyramus and Thisbe (taken from the last act of *A Midsummer Night's Dream*) is performed. This version, first staged in 1723 at Drury Lane, was revived in 1740 and flourished during the rest of the eighteenth century. But *As You Like It* was also produced pretty much as Shakespeare wrote it, though with some amplification of Jaques's part, and with the addition of "When daisies pied and violets blue" from the last act of *Love's Labor's Lost*.

The play was popular throughout the nineteenth century, for instance in productions by William Charles Macready (1837 and 1842, with Ada Nisbett as Rosalind), and especially in productions by Augustin Daly (in New York in 1889, and in London in 1890, with Ada Rehan as Rosalind). Daly cut about four hundred lines from the text, deleted what seemed to be bawdry and blasphemy ("bastard" becomes "little child," and "God" becomes "Heaven"), and rearranged some scenes in order to provide Rehan with curtain speeches, but these alterations were relatively minor, especially when compared to some of the alterations made today by advocates of director's theater.

Of the earliest twentieth-century productions, the most notable is that in 1907 by Oscar Asche, who made a forest of two thousand pots of ferns, cartloads of leaves, and moss-covered logs (renewed weekly). This production was in the nineteenth-century tradition of elaborate, illusionistic settings, and by 1907 (although Max Beerbohm found Asche's production "an awfully jolly affair") it was decidedly old-fashioned. Beerbohm said Asche's Arden "is a very beautiful place. But it is not, like Shakespeare's Arden, an enchanted place. One feels that it is mentioned by Baedecker, and reproduced in color on picture postcards." A moment later he adds, "Things have come to a pretty pass when we bother our heads about verisimilitude for such a dream as *As You Like It*." Still, what can be thought of as the first modern production—a production in which verisimilitude was jettisoned—did not take place until 1919, when Nigel Playfair staged *As You Like It* at Stratford and then a little later at the Lyric Theatre in London, with Athene Seyler as Rosalind. Playfair describes this remarkable production at some length, and illustrates two costumes and a set (the designer was Claud Lovat Fraser), in *The Story of the Lyric Theatre*. (It is also described, more briefly, but with illustrations of two costumes, in J. L. Styan, *The Shakespeare Revolution*.) The sets (bright pillars and medieval turrets for the court, loops of foliage for the forest) were alleged to be derived from fourteenth-century missals and tapestries, and doubtless Playfair and Fraser were sincere in referring to these sources, but it is evident to anyone familiar with, say, Picasso's harlequins and his designs (1917–19) for the Russian ballet that the critics were right to howl that Fraser was bringing in "modernistic"—even "futuristic" and "Bolshevik"—ideas. The costumes were particolored and vivid (emerald-green, lemon-yellow, ultramarine-blue); the men wore tunics and hose, the women wore high-waisted dresses with full skirts. Even more offensive to traditional taste than the unusual costumes was the sprightly pace at which the play was given, and most offensive of all was the omission of the stuffed stag. Back in 1879, in the opening season of the Shakespeare Memorial Theatre in Stratford-upon-Avon, a stag from the herd at Charlecot, where according to tradition Shakespeare had poached, was killed in the morning and used in a performance of *As You Like It*, in 4.2, when performers sing, "What shall he have that killed the deer?" In succeeding years the deer—which had been stuffed and preserved in the local museum—was regularly propped up in Stratford productions of the pastoral scenes. But by 1919 the creature was moth-eaten, and in any event this sort of stodgy realism was not to Playfair's taste. Rather, his production—entirely faithful to the text in that nothing was cut—was something of a musical comedy (musicians dressed as pages sat in front of the curtain before the play began, and then took their place on stage), with Elizabethan settings for the songs. Bright and lively rather than dull and slow, this production seemed intolerable to some critics. In his book Playfair quotes, at length, an unfavorable review, and then counters it with a favorable one. There is space here to quote only a small part of the second review. It rings true:

> It is difficult to know where to begin to particularize in praise. Was it the dress or the acting that pleased most, the music or the scene? Or was it a certain extraordinary impression of vitality and sensibility? In the first place, Mr. Nigel Playfair's methods succeed in leaving the audience with the impression that *As You Like It* is almost the greatest of Shakespeare's plays. Its humanity and sympathy and its charm are unrivalled. Its poetry is limpid and exquisite, like that of *The Tempest*; it is as well constructed as *Macbeth*, and almost as metaphysical as *Hamlet*, while in humor it equals *Twelfth Night*. These facts are not, I think, striking to a reader of the play, but I think that anyone who had been to the [theater] would agree to this evaluation. Miss Athene Seyler as Rosalind and Mr. Herbert Marshall as Jaques made us conscious of the deep current of the philosophy of life which runs under the play, bearing up its exquisite fragility. Their acting was raised above that of an extraordinarily good cast by their remarkable perception of this inner play. Rosalind and Jaques, they made us feel, were the two clairvoyants of the "Golden World"—optimist and pessimist philosophers. Like Hamlet, they hear the august harmonies of the lives of men and women, and are respectively moved to pity or stung to contempt for themselves and for those of less vision. But her finer conception does not cut Rosalind off from her kind. Unlike Jaques, she is more of an actor than an onlooker, and her active, restless spirit and her vivid sense of humor lead her inevitably into the part of *dea ex machina*.

The next *As You Like It* that requires mention is Esme Church's production at the Old Vic in 1936–37, with Edith Evans (Rosalind) costumed rather like Gainsborough's "Blue Boy." Another way of putting it is to say that the scenes and costumes evoked the world of Watteau; that is, for English pastoralism of the Renaissance the designer substituted the more familiar rococo artificiality of the *fêtes galantes* of the French eighteenth century, and in fact this sort of decor, with its parklike setting of arching boughs beneath which move figures in silvery silk and satin, has proved popular (and effective) in later productions. There is no need to discuss Church's *As You Like It* at greater length, since a reviewer's comment says it all: Edith Evans "made the audience one Orlando."

When one thinks casually of *As You Like It*, one thinks of only two settings, court versus country—and these suggest the artificial versus the natural. Moreover, one is inclined to think of the country scenes as taking place in the spring:

> It was a lover and his lass,
>   With a hey, and a ho, and a hey nonino,
> That o'er the green cornfield did pass
>   In springtime, the only pretty ringtime,
> When birds do sing, hey ding a ding, ding.
> Sweet lovers love the spring.   (5.3.13–18)

But this delightful song does not occur until late in the play; earlier we get references to the "cold," the "icy fang / And churlish chiding of the winter's wind," and to "winter and rough weather." Consequently, for several decades directors have been inclined to darken even the country setting, at least in the first half of the play, so that the play may move from winter to spring. Thus, in Glen Byam Shaw's production in Stratford in 1952, with Margaret Leighton as Rosalind, in the early country scenes the set suggested winter. In Michael Elliott's production at Stratford in 1961, with Vanessa Redgrave as Rosalind, the great oak that dominated the set (it served as Oliver's orchard, Duke Frederick's back lawn, and the Forest of Arden) was leafless at the start but green at the end. Similarly, in Terry Hands' production at Stratford, 1980, the wintry atmosphere of the first part of the play (snow and white furs—even Rosalind and Celia wore black velvet edged with white fur) changed to a warmer world of browns and-greens, and at the end there was a garlanded cart for the weddings. Some directors, however, are reluctant even at the end to bring in the spring. David Jones' 1967 production at Stratford, with the Royal Shakespeare Company—Dorothy Tutin played Rosalind—was fairly somber throughout, with two rather sinister trees at the back of the stage. (The production was "dark" in yet other ways; for instance, the hunters ritually stained each other with the blood of the deer. A few years later, in Terry Hands' 1980 production, we had other sorts of darkness: Frederick and Oliver seemed almost crazed; and Touchstone, having stepped in sheep dung, wiped off his shoe with one of Orlando's poems, and then tossed the paper out into the audience.)

We have already glanced at the brown tree, decked with melancholy Spanish moss, that characterized a production in Minneapolis in 1966; perhaps now we can generalize, and say that from the late 1960s to the early 1980s, *As You Like It* was sometimes seen not chiefly as a happy pastoral play but as a Chekhovian play, or even something much darker. Thus Frederick, Oliver, and Jaques were sometimes depicted as neurotics, and the play was interpreted as a study of power struggles. No one, not even Rosalind, escaped a severe judgment. For instance, Ralph Berry, in a book called *Shakespeare's Comedies,* said that Rosalind is "motivated above all by a will to dominate." One understands what he means, for it is true that she is the agent who brings four couples to the nuptial dance in the fifth act, but it is sobering to recall that earlier commentators used such words as "buoyant," "energetic," "lively," "witty," "high-spirited," and "intelligent."

Another device to darken the work is the use of the same actor to play Duke Senior and Duke Frederick, thus implying that Arden is as corrupt as the court. Liviu Ciulei used this device in a 1982 production at the Guthrie Theater in Minneapolis; it was also used, in the same year, in a

Munich production. On the other hand, sunny versions of *As You Like It*, or at least versions in which the wintry spirit is by the end dispelled in an atmosphere of spring and love, occasionally were staged even in the 1960s and 1970s.

One of the most unusual productions since World War II was the all-male version done in England by the National Theatre (directed by Clifford Williams) in 1966, and brought to the United States in 1974. This was not intended as a mere novelty (such as the all-female version, with some women in false beards, staged in America in 1893), nor was it intended as an experiment based on the Elizabethan practice of using boy actors to perform female roles. (Ben Greet in 1920 had staged an all-male *As You Like It*; it was regarded uneasily before it opened, but was found in production to be thoroughly chaste.) The germ for Williams' version can be found in Jan Kott's long essay on *As You Like It*, "Shakespeare's Bitter Arcadia," in *Shakespeare Our Contemporary*. Kott explores the idea that this play is rich in sexual ambiguity, since (in the original productions) a boy actor played Rosalind. Thus, a boy (the actor) plays a girl (Rosalind) who plays a role in which she disguises herself as a boy (Ganymede) and in the course of this disguise plays a girl (Ganymede invites Orlando to think of Ganymede as Rosalind). So, Kott says, "Everything is real and unreal, false and genuine at the same time." The meaning of disguise in the Renaissance, he says, was "an attempt at eroticism free from the limitations of the body. It was also a dream of love free from the limitations of sex, of love pervading the bodies of boys and girls, men and women, in the way light penetrates through glass."

Kenneth Tynan, then the National Theatre's literary manager, called the company's attention to Kott's essay and asked John Dexter to produce an all-male version; Dexter passed the idea on to Clifford Williams. At first Williams was not enthusiastic, but later he warmed to the idea, though he continued to insist (even after quoting in the program some of Kott's remarks about sexual ambiguity) that his production did not seek merely to put Kott's ideas on the stage. In the program note Williams also declared that his purpose was not "to reintroduce the convention of boys acting women"; rather, it was to help the viewer experience the greatness of *As You Like It* by preventing us from being attracted only to its surface, its seeming story of sexual love:

> The examination of the infinite beauty of Man in love— which lies at the very heart of *As You Like It*—takes place in an atmosphere of spiritual purity which transcends sensuality. . . . It is for this reason that I employ a male cast; so that we shall not—entranced by the surface reality—miss the interior truth.

This all sounds rather like Brecht's "alienation effect," which, keeping the audience alert by preventing any emotional involvement, seeks to arouse the audience's detached thought. By using men to play the women's parts— especially by using lanky, hawk-nosed Ronald Pickup to play Rosalind—Williams prevented his spectators from experiencing any sort of merely sexual infatuation or making any sort of physical identification with these lovers, in whose love, Williams said in an interview, there is "an incredible incandescent purity." The set, too, by Ralph Koltai, had an alienating effect. In 1919 Nigel Playfair had banished the stuffed deer and had substituted a stylized forest for the traditional, supposedly realistic forest, but his forest still could immediately be recognized as a forest, however stylized the leaves were. At first Williams thought of setting the play in a prisoner-of-war camp (this would explain why all of the roles were taken by men), then of setting it in a Roman mansion inhabited by persons who live *la dolce vita*, but he finally chose a dreamlike set, consisting of hanging Plexiglas tubes that served as foliage, and translucent Plexiglas cubes and pyramids that served as trees, rocks, and stools. These were chiefly gray, silver, and white. Somewhat cold, and not at all the happy greenwood of the hey-ding-a-ding world, they kept the viewer from slipping into easy, standard emotions. What love there was in this wood was in the words and the actions, not in the setting, with its psychedelic lighting.

Some viewers saw Williams' production as campy, others saw it (in the spirit of the director) as a profound vision of sensual and spiritual love. Twenty-five years later another all-male production (1991–95), this one by a company called Cheek by Jowl, received similarly mixed reviews. The play began with actors, uniformly dressed in black trousers and white collarless shirts, standing in a group while some lines from 2.7 were recited: "All the world's a stage, / and all the men"—at this point all but two of the performers moved stage right—"and women"—at this point the two performers who would play Rosalind and Celia moved downstage left—"merely players." Costumes were Edwardian and modern (evening dress for the court scenes, colorful costumes for the forest scenes), with Rosalind and Celia at first wearing long dresses (but no bosom padding). The set was simple, walls covered with white canvas for the court, and for the forest scenes some hanging strips of green, lowered from the flies; the journey to Arden was made by walking around the stage. Although some reviewers said that after the initial shock they put aside all thoughts of a man wooing a man, others saw the play largely as an exploration of homosexual and homosocial relationships, and there was considerable talk about the construction of gender. Jacques was clearly a repressed homosexual, and Le Beau an overt one (he pawed Orlando at "I shall desire more love and knowledge of you"—1.2.275), but it should be mentioned that even in many straight modern productions, Le Beau is campy. It should also be mentioned that Rosalind was played by a black performer, Adrian Lester, whose performance in particular was much praised.

Still, what is one to make out of an all-male *As You Like It*? As we have seen, such a production can be offered for at least two very different reasons: to imitate the Elizabethans, with their boy actors, or to make the play strange and therefore somewhat fresh to the audience. Notice that the first of these reasons, imitation of Elizabethan theatrical companies, has an historical justification, but it should be made clear that the use of boy actors does not, or at least did not in Shakespeare's day, serve to make the play unrealistic. The boys were highly skilled performers, and no one seems to have thought they were at all deficient in representing women. When Thomas Coryot, an Englishman who visited

Italy in 1608, saw his first actresses, he remarked with some surprise that they were just as skillful as the performers he saw in England. That is, even when Coryot saw actresses, he did not then find the custom of boys playing female roles absurd.

It's difficult to talk sensibly about Elizabethan use of boy actors. Obviously we can never recover the Elizabethan experience; we cannot—even if we see the play done with boy actors—experience *As You Like It* as the Elizabethans did. But perhaps a few points can be made. First, strange though it may seem to us today, living in a world of semiotics, psychoanalysis, gay liberation, feminism, structuralism, and post-structuralism, it is likely that the Elizabethans didn't give a thought to the convention of boys playing women. *Convention* is the key term here. A convention—such as the photographer's use of black and white to represent a reality that is multicolored—is, when really a successful convention, unnoticed. Thus, when we see a photograph in the newspaper, our minds do not think of the absent colors, or that the person pictured is only a couple of inches tall whereas the real man or woman may be six feet. Nor, when we see a photograph of a head, do we say, "Oh, but there must be a body attached to this head." Similarly, when we attend a performance of *Julius Caesar* we do not wonder why these Romans are speaking English; nor do we, when we see what looks like a room on the stage, wonder why the fourth wall is missing, or marvel that the actors take no notice of us. A convention is *un*questioned, *un*noticed. We take what we get, instantly, unthinkingly, and we do not surround the perception with clouds of thought. But some critics today proceed differently, assuming that a dramatic convention is not so much a way of communicating a meaning but is itself a large part of the meaning of the play. Thus, they cannot make the simpleminded assumption that the actor represents Rosalind, and that Rosalind represents a woman; rather, they see Rosalind as, say, the playwright's way of getting a boy actor before the audience.

To talk a bit further about the convention in question: Lisa Jardine, in a recent book entitled *Still Harping on Daughters: Women and Drama in the Age of Shakespeare*, says that the boy players in female roles conveyed homoerotic (rather than heterosexual) appeal to the men in the audience. (What evidence does she cite? Chiefly the words of the bitterly anti-theatrical John Rainolds, an Oxford theologian who in 1592–93 gave the standard Puritan arguments against acting, such as the injunction in Deuteronomy against transvestism.) For Jardine, "the resulting eroticism is to be associated with their maleness rather than with their femaleness." Such a view assumes that the audience is more attentive to the performer than to the role being performed. Of course, while watching a play we sometimes *do* let our minds dwell on the performer ("Tom Hanks doesn't seem right for this role"), but for the most part, when the production is going well, our minds are focused on the make-believe world on the stage, not on the real world of the actors who provide the make-believe. Thus, at a successful performance of *As You Like It* most of us probably regard Rosalind not as an actress (or as a boy actor) playing a young woman, but simply as Rosalind. We think of her this way throughout the play—whether or not she is disguised as the youth Ganymede, and whether or not Ganymede is (in Orlando's presence) playing the role of Orlando's beloved. It is clear from the text that Shakespeare wanted his audience to see Rosalind as Rosalind, and not as a boy. He makes it easy for us to think of Rosalind *always* as a young woman, except in the epilogue, when the performer says, "If I were a woman." On several occasions Shakespeare causes Rosalind's femininity to break through her masculine attire. Thus, in 2.4 when she first appears disguised as a male, she says,

> I could find in my heart to disgrace my man's apparel and to cry like a woman; but I must comfort the weaker vessel, as doublet and hose [i.e., male attire] ought to show itself courageous to petticoat. Therefore, courage, good Aliena.
>
> (4–8)

We need look at only two additional examples. In 3.2 Celia teases Rosalind, alluding to a man who writes poems about one Rosalind, but not directly naming this man as Orlando. Rosalind cannot contain her excitement:

> Dost thou think, though I am caparisoned like a man, I have a doublet and hose in my disposition?   (193–95)

Surely if the thoughtful spectator were to think, "Well, yes, you are a male playing the role of Rosalind, so indeed you *do* have 'a doublet and hose' [i.e., maleness] in your nature," all of the fun would be lost. The delight is in seeing Rosalind *as a woman,* despite her costume; thoughts of the gender of the performer are irrelevant. One more example: In 4.3, after Rosalind—still disguised as a male—recovers from fainting at the sight of blood, Oliver says, "Be of good cheer, youth. You a man! You lack a man's heart." Rosalind replies,

> I do so, I confess it. Ah, sirrah, a body would think this was well counterfeited. I pray you tell your brother how well I counterfeited. Heigh-ho!   (164–68)

The emphasis here is entirely on Rosalind *as a woman;* if we say to ourselves, "But of course the speaker *really is* a male, a boy actor," the charm of the passage is utterly lost. (Rosalind is confessing that she lacks a man's heart, as she literally does, and at the same time is trying—with that preposterously casual "Heigh-ho"—to seem masculine.)

Finally, a few words about the BBC TV production (1978), directed by Basil Coleman, with Helen Mirren (Rosalind), Brian Stirner (Orlando), and Richard Pasco (Jacques). The play was filmed on location, at Glamis Castle, Scotland, and the director uttered some politically correct comments in *The BBC TV Shakespeare* edition of the play, to the effect that *As You Like It* is "an anti-materialist play about rediscovering Nature and our dependence on it. It touches on our responsibility to the environment." Fortunately, this conception is not evident in the production, which has the virtue of being fairly traditional, or, rather, in the newish tradition of a somber, Chekhovian vision.

The chief problem is rooted in the producer's decision to film the play in a real landscape rather than in a theatrical set. *As You Like It* is, after all, a pastoral play, and pastoral offers us an *un*natural world. Pastoral, contrary to the director's statement, is not about discovering our dependence on nature but is rather about states of mind. The pastoral world is not "real" nature; rather, it is an allegorical representation of a period of retreat that helps the participants to form a new perspective on social relationships. After all, the events in a pastoral poem or play are largely *un*natural, for instance Orlando's defeat of the professional wrestler Charles, or Oliver's and Duke Frederick's instant conversions. In a theatrical production, the set, even if it is relatively naturalistic, does not imply that the natural world is a large part of the meaning of the play. But television audiences, used to far-flung camera crews, are said to want the real thing—not landscape fabricated in a studio, but a real landscape populated by players. The conflict between the artificial play and the natural setting is evident almost everywhere in this television version, but perhaps especially in the scene with Hymen, where a laurel-wreathed man in an odd costume moves in an all-too-real setting. Still, despite the problem caused by shooting the play in the real world—and by an utterly unlovable Orlando and a perhaps too morose Rosalind—one is grateful that the play is offered with only a very few cuts.

Suggested References

The number of possible references is vast and grows alarmingly. (The *Shakespeare Quarterly* devotes one issue each year to a list of the previous year's work, and *Shakespeare Survey*—an annual publication—includes a substantial review of biographical, critical, and textual studies, as well as a survey of performances.) The vast bibliography is best approached through James Harner, *The World Shakespeare Bibliography on CD-Rom: 1900–Present.* The first release, in 1996, included more than 12,000 annotated items from 1990–93, plus references to several thousand book reviews, productions, films, and audio recordings. The plan is to update the publication annually, moving forward one year and backward three years. Thus, the second issue (1997), with 24,700 entries, and another 35,000 or so references to reviews, newspaper pieces, and so on, covered 1987–94.

Though no works are indispensable, those listed below have been found especially helpful. The arrangement is as follows:

1. Shakespeare's Times
2. Shakespeare's Life
3. Shakespeare's Theater
4. Shakespeare on Stage and Screen
5. Miscellaneous Reference Works
6. Shakespeare's Plays: General Studies
7. The Comedies
8. The Romances
9. The Tragedies
10. The Histories
11. *As You Like It*

The titles in the first five sections are accompanied by brief explanatory annotations.

1. Shakespeare's Times

Andrews, John F., ed. *William Shakespeare: His World, His Work, His Influence,* 3 vols. (1985). Sixty articles, dealing not only with such subjects as "The State," "The Church," "Law," "Science, Magic, and Folklore," but also with the plays and poems themselves and Shakespeare's influence (e.g., translations, films, reputation)

Byrne, Muriel St. Clare. *Elizabethan Life in Town and Country* (8th ed., 1970). Chapters on manners, beliefs, education, etc., with illustrations.

Dollimore, John, and Alan Sinfield, eds. *Political Shakespeare: New Essays in Cultural Materialism* (1985). Essays on such topics as the subordination of women and colonialism, presented in connection with some of Shakespeare's plays.

Greenblatt, Stephen. *Representing the English Renaissance* (1988). New Historicist essays, especially on connections between political and aesthetic matters, statecraft and stagecraft.

Joseph, B. L. *Shakespeare's Eden: the Commonwealth of England 1558–1629* (1971). An account of the social, political, economic, and cultural life of England.

Kernan, Alvin. *Shakespeare, the King's Playwright: Theater in the Stuart Court 1603–1613* (1995). The social setting and the politics of the court of James I, in relation to *Hamlet, Measure for Measure, Macbeth, King Lear, Antony and Cleopatra, Coriolanus,* and *The Tempest.*

Montrose, Louis. *The Purpose of Playing: Shakespeare and the Cultural Politics of the Elizabethan Theatre* (1996). A poststructuralist view, discussing the professional theater "within the ideological and material frameworks of Elizabethan culture and society," with an extended analysis of *A Midsummer Night's Dream.*

Mullaney, Steven. *The Place of the Stage: License, Play, and Power in Renaissance England* (1988). New Historicist analysis, arguing that popular drama became a cultural institution "only by . . . taking up a place on the margins of society."

Schoenbaum, S. *Shakespeare: The Globe and the World*

(1979). A readable, abundantly illustrated introductory book on the world of the Elizabethans.

Shakespeare's England, 2 vols. (1916). A large collection of scholarly essays on a wide variety of topics, e.g., astrology, costume, gardening, horsemanship, with special attention to Shakespeare's references to these topics.

2. Shakespeare's Life

Andrews, John F., ed. *William Shakespeare: His World, His Work, His Influence,* 3 vols. (1985). See the description above.

Bentley, Gerald E. *Shakespeare: A Biographical Handbook* (1961). The facts about Shakespeare, with virtually no conjecture intermingled.

Chambers, E. K. *William Shakespeare: A Study of Facts and Problems,* 2 vols. (1930). The fullest collection of data.

Fraser, Russell. *Young Shakespeare* (1988). A highly readable account that simultaneously considers Shakespeare's life and Shakespeare's art.

———. *Shakespeare: The Later Years* (1992).

Schoenbaum, S. *Shakespeare's Lives* (1970). A review of the evidence and an examination of many biographies, including those of Baconians and other heretics.

———. *William Shakespeare: A Compact Documentary Life* (1977). An abbreviated version, in a smaller format, of the next title. The compact version reproduces some fifty documents in reduced form. A readable presentation of all that the documents tell us about Shakespeare.

———. *William Shakespeare: A Documentary Life* (1975). A large-format book setting forth the biography with facsimiles of more than two hundred documents, and with transcriptions and commentaries.

3. Shakespeare's Theater

Astington, John H., ed. *The Development of Shakespeare's Theater* (1992). Eight specialized essays on theatrical companies, playing spaces, and performance.

Beckerman, Bernard. *Shakespeare at the Globe, 1599–1609* (1962). On the playhouse and on Elizabethan dramaturgy, acting, and staging.

Bentley, Gerald E. *The Profession of Dramatist in Shakespeare's Time* (1971). An account of the dramatist's status in the Elizabethan period.

———. *The Profession of Player in Shakespeare's Time, 1590–1642* (1984). An account of the status of members of London companies (sharers, hired men, apprentices, managers) and a discussion of conditions when they toured.

Berry, Herbert. *Shakespeare's Playhouses* (1987). Usefully emphasizes how little we know about the construction of Elizabethan theaters.

Brown, John Russell. *Shakespeare's Plays in Performance* (1966). A speculative and practical analysis relevant to all of the plays, but with emphasis on *The Merchant of Venice*, *Richard II*, *Hamlet*, *Romeo and Juliet*, and *Twelfth Night*.

———. *William Shakespeare: Writing for Performance* (1996). A discussion aimed at helping readers to develop theatrically conscious habits of reading.

Chambers, E. K. *The Elizabethan Stage*, 4 vols. (1945). A major reference work on theaters, theatrical companies, and staging at court.

Cook, Ann Jennalie. *The Privileged Playgoers of Shakespeare's London, 1576–1642* (1981). Sees Shakespeare's audience as wealthier, more middle-class, and more intellectual than Harbage (below) does.

Dessen, Alan C. *Elizabethan Drama and the Viewer's Eye* (1977). On how certain scenes may have looked to spectators in an Elizabethan theater.

Gurr, Andrew. *Playgoing in Shakespeare's London* (1987). Something of a middle ground between Cook (above) and Harbage (below).

———. *The Shakespearean Stage, 1579–1642* (2nd ed., 1980). On the acting companies, the actors, the playhouses, the stages, and the audiences.

Harbage, Alfred. *Shakespeare's Audience* (1941). A study of the size and nature of the theatrical public, emphasizing the representativeness of its working class and middle-class audience.

Hodges, C. Walter. *The Globe Restored* (1968). A conjectural restoration, with lucid drawings.

Hosley, Richard. "The Playhouses," in *The Revels History of Drama in English*, vol. 3, general editors Clifford Leech and T. W. Craik (1975). An essay of a hundred pages on the physical aspects of the playhouses.

Howard, Jane E. "Crossdressing, the Theatre, and Gender Struggle in Early Modern England," *Shakespeare Quarterly* 39 (1988): 418–40. Judicious comments on the effects of boys playing female roles.

Orrell, John. *The Human Stage: English Theatre Design, 1567–1640* (1988). Argues that the public, private, and court playhouses are less indebted to popular structures (e.g., innyards and bear-baiting pits) than to banqueting halls and to Renaissance conceptions of Roman amphitheaters.

Slater, Ann Pasternak. *Shakespeare the Director* (1982). An analysis of theatrical effects (e.g., kissing, kneeling) in stage directions and dialogue.

Styan, J. L. *Shakespeare's Stagecraft* (1967). An introduction to Shakespeare's visual and aural stagecraft, with chapters on such topics as acting conventions, stage groupings, and speech.

Thompson, Peter. *Shakespeare's Professional Career* (1992). An examination of patronage and related theatrical conditions.

———. *Shakespeare's Theatre* (1983). A discussion of how plays were staged in Shakespeare's time.

4. Shakespeare on Stage and Screen

Bate, Jonathan, and Russell Jackson, eds. *Shakespeare: An Illustrated Stage History* (1996). Highly readable essays on stage productions from the Renaissance to the present.

Berry, Ralph. *Changing Styles in Shakespeare* (1981). Discusses productions of six plays (*Coriolanus*, *Hamlet*, *Henry V*, *Measure for Measure*, *The Tempest*, and *Twelfth Night*) on the English stage, chiefly 1950–1980.

————. *On Directing Shakespeare: Interviews with Contemporary Directors* (1989). An enlarged edition of a book first published in 1977, this version includes the seven interviews from the early 1970s and adds five interviews conducted in 1988.

Brockbank, Philip, ed. *Players of Shakespeare: Essays in Shakespearean Performance* (1985). Comments by twelve actors, reporting their experiences with roles. See also the entry for Russell Jackson (below).

Bulman, J. C., and H. R. Coursen, eds. *Shakespeare on Television* (1988). An anthology of general and theoretical essays, essays on individual productions, and shorter reviews, with a bibliography and a videography listing cassettes that may be rented.

Coursen, H. P. *Watching Shakespeare on Television* (1993). Analyses not only of TV versions but also of films and videotapes of stage presentations that are shown on television.

Davies, Anthony, and Stanley Wells, eds. *Shakespeare and the Moving Image: The Plays on Film and Television* (1994). General essays (e.g., on the comedies) as well as essays devoted entirely to *Hamlet, King Lear*, and *Macbeth*.

Dawson, Anthony B. *Watching Shakespeare: A Playgoer's Guide* (1988). About half of the plays are discussed, chiefly in terms of decisions that actors and directors make in putting the works onto the stage.

Dessen, Alan. *Elizabethan Stage Conventions and Modern Interpretations* (1984). On interpreting conventions such as the representation of light and darkness and stage violence (duels, battles).

Donaldson, Peter. *Shakespearean Films/Shakespearean Directors* (1990). Postmodernist analyses, drawing on Freudianism, Feminism, Deconstruction, and Queer Theory.

Jackson, Russell, and Robert Smallwood, eds. *Players of Shakespeare 2: Further Essays in Shakespearean Performance by Players with the Royal Shakespeare Company* (1988). Fourteen actors discuss their roles in productions between 1982 and 1987.

————. *Players of Shakespeare 3: Further Essays in Shake-

spearean Performance by Players with the Royal Shakespeare Company (1993). Comments by thirteen performers.

Jorgens, Jack. *Shakespeare on Film* (1977). Fairly detailed studies of eighteen films, preceded by an introductory chapter addressing such issues as music, and whether to "open" the play by including scenes of landscape.

Kennedy, Dennis. *Looking at Shakespeare: A Visual History of Twentieth-Century Performance* (1993). Lucid descriptions (with 170 photographs) of European, British, and American performances.

Leiter, Samuel L. *Shakespeare Around the Globe: A Guide to Notable Postwar Revivals* (1986). For each play there are about two pages of introductory comments, then discussions (about five hundred words per production) of ten or so productions, and finally bibliographic references.

McMurty, Jo. *Shakespeare Films in the Classroom* (1994). Useful evaluations of the chief films most likely to be shown in undergraduate courses.

Rothwell, Kenneth, and Annabelle Henkin Melzer. *Shakespeare on Screen: An International Filmography and Videography* (1990). A reference guide to several hundred films and videos produced between 1899 and 1989, including spinoffs such as musicals and dance versions.

Sprague, Arthur Colby. *Shakespeare and the Actors* (1944). Detailed discussions of stage business (gestures, etc.) over the years.

Willis, Susan. *The BBC Shakespeare Plays: Making the Televised Canon* (1991). A history of the series, with interviews and production diaries for some plays.

5. Miscellaneous Reference Works

Abbott, E. A. *A Shakespearean Grammar* (new edition, 1877). An examination of differences between Elizabethan and modern grammar.

Allen, Michael J. B., and Kenneth Muir, eds. *Shakespeare's Plays in Quarto* (1981). One volume containing facsimiles of the plays issued in small format before they were collected in the First Folio of 1623.

Bevington, David. *Shakespeare* (1978). A short guide to hundreds of important writings on the subject.

Blake, Norman. *Shakespeare's Language: An Introduction* (1983). On vocabulary, parts of speech, and word order.

Bullough, Geoffrey. *Narrative and Dramatic Sources of Shakespeare*, 8 vols. (1957–75). A collection of many of the books Shakespeare drew on, with judicious comments.

Campbell, Oscar James, and Edward G. Quinn, eds. *The Reader's Encyclopedia of Shakespeare* (1966). Old, but still the most useful single reference work on Shakespeare.

Cercignani, Fausto. *Shakespeare's Works and Elizabethan Pronunciation* (1981). Considered the best work on the topic, but remains controversial.

Dent, R. W. *Shakespeare's Proverbial Language: An Index* (1981). An index of proverbs, with an introduction concerning a form Shakespeare frequently drew on.

Greg, W. W. *The Shakespeare First Folio* (1955). A detailed yet readable history of the first collection (1623) of Shakespeare's plays.

Harner, James. *The World Shakespeare Bibliography*. See headnote to Suggested References.

Hosley, Richard. *Shakespeare's Holinshed* (1968). Valuable presentation of one of Shakespeare's major sources.

Kökeritz, Helge. *Shakespeare's Names* (1959). A guide to pronouncing some 1,800 names appearing in Shakespeare.

———. *Shakespeare's Pronunciation* (1953). Contains much information about puns and rhymes, but see Cercignani (above).

Muir, Kenneth. *The Sources of Shakespeare's Plays* (1978). An account of Shakespeare's use of his reading. It covers all the plays, in chronological order.

Miriam Joseph, Sister. *Shakespeare's Use of the Arts of Language* (1947). A study of Shakespeare's use of rhetorical devices, reprinted in part as *Rhetoric in Shakespeare's Time* (1962).

The Norton Facsimile: The First Folio of Shakespeare's Plays (1968). A handsome and accurate facsimile of the first collection (1623) of Shakespeare's plays, with a valuable introduction by Charlton Hinman.

Onions, C. T. *A Shakespeare Glossary*, rev. and enlarged by

R. D. Eagleson (1986). Definitions of words (or senses of words) now obsolete.

Partridge, Eric. *Shakespeare's Bawdy*, rev. ed. (1955). Relatively brief dictionary of bawdy words; useful, but see Williams, below.

Shakespeare Quarterly. See headnote to Suggested References.

Shakespeare Survey. See headnote to Suggested References.

Spevack, Marvin. *The Harvard Concordance to Shakespeare* (1973). An index to Shakespeare's words.

Vickers, Brian. *Appropriating Shakespeare: Contemporary Critical Quarrels* (1993). A survey—chiefly hostile—of recent schools of criticism.

Wells, Stanley, ed. *Shakespeare: A Bibliographical Guide* (new edition, 1990). Nineteen chapters (some devoted to single plays, others devoted to groups of related plays) on recent scholarship on the life and all of the works.

Williams, Gordon. *A Dictionary of Sexual Language and Imagery in Shakespearean and Stuart Literature*, 3 vols. (1994). Extended discussions of words and passages; much fuller than Partridge, cited above.

6. Shakespeare's Plays: General Studies

Bamber, Linda. *Comic Women, Tragic Men: A Study of Gender and Genre in Shakespeare* (1982).

Barnet, Sylvan. *A Short Guide to Shakespeare* (1974).

Callaghan, Dympna, Lorraine Helms, and Jyotsna Singh. *The Weyward Sisters: Shakespeare and Feminist Politics* (1994).

Clemen, Wolfgang H. *The Development of Shakespeare's Imagery* (1951).

Cook, Ann Jennalie. *Making a Match: Courtship in Shakespeare and His Society* (1991).

Dollimore, Jonathan, and Alan Sinfield. *Political Shakespeare: New Essays in Cultural Materialism* (1985).

Dusinberre, Juliet. *Shakespeare and the Nature of Women* (1975).

Granville-Barker, Harley. *Prefaces to Shakespeare*, 2 vols. (1946–47; volume 1 contains essays on *Hamlet, King*

Lear, Merchant of Venice, Antony and Cleopatra, and *Cymbeline*; volume 2 contains essays on *Othello, Coriolanus, Julius Caesar, Romeo and Juliet, Love's Labor's Lost*).

———. *More Prefaces to Shakespeare* (1974; essays on *Twelfth Night, A Midsummer Night's Dream, The Winter's Tale, Macbeth*).

Harbage, Alfred. *William Shakespeare: A Reader's Guide* (1963).

Howard, Jean E. *Shakespeare's Art of Orchestration: Stage Technique and Audience Response* (1984).

Jones, Emrys. *Scenic Form in Shakespeare* (1971).

Lenz, Carolyn Ruth Swift, Gayle Greene, and Carol Thomas Neely, eds. *The Woman's Part: Feminist Criticism of Shakespeare* (1980).

Novy, Marianne. *Love's Argument: Gender Relations in Shakespeare* (1984).

Rose, Mark. *Shakespearean Design* (1972).

Scragg, Leah. *Discovering Shakespeare's Meaning* (1994).

———. *Shakespeare's "Mouldy Tales": Recurrent Plot Motifs in Shakespearean Drama* (1992).

Traub, Valerie. *Desire and Anxiety: Circulations of Sexuality in Shakespearean Drama* (1992).

Traversi, D. A. *An Approach to Shakespeare*, 2 vols. (3rd rev. ed, 1968–69).

Vickers, Brian. *The Artistry of Shakespeare's Prose* (1968).

Wells, Stanley. *Shakespeare: A Dramatic Life* (1994).

Wright, George T. *Shakespeare's Metrical Art* (1988).

7. The Comedies

Barber, C. L. *Shakespeare's Festive Comedy* (1959; discusses *Love's Labor's Lost, A Midsummer Night's Dream, The Merchant of Venice, As You Like It, Twelfth Night*).

Barton, Anne. *The Names of Comedy* (1990).

Berry, Ralph. *Shakespeare's Comedy: Explorations in Form* (1972).

Bradbury, Malcolm, and David Palmer, eds. *Shakespearean Comedy* (1972).

Bryant, J. A., Jr. *Shakespeare and the Uses of Comedy* (1986).

Carroll, William. *The Metamorphoses of Shakespearean Comedy* (1985).

Champion, Larry S. *The Evolution of Shakespeare's Comedy* (1970).

Evans, Bertrand. *Shakespeare's Comedies* (1960).

Frye, Northrop. *Shakespearean Comedy and Romance* (1965).

Leggatt, Alexander. *Shakespeare's Comedy of Love* (1974).

Miola, Robert S. *Shakespeare and Classical Comedy: The Influence of Plautus and Terence* (1994).

Nevo, Ruth. *Comic Transformations in Shakespeare* (1980).

Ornstein, Robert. *Shakespeare's Comedies: From Roman Farce to Romantic Mystery* (1986).

Richman, David. *Laughter, Pain, and Wonder: Shakespeare's Comedies and the Audience in the Theater* (1990).

Salingar, Leo. *Shakespeare and the Traditions of Comedy* (1974).

Slights, Camille Wells. *Shakespeare's Comic Commonwealths* (1993).

Waller, Gary, ed. *Shakespeare's Comedies* (1991).

Westlund, Joseph. *Shakespeare's Reparative Comedies: A Psychoanalytic View of the Middle Plays* (1984).

Williamson, Marilyn. *The Patriarchy of Shakespeare's Comedies* (1986).

8. The Romances (*Pericles, Cymbeline, The Winter's Tale, The Tempest, The Two Noble Kinsmen*)

Adams, Robert M. *Shakespeare: The Four Romances* (1989).

Felperin, Howard. *Shakespearean Romance* (1972).

Frye, Northrop. *A Natural Perspective: The Development of Shakespearean Comedy and Romance* (1965).

Mowat, Barbara. *The Dramaturgy of Shakespeare's Romances* (1976).

Warren, Roger. *Staging Shakespeare's Late Plays* (1990).

Young, David. *The Heart's Forest: A Study of Shakespeare's Pastoral Plays* (1972).

9. The Tragedies

Bradley, A. C. *Shakespearean Tragedy* (1904).

Brooke, Nicholas. *Shakespeare's Early Tragedies* (1968).

Champion, Larry. *Shakespeare's Tragic Perspective* (1976).

Drakakis, John, ed. *Shakespearean Tragedy* (1992).

Evans, Bertrand. *Shakespeare's Tragic Practice* (1979).

Everett, Barbara. *Young Hamlet: Essays on Shakespeare's Tragedies* (1989).

Foakes, R. A. *Hamlet versus Lear: Cultural Politics and Shakespeare's Art* (1993).

Frye, Northrop. *Fools of Time: Studies in Shakespearean Tragedy* (1967).

Harbage, Alfred, ed. *Shakespeare: The Tragedies* (1964).

Mack, Maynard. *Everybody's Shakespeare: Reflections Chiefly on the Tragedies* (1993).

McAlindon, T. *Shakespeare's Tragic Cosmos* (1991).

Miola, Robert S. *Shakespeare and Classical Tragedy: The Influence of Seneca* (1992).

———. *Shakespeare's Rome* (1983).

Nevo, Ruth. *Tragic Form in Shakespeare* (1972).

Rackin, Phyllis. *Shakespeare's Tragedies* (1978).

Rose, Mark, ed. *Shakespeare's Early Tragedies: A Collection of Critical Essays* (1995).

Rosen, William. *Shakespeare and the Craft of Tragedy* (1960).

Snyder, Susan. *The Comic Matrix of Shakespeare's Tragedies* (1979).

Wofford, Susanne. *Shakespeare's Late Tragedies: A Collection of Critical Essays* (1996).

Young, David. *The Action to the Word: Structure and Style in Shakespearean Tragedy* (1990).

———. *Shakespeare's Middle Tragedies: A Collection of Critical Essays* (1993).

10. The Histories

Blanpied, John W. *Time and the Artist in Shakespeare's English Histories* (1983).

Campbell, Lily B. *Shakespeare's "Histories": Mirrors of Elizabethan Policy* (1947).

Champion, Larry S. *Perspective in Shakespeare's English Histories* (1980).

Hodgdon, Barbara. *The End Crowns All: Closure and Contradiction in Shakespeare's History* (1991).

Holderness, Graham. *Shakespeare Recycled: The Making of Historical Drama* (1992).

———, ed. *Shakespeare's History Plays: "Richard II" to "Henry V"* (1992).

Leggatt, Alexander. *Shakespeare's Political Drama: The History Plays and the Roman Plays* (1988).

Ornstein, Robert. *A Kingdom for a Stage: The Achievement of Shakespeare's History Plays* (1972).

Rackin, Phyllis. *Stages of History: Shakespeare's English Chronicles* (1990).

Saccio, Peter. *Shakespeare's English Kings: History, Chronicle, and Drama* (1977).

Tillyard, E. M. W. *Shakespeare's History Plays* (1944).

Velz, John W., ed. *Shakespeare's English Histories: A Quest for Form and Genre* (1996).

11. *As You Like It*

In addition to the titles listed above in Section 7, The Comedies, see the following:

Barnet, Sylvan. "Strange Events: Improbability in *As You Like It*." *Shakespeare Studies* 4 (1969): 119–31.

Dusinberre, Juliet. "*As Who* Liked It?" *Shakespeare Survey* 46 (1993): 9–21.

Frey, Charles. "The Sweetest Rose: *As You Like It* as Comedy of Reconciliation." *Comedy: New Perspectives*, ed. Maurice Charney (1978), pp. 167–83.

Halio, Jay, and Barbara C. Millard. *"As You Like It": An Annotated Bibliography, 1940–1980* (1985).

Hayles, Nancy K. "Sexual Disguise in *As You Like It* and *Twelfth Night*." *Shakespeare Survey* 32 (1979): 63–72.

Knowles, Richard, ed. *"As You Like It": A New Variorum Edition of Shakespeare* (1977).

Montrose, Louis A. " 'The Place of a Brother' in *As You Like It*: Social Process and Comic Form." *Shakespeare Quarterly* 32 (1981): 28–54.

Tomarken, Edward, ed. *"As You Like It" from 1600 to the Present: Critical Essays* (1997).

Traub, Valerie. "Desire and the Differences It Makes," in *The Matter of Difference: Materialist Feminist Criticism of Shakespeare*, ed. Valerie Wayne (1994), pp. 81–114.

Wilson, Richard. *Will Power* (1993).

Wofford, Susanne L. " 'To You I Give Myself, For I Am Yours': Erotic Performatives in *As You Like It*." *Shakespeare Reread*, ed. Russ McDonald (1994), pp. 147–69.

Young, David P. *The Heart's Forest: A Study of Shakespeare's Pastoral Plays* (1972).